T R A D I T I O N

AKASHIC
BROTHERHOOD™

XI

眞屍龍拳

眞空波動拳

JUSTICE.

By Malcolm Sheppard

CREDITS

Author: Malcolm Sheppard
Development: Jess Heinig
Editing: James Stewart
Art Direction: Aileen E. Miles
Interior Art: Langdon Foss, Leif Jones, Drew Tucker, Melissa Uran
Cover Art: Christopher Shy
Cover Design, Layout & Typesetting: Aileen E. Miles
Playtesting: Henry and Mindy Walsh

AUTHOR'S DEDICATION

I give a threefold thanks to:

Dave MacIssac and the staff at the Lazy Dragon Pub, for feeding me and providing moral support,

Jess Heinig, for reading a message sent on a sleepless night, and giving me the opportunity to write this book,

And Jennifer Booth, for keeping me safe in the cold Peterborough winter.

EDITORS' MAFIA SPECIAL THANKS

Fred "Screw 'em" **Yelk**, for being to most corrupt commissioner in the history of the sport.

Ken "Loan Shark" **Cliffe**, for charging no points on the vig.

Geoff "Thug" **Grabowski**, for describing what sort of people run the World of Darkness these days.

John "Women Behind Bars" **Chambers**, for finding the most available of ladies.

Ed "Criminal Mastermind" **Hall**, for knowing who the real crooks are.

Carl "Biscuits No Love" **Bowen**, for holding up under months of Kool Keith torture.

Tim "Never Do the Right Thing" **Avers**— like the guy at the Decatur courthouse said, "I know *that's* right...."

Matt "Gimme a Solid Dollah" **O'Connor**, for resisting the corruption that overwhelmed other interns.

Ethan "Eliot Ness" **Skemp**, for shutting down the racket before it reached its insidious bloom.

In the crossfire, we lost a friend of outy. On October 20, 2000, **Kraig Blackwelder** died in a hail of bullets as he left the Watershed. Please send no flowers; we prefer to think that he's just on the lam.

735 PARK NORTH BLVD.
SUITE 128
CLARKSTON, GA 30021
USA

WHITE WOLF
GAME STUDIO

TRADITION BOOK: AKASHIC BROTHERHOOD

CONTENTS

PROLOGUE: ASHES AND RAIN

This manifest world, visible to the naked eye and felt with the five senses, is not God's creation. I was greatly mistaken in accusing and judging God.
— Taniguchi Masaharu

SMOKE TIGER:
BANGKOK, THAILAND

They say every drop of rain that strikes the earth was once part of a living being; blood, piss, sap and bile rot their way through the Wheel, burn out of the earth and fall from the sky, purified. At the end of our lives, our bodies will boil to the heavens and erode into the earth, and all that will be left is earth, water and wind.

I have been a man, a woman, a corpse and a cloud far too many times, I think.

It's the rainy season, and everything in Bangkok is muted by the storm, as if enough falling water could wash out the neon and reduce it all to the blue-gray of an ink-brush painting. Bored girls smoke cigarettes under metal eaves that ring with the rain. I huddle beside a cluster of them.

My own composure is fraying. *He* is here, his presence skirting the very edge of my awareness, teasing me with visions of his new face and his pale arms. With every breath of mine, a tiger stirs. My legs stretch as he awakens, my stomach trembles with his pacing and his growling rises to the back of my throat. *Let me stalk him, and we will exact vengeance together.* I can see him pacing. My calves tense like a sprinter's.

"No." The girls look at me startled. I'm embarrassed to find that I've spoken aloud. *You're an animal playing at a person's game. I've got to subdue you, Tiger. With all of your shouting my Bodhicitta can barely be heard.* So I set the great cat to warring with a crane in my mind, and as my hand traces the proper mudra to gaze on Indra's Net, the animals dance my surroundings into being. The pattern becomes the city streets; no crevice or alley in a hundred feet is hidden to me.

In this mandala of corrugated tin and bamboo, I see a stream of red.

In the hidden places, corpses wait for me.

PETER: LHASA, TIBET.

"Sifu?"

Raging Eagle opened his eyes and looked up at Peter. His student rubbed his hands together, shivering in the stone courtyard.

"They're going to cremate Gentle Mountain now. I thought you might want to be there."

"I know," he said, slapping the dust off of his robes and standing. "Stop playing with that scarf. It binds hands that should be free to act."

Peter tucked it in his parka, doubly self-conscious that the bulky coat made him stand out among these people. By contrast, Raging Eagle never seemed to get the same sidelong glances from the Tibetans, despite the fact that he looked just as Caucasian and all the more bizarre with his shaved head and his thin red robes.

And how the hell could he stand the cold? Tumo yoga? Peter made a mental note to ask about it later.

"You're looking inward." Raging Eagle caught Peter's gaze with his own. "I need you to be aware of your surroundings, Peter. We'll be leaving tomorrow."

"No, Sifu. Please don't cut things short on my account. I can get used to things around here." Gentle Mountain's arrival and funeral had consumed most of their time. Peter knew that Sigung Jou Shan and Raging Eagle had been close friends, perhaps through many lives.

In his master's shoes, Peter would have spent a few days here to regain his composure. He hated to think that his own awkwardness was keeping Raging Eagle from doing that. But how could he know? The man never seemed happy or sad.

"That's all right. We've been given an important mission by the Sangha and we have to leave immediately." As if to emphasize the point, he started walking toward their quarters immediately. Peter had to jog to keep up with the long strides.

"What? Where are we going?"

"Thailand. Bangkok. To apprehend two Awakened fugitives."

"But why us?" Peter felt the sweat bead on the back of his neck. "I mean, I've only been with the Sangha for five years now."

"I was asked because I have done this before. You are coming with me to learn as you work. More Brothers will join us when we get there. Pay attention to them — you could do with some training outside the Kannagara."

Peter ducked through a low doorway and just missed headbutting his own luggage, which Raging Eagle held out for him, packed and ready to carry.

"I won't lie to you," he continued. "This will be dangerous. Follow my instructions and remember your training, and we'll all be safe.

"Mitchell Pratts and Ming Wong are skilled mages and wily fighters, but that isn't all that matters when the Awakened must fight. In an instant, the life span of a dewdrop, you could cultivate the things that they, in a thousand lives, could never learn."

"What are those things?" Peter accepted another bag from Raging Eagle's muscular hands.

"Peace, Peter. They want power to sate a craving for Self. It's a madness that can't be satisfied with mountains of gold, the sharpest swords or the greatest magical secrets. It blinds them to the flaws that creep in and the possibilities that arise from the simplest things. There, in those hidden, weak places, you will succeed where they fail."

"Wait, Sifu, I don't understand."

"Do your parka up. We have a plane to catch."

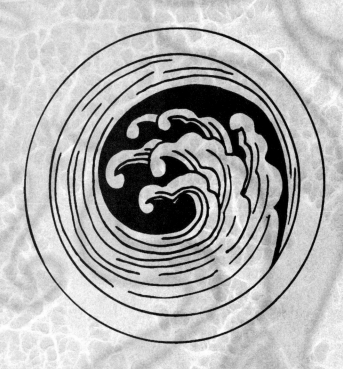

INTRODUCTION: ENTERING THE STREAM

Describe your face before your parents were born.
— Zen koan

The quote above describes the problems one encounters when trying to describe the Akashic Brotherhood. You search for bedrock, a solid foundation to rest a thousand layers of belief about life, magic and the nature of being.

There's no such thing.

The true "face" of the Brotherhood is the idea that the world doesn't have a foundation stone, and neither do people. Reality is more than the laws laid down by the Consensus. Even paradigms bow to the cycle of karma, growing, changing, and dying in an endless dance of passion and misery. For the Akashic Brotherhood, the trick is to see through the illusion of fixed ideas, because beyond the Great Wheel of actions and consequences, miracles can occur.

Thus, reality rides on a swiftly moving razor's edge, and Chi'n Ta, or mages, learn to strike a balance in the midst of the fury — or to step out of the cycle completely and detach themselves from the karmic chains that bind her to ignorance and suffering.

So Akashayana (the Sanskrit name for the Brotherhood and its members) dance the Great Wheel in a variety of guises. You've heard of the Shaolin monks and of samurai who can read the subtlest intentions of an enemy. Or maybe you've listened to whispered rumors about dark sorcery that throws the body and spirit out of balance, where long manicured fingernails direct streams of black power.

All of these exist, but the reasons are more important than the forms.

THEME: DISCIPLINE AND CHANGE

The Akashic path is perhaps the most demanding of any Tradition. While others may separate their personal and magical lives, the Brotherhood demands a discipline that affects everything from speech, to breathing, to diet. Many Brothers are overwhelmed by the demands put on their private lives, and give up their jobs and relationships to pursue magical prowess and enlightenment. Others turn their back on magic and close the door on destinies that might have been a thousand lifetimes in the making.

Aside from this problem, Akashic discipline also has the potential to turn against the very ideals that the Harmonious Brothers stand for. Many Akashayana become set in their ways. A routine of constant training and ritual turns a vigorous quest for truth into empty, meaningless habit. When they look for guidance from their superiors, they are invariably told that the answer is "more training." Disciplines designed to free them from the vicissitudes of the Great Wheel and strike an internal balance become routines that bind them to karma and imbalance their lives, as perfection of the mind and body become obsessive goals.

Some sort of resolve and practice is needed to preserve their special insights into existence, but the old ways work for fewer and fewer disciples. Perhaps the solution is to act instead of practice? The Brotherhood has always seen the value of the smallest things in life — even washing your clothes can be an act of Do — but they have been less involved with the larger struggles of the world. War, poverty, and famine rip through many of the nations where the Akashayana is strong. Now that

they need not commit all of their numbers to the Ascension War, they can discipline themselves in the forge of change itself. In the real world, there is always a new challenge.

MOOD: PEACE AND POWER

Detractors call the Brotherhood the "Warring Fist," and despite the efforts of diplomats and pacifists, it has become a fitting moniker to describe some aspects of Akashic life. The Akashayana have fought bloody wars and then withdrawn at the eve of victory. They've encouraged the growth of pacifistic faiths but have trained thousands in the killing arts.

The Akashic Brotherhood does not view this as hypocritical or contradictory. Akashics believe that everyone has his own path to travel, and that the validity of an ideal, even peace, can

LEXICON

Akasha: 1. The fifth element (after Earth, Water, Fire and Air) in Hindu and Buddhist metaphysics, which only exists relative to (and is necessary to the existence of) the other four. 2. An honorific given to the Ascended of the Brotherhood, who are considered to have merged with this element. 3. Ascension, the union with Akasha, the energy of impermanence and interconnectedness.

Akashi: The name used by the Akashic Brotherhood until the Himalayan Wars, when they changed it to emphasize that they were a different "vehicle" (yana) to enlightenment than other sects.

Akashakarma: 1. The impressions all beings make upon the fabric of the Tapestry with their actions; magic makes these tangible to the Akashayana. Called the Akashic Record by Western Brothers. 2. The passive (Yin) principle of Akashic philosophy, similar to the Taoist wu-wei.

Akashayana Sangha: "The Order of the Vehicle of Akasha." The name the Tradition uses for itself. "Sangha" more strictly refers to the Kannagara monastic order. "Akashayana" is used on its own as well, to emphasize that each Brother is a vehicle for the Akasha, in a singular or plural fashion.

Bodhicitta: The Avatar. Not an indestructible soul, but a concept and feeling of enlightenment that speaks to the mage.

Bodhisattva: In Akashic usage, an Oracle; one who has refused final enlightenment to help others attain Samadhi.

Bodhimandala: Also Tao Chang, Dojo or Dojang. A Chantry.

Chi: Quintessence.

Chi'n Ta: An Asian mage

Dharma: 1. In Hindu belief, a set of social mores and ritual behaviors that one must follow to live a good life. 2. In Buddhism, an ultimate truth about the nature of wisdom and the universe. 3. In Akashic terminology, a core magical principle or field, often used to refer to the Spheres.

Dragon: One of the Three Ministers of the Sam Chien. Entropy in the Metaphysic Trinity. Associated with Yin.

dragon nest: A Node.

Drahma: The short form of Draladharma, hybridized term derived from Tibetan and Sanskrit meaning, "the law of transcending the enemy." The active (Yang) principle in Akashic philosophy.

Lung-ta: Also called the Kai-lin, or Windhorse. A spirit aligned with the Li-Hai and some hengeyokai, associated with the Maya Realm, the stars and enigmas.

Lin Shen: "Forest Spirit." A Jnani hermit. Sometimes a euphemism for a Brotherhood assassin.

Meru'ai: The people of Meru, the oldest name for the Akashayana.

mudra: A hand gesture used to invoke and direct spiritual energy. Among the Akashic Brotherhood, it also serves as a sophisticated sign language.

Phoenix: One of the Three Ministers of the Sam Chien. Stasis in the Metaphysic Trinity. Associated with Heaven.

Phoenix Robes: Alternate name for the Kannagara.

rinpoche: A title for a Brother who was a Brother in a previous life. Also called a **tulku.**

Samadhi: Ascension.

Sam Chien: "Triple Struggle," called Trican in Sanskrit. The Metaphysic Trinity, both as an internal cycle and as the cosmic forces of Tiger, Dragon and Phoenix.

Santana: The self. Literally, "stream." The Akashayana believes that self is in constant flux and intertwined with the Ten Thousand Things, such that it cannot be said to have an independent existence.

Sifu: A Master.

Sigung: An Archmage.

Sihing: "Elder Brother." An Adept.

Tao-shih: "Way Scholar/Warrior." A Do specialist within the Brotherhood.

Tiger: One of the Three Ministers of the Sam Chien. Dynamism in the Metaphysic Trinity. Associated with Yang.

Warring Fist: 1.Wu Chuan, the martial art of the Vajrapani. 2. A derogatory nickname for the Vajrapani and the Brotherhood as a whole.

only be verified through experience. Contrary to the stereotype of cloistered, repressed monks, many Brothers deliberately seek out the things that turn life upside down and learn to adapt to them. Unlike the Cult of Ecstasy, Akashayana don't look for pleasure or pain per se, but try to see their lives as representative of a larger dynamic principle.

Even with these noble motives in place, it's hard to renounce those experiences when the time comes to move on. Combine these life-shaping experiences with the comfortable prowess that Akashic brothers develop in Do, and many are reluctant to leave behind a lifestyle they've spent years, decades, or lifetimes investigating and perfecting. As the Shaolin Temple showed, warriors don't always make the best monks. At its core, the Akashic ethic is strongly nonviolent, but the Brotherhood believes just as strongly that it would be a hollow code unless its members struggled to embrace it with their hearts instead of simply repeating an empty creed.

CONTENTS

As with any ancient and complex set of beliefs, the Akashic Brotherhood's philosophy, traditions and practices can't fit into one volume. Storytellers might research the beliefs that influenced the Brotherhood, and elaborate and modify what appears herein to immerse Akashic characters and visitors in a vivid environment that brings home their importance to the Traditions and to the world at large. This book gives you a place to start.

Chapter 1: Heaven and Earth recounts the history, philosophy and beliefs of the Akashic Brotherhood from the perspective of the Brothers themselves, covering infamous events such as the Himalayan War, their modern relationship with the other Traditions, and their place in Eastern and Western societies.

Chapter 2: The Way and the Law reveals the internal organization, politics, and practices of the modern Brotherhood. Each sect and position within the Tradition is described, including their new alliance with the proud and powerful Wu Lung. You'll learn about Akashic magic, from the paradigm that inspires it to the powers that manifest on the journey to enlightenment. Do, the mysterious and potent martial art of the Brotherhood, is given a full treatment — from techniques to magical forms.

Chapter 3: Sages and Warriors, discusses the role of the Akashic Brotherhood in a **Mage** chronicle. Advice on using all-Akashic cabals, sample characters and templates are presented to make it easy and rewarding to use Akashic characters in a game. Famous Brothers and ancient legends provide story hooks for your **Mage** chronicle.

CHAPTER ONE: HEAVEN AND EARTH

The world itself is, essentially speaking, in everlasting Enlightenment.
— Wonhyo

THE DISCIPLE'S DREAM: HISTORY

Peter slept, and visions came to him.

He was running in the rain, cloth shoes plowing through the yellow mud. A sword was in his hand.

"General!"

He pivoted, a blade ready; Zhen Ba faced off against two Handura. Karma bent, and Zhen's staff rotted into useless fragments. Peter leaped to him, but the Jnani was already dying. A knotted cord strangled him while the other death-priest chanted.

I'm enmeshed in illusion, he thought. *I am not a separate thing, different from the stones or the water. I can be everywhere at once. Yes.* The mandala formed in his mind and movements.

As Zhen Ba fell, a pale corpse, the Handura turned, frowning, to face him. Eight swordsmen, formed from the stones, the rain, and the air, surrounded them.

In eight bodies, Peter dashed the weapons from their hands, and started cutting, and cutting, and cutting.

He sat up with a start, waking up to enough turbulence to throw him toward the seat in front of him, which he clutched with both hands. Cold sweat stung his eyes. He was on a plane. China Air. His fourth connecting flight in the five days since they had left Lhasa.

"You were dreaming." Raging Eagle looked at him with narrowed eyes. "What is wrong?"

"Was it one of my past lives? I'm not certain."

"You know I can't tell you that, Peter. Right now, it would weaken your ability to discover the truth for yourself."

"Please. It was terrible." The image of a severed arm slid, unbidden, into his mind. Blood darkened the damp earth of his dreams.

"I can tell you about our history, Peter. Perhaps you'll recognize something that will calm your spirit. Close your eyes. Breathe. I will guide you through the Record."

THE ANCIENT CYCLE

There was only the darkness of his closed eyes, and Raging Eagle's gentle voice.

"We are not like the other Traditions. They look to beginnings, to something that will anchor them to the past and give them the comfort of ancient things, marks that they've made in the earth that will last forever.

"But there is no beginning, Peter. No beginning and no end. All Dharmas, even Drahma, perpetuate themselves in the Great Cycle. If we come from a beginning, it is also an ending."

Peter saw shapes in the darkness. Most were men and women, but he thought he saw the coils of a dragon in the corner of his eye. They danced, weaving circular paths in and out of the shadows.

"An ending, indescribable and mysterious. Before the cosmos we know now, there was another, as full of division and suffering as ours is now. The Wheel turns, and compassion and balance grow. Things become One again, and are subsumed by the emptiness of Akasha."

The rioting shadows spun together into a disk of gray light. Peter knew it from the Bardo Thodol, the Tibetan Book of the Dead, where it symbolized the true self, freed from conditioning and egotism.

"Only a few beings remain from the previous age. They are fully enlightened, 'Ascended,' and have made themselves a place in the center of the Wheel. The Tibetans remember it as Shambhala, the Indians as Golconda. Even in the West, we think of Avalon. All of these are dull memories of Meru, where the sages created paradise — a place immune to the ravages of karma, duality and death.

"The cosmos creates itself again. It takes the shape of a human being. Pangu and Purusa are names used to describe him. Listen to this:

"'From his navel the middle realm of space arose; from his head the sky evolved. From his two feet came the earth, and the quarters of the sky from his ear. Thus they set the worlds in order.'

"That 's from the Rig Veda. It is one version of the truth. The world comes from the Cosmic Body divided. Yin and Yang and Heaven and Earth separate and commingle. Their interaction forms trigrams, characters, language and form. The greatest of these beings are Tiger, Dragon and Phoenix, ministers of Heaven who have been charged with the turning of the Wheel itself. Under their care the Sam Chien begins, and the world unfolds into a great mandala whose four quarters are Pangu's limbs and whose atmosphere is his very breath."

Before Peter, the gray circle spun and darkness coalesced into the black fish of Yin, clasped to brilliant, white Yang. The symbol of the Tao expanded, threads from each side weaving into the other. A swastika became a map of the world, and guardian spirits arose on each continent. In the center, a great mountain flared with blazing light.

"At the axis of the Wheel, the village of the sages remains. It is Meru, the mountain at the center of creation. Below the summit where the Meru'ai dwell, gods, women, men, animals and ghosts arise, populating the four quarters of the world. The Wall separating spirit and flesh doesn't exist, and gods and spirits walk among the people. Some become Sheng, Awakened sages who climb Meru and discover sacred wisdom. They return with the secrets of fire, agriculture and alchemy.

"Heaven gives each being a place. The Wan Xian are charged with safeguarding Chi, the shapeshifters promote harmony and balance in the natural world, and the gods work to defend the righteous and balance the cosmic furies.

"They fail."

The Vow of the Meru'ai

"The nature of the world leads us to believe that we're separate beings, and not part of a greater whole. When we are called on to make sacrifices or let go of our desires, we find that

we can't, because we won't admit that our inner lives are no different from the chaos of the external world. Both flow, change, die and are reborn. Nothing is permanent.

"The gods make this mistake as well. The servants of Dragon rebel, and call themselves the Yama Kings. Though they fancy themselves the rulers of death, they are preoccupied with perpetuating their existence. The Chi they steal is used to prolong their lives and resist the turn of the Wheel. The Wan Xian follow in the Yama Kings' footsteps. They steal Chi from the land and its people. Enraged shapeshifters attack them, but become attached to their own anger and lose sight of their divine portfolios. As each being embraces the lie of the self, they invent other lies: that they have an immortal soul, or that everything they do is determined by a God or Goddess, or that the earthy passions of living are all that a human being is capable of. Even the Sheng forget the source of their wisdom. Few reach Samadhi. Deceived by materialism and faith, some go so far as to kowtow to the Yama Kings themselves."

Wars erupted before Peter's eyes. Half-human creatures drank the life out of crying children. Priests ordered their people to cover altars in useless, beautiful metals, for gods who showered them with thunder and famine.

"The Meru'ai cannot ignore this. Filled with compassion, they decide to enter the world, refusing to return to the mountain until all suffering beings are saved. Heaven destroys Meru then, and humanity replaces Heaven's will with the Wall, to separate Samara, the world of illusion and selfishness, from the true world beyond."

"Wait," Peter said, "Is this really true? Did Meru really exist, or is this a myth or an allegory?"

"That's Technocratic thinking, to say that the myths are somehow less 'true' than the material. Magic is a mythical meaning given form by enlightenment, Peter. Why should this be any different?"

"But it is! I mean, when I sense a man behind me, or practice with you wearing a blindfold, I can see and feel that something is really happening. In this sense, did we really come from Meru?"

"Is something you can see and feel real, Peter, or is it just a way for you to show yourself that you really exist?"

"What?"

"*You* are doing the seeing and the feeling. You're proving to yourself that you're a separate being, apart from all of these phenomena."

"And that's bad, I know."

"It's the legacy of the Ascension War. The most important things in the world have become imaginary, and the illusions have become real."

GARUDA'S CHILDREN

"In the beginning, the Meru'ai lived in the Garuda Valley, west of Mount Kailas. Let me show you."

A sudden lurching, a spinning, and the great mandala became a cliff side, honeycombed with tunnels. The symmetrical pattern of the holes reminded Peter of a high-rise apartment. For a moment he missed his old bachelor pad in Toronto, when all he had to do was pay the rent and the dojo, and his life was his own.

It was cold. Even in his dreams, Tibet was too cold. Smoke curled toward the sky; it drifted from the caves, carrying the smell of butter and millet. On the valley floor, a hundred men and women sat in silence around an empty bench. Peter could hear their breaths

rise and fall together. Behind them, sweet smoke wafted from a squat stone building. Carved cats guarded the entrance.

"Hello!" The voice was off to his left.

A short, weathered man waved to him from a nearby cave. Peter became aware of the presence of his body even as he walked toward the entrance.

"Who are you?"

"Right now, I'm Moy. Later, I'll be named a number of things, including Cheng Sa."

"Cheng Sa! How can you be talking to me? You're in Detroit."

"Oh no. I'm not the shell of matter and thought that calls itself the Cheng Sa that you know. I'm the imprint of his karma upon the Akashic Record. You do know that the Tapestry records even the movement of a particle of dust?"

"Yes, you told me, before I left for Tibet."

"The people here don't have the same names for these ideas, but they have them, nonetheless. They're strong and contemplative, these ones. The other tribes call them the tulku, which means 'old ones' in the language many of them speak. The meaning of the word will change with time, but right now it serves to mark them as wise, slow to violence and set in their ways.

"They, of course, just call themselves 'people.'

"They have one law: that no one may enter the valley from the outside world. They consider outsiders to be 'barbaric,' because they live in tents and can't excavate caves or build temples. They kill all intruders.

"Today is different. The intruder is a man who left the valley years ago. Here, come into my home."

Peter sat on a wooden stool and leaned close to Moy's fire.

"When he comes out, he will speak for three consecutive days. On the first day, he will tell them that they cannot separate themselves from the world, and must leave the valley or perish because of forces they will never see or understand. On the second day, he will tell them the true nature of reality, that it is an illusion created by our greed, ignorance and hatred. On the third day, he will teach the way to know reality as it is.

"Then he will cut himself to pieces with a bronze knife before the waterfall. He'll attain final Samadhi, with this — a sacrifice that shows us that our lives are one with the Wheel and that death is an illusion. He reveals Akashakarma, the record of all that flows through the Tapestry."

"What, you mean the first Akasha? He's about to speak, right now?"

"Yes, he called himself that, because he wishes to be the embodiment of emptiness and enclose the whole universe. After Akasha, we will give his name to anyone who attains his oneness. We will record his teachings in the Stone Sutra by using the symbols he has brought back from Heaven."

"So what you're saying is," Peter was shaking with excitement, "what you're saying is I could walk outside and see and hear the founder of our Tradition?"

"No," said Moy.

And Peter's world spun again.

The Wandering Akashi

Peter was in the jungle, now. The Tibetan chill gave way to the sauna warmth of Southern India. Peter knew the place instantly. He'd lived here for over a year, looking for a guru, before the Brotherhood had picked him up.

"It's a thousand years before the Common Era." Peter tensed at the sound of Raging Eagle's long absent voice, and the sudden reminder that he *was* on a plane bound for Bangkok. "We have followed the Stone Sutra to many lands. China, Korea and Southeast Asia all know the name of the Akashi. We still have hermits in our midst, but they are supported by shamans and healers who bring the Drahma to ordinary people, and strong warriors who protect us from harm.

"We've become dangerous people as well. We believe that we should perfect any necessary task as a tool for Awakening, and encountering violence and injury, we seek to master war and medicine. We gain some cold-hearted soldiers but also sudden insights on the relationship between the mind and body. This form of training is so successful that its practitioners are known as Vajrapani, the 'hand of the thunderbolt.' The Kannagara and Jnani grow out of our ascetics and shamans."

Rounding a bend in the trail, Peter came upon perhaps a dozen people sitting idly in the sun, their dark brown and golden skin sporting a sheen of sweat. As they were eating and chatting, Peter noticed that some of them bore the arms and armor he remembered from his dream. For a second, the memory of those swords in action overwhelmed him, and he shook uncontrollably.

"Sifu? Who are these people?"

"They are all priests of the Wheel. This is a historic meeting, for they have each shared their greatest insights. One group taught that the idea of karma, fate and luck are one. The other reveals the truth of formless creation."

"Formless creation? Akasha? So those would be us. But who are the others?"

"Those would be the Euthanatos."

SMOKE TIGER: THE WHEEL OF BLOOD

With his throat neatly slit, the body puts me in a kind of reverie.

Ranjit has laid him out perfectly for me. Even in a back alley, strewn with cardboard and broken glass, it evokes that memory. The head is tilted perfectly, and the hands curl forward at the wrists as if groping for something in the dark, just as if it had happened then, before the war.

I remember the plague years. We had developed a close bond with the Handura, who shared our practical sensibilities and agreed that the body was just as important as the self was. When the disease hit, we acted as one people, not two. Ranjit was a powerful healer, but he opened himself to my insights about the body.

Still, there were those we had to burn. You must understand that I never doubted that. But when I saw them, laid like still bundles of wood, the blood fresh, the cuts looking like a ragged parody of a smile, I was enraged, ready to kill. I spun Ranjit around by the edge of his cloak.

"What are you doing? You killed them!"

"Yes." Ranjit's voice, always so calm. "They could not live through the treatment." He smiled, as if to acknowledge that we both knew he was lying.

"I know why we're going to the villagers one by one, when together, we could have cured them all at once. We've worked together long enough; I *know* we could have performed a rite to heal them all from the Ganges."

I don't think he had lived in human flesh for very long. His eyes were young. They seemed too soft for his craft.

"You've come to judge them, haven't you?" I said. "The worthy will be allowed to grow, and fulfil the Dharma that allows them to move into a higher jat, a higher caste of existence, and the unworthy will meet your knife."

He turned to the next patient, so I killed him.

THE WARRING FIST STRIKES

Chan Ng met me thirty days later. The Handura guard gave me to his soldiers without a word. In the next hour, I was in his chambers, my shackles removed and a fresh robe on my back.

Chan spoke to me for a full day. The Handura, he said, were only part of the problem. The cults of death and judgement infested this country, from the Dacoits in the south to the wandering Idrans.

War is not our way. I remember telling him that. But he was General Chan now, and not some humble caretaker for the Kannagara.

A great mandala was carved into the rock nearby. In the center, Chan could lead the efforts of Akashi in all ten directions. Our minds united, we struck all of the death cults at once, from the mountains to the southernmost jungles.

The Chakravanti have their songs and legends, as epic as the Mahabharata, where we cross bronze and iron blades in noble combat, but we had more to fear at night in those days, when the death-priests would sneak into our camp with knife and strangling cord in hand. They fought well on the field, but we were the Akashi. As great as their warriors were, they were like children next to us.

We gave them a mountain of cutthroats. This was slaughter, not war.

I noticed a pattern in the fighting. Chan Ng harried groups like the Idran and pushed them into the Handura. In each case, they quickly joined forces and drove us off. By my third life in the war, allied camps of Chakravanti guarded the Ganges.

I remember storming into the general's tent, demanding to know why he had strengthened our enemies instead of defeating them.

Now that I know the reasons why, I think perhaps I killed the wrong man. Perhaps, here in this city, now, I will kill the wrong man again.

That man is close to me now. I know that he's watching me hunt him.

PETER: FIVE HUNDRED YEARS AND THE NIGHT OF FANA

Why won't he let me see the war? Peter was wrapped in the gray primordial light again.

"The Himalayan War prolonged itself out of our own error," said Raging Eagle. "A quick strike to liberate India degenerated into the feuds of Akashi and Chakravanti who refused to let death deny them victory. Generals and assassins quickly reincarnated. As children, bloodthirsty beyond their years, they urged us forward with tactical secrets gleaned from their past lives."

"Show me."

"I can't."

"You can't, or you won't?" Peter was shouting now, to get past the deferential fear that always came when he spoke to his Sifu. "What are you—what is the Brotherhood hiding from me?"

"All right then." The sound of a long inhalation echoed through the gray brilliance. "The truth is that I won't. It wasn't a proud time for the Euthanatoi or us. Toward the end, our leaders were children bearing the vendettas of a dozen lives. Demons whispered to us in our sleep, but we still fought and killed. The terrible karma generated by those times still troubles both Traditions. I won't burden you with it until you're ready."

"Well, how did it end then?"

Suddenly, Peter was floating over a desert, flying low like a soaring bird. Faint music grew louder as he approached campfires in the distance. He swooped ever lower, until a circle of tents surrounded him. Dancing, hooded men and women spun sabers in intricate arcs. Peter recognized one pattern from his own Shastamarga training, but the rest were new to him.

"You have quite an imagination!" A woman in a dusty robe, swathed in a scarf, said this to him as he drifted down towards the camp. "My name is Hundred Killer, or Battering Ram. It's a very special night!"

"Um, thanks. Why?"

"We're free now! Three days ago, the Night of Fana swept this place." She swung her arm across the desert vista for emphasis. "My friends and I were set upon by Handura warriors. A few of us escaped. Our group formed to harass pursuers, and the rest took sanctuary with the Darwushin."

Peter nodded. He knew the name of this Ecstatic sect from Cheng Sa's lectures.

"That night, an amazing thing happened. The two groups reached Samadhi together. Their fused form became an Akasha, and taught a new Dharma."

"The Khwaja al-Akbar. The Doctrine of Unity." He remembered this from his lessons.

"Yes! A new Dharma has entered the world. Now the war can end!"

"What? No, that's not true. It goes on for more than a hundred years after this."

Battering Ram frowned and shot him an angry look. "Why? We've done it! I've died so often so that this day could come, General. What more do you want? End it. My Brothers are tired."

"No!" Peter was surprised at the angry edge in his voice. "It won't happen that way. It *can't* happen that way." *Wait. She called me "General," like the dream.* "Who am I, Battering Ram?"

She smiled. "You're deceived by appearances. This really isn't Afghanistan. You're treading Akashakarma, Peter. It can tell you no more than what your Bodhicitta will reveal."

The Dragon River War

The sand turned from black to brown, and a river carved its way across the plain. "You are in China now," said Raging Eagle, "about two and a half millennia ago. The land is recovering from the Dragon River War, waged a decade earlier.

"It started when a group of Wan Xian, led by Hon Li of the Searing Wind, seized Mount Kailas for themselves. Aside from being close to the Garuda Valley, the mountain is one of the few

true earthly reflections of Mount Meru. It is literally a stone that pins the tails of the dragons, and directs their Chi, like rivers flowing from the mountain snow."

Peter saw a farmhouse, nearby, behind a withered stand of cherry trees. He started for it.

"We repelled them easily enough, but in revenge, they formed an alliance with Yi Han, an evil and strong Wu Lung. The wizard directed the Chi of Hon Li's allies into ten suns that blazed in the sky. The suns reduced the rivers to cracked clay beds and drove thousands to thirst and famine. We starved with the people and fought the evil when we could.

In the end, it was Yi the Excellent Archer who banished the false suns. We offered him a place in the Akashayana, but he would have nothing to do with wizards' politics. His servants, the Shih, still walk the earth. Like us, they train in the martial arts. Do is a mighty art, but these warriors possess a rare dedication that makes their methods just as deadly. Aid them when they'll allow it and pray that you never commit a sinful deed while they're watching you."

"But this all happened in the past," said Peter. "Why am I here?" He entered the courtyard of the farmhouse. A horse was tied outside, and he could smell rice cooking behind the door.

It opened. A man in a leather apron bowed to him. Behind, a bowl of rice awaited him on a table laden with iron tools and fabulous bronze machines. A metal dragon swam in a wooden bowl.

"Because you are meeting one of the first Technocrats."

A Hundred Schools

"The people are tired of shamans and sorcerers telling them what to do. The Dragon River War showed them that the affairs of the Chi'n Ta were as flawed as their own. By the time of the Chou dynasty, many nobles are sponsoring scholars who can find the answers without looking to Heaven. Those who master the material world form the Dalou'laoshi — China's first Technocrats. At the fall of the Chou, the Wu Lung war upon each other. Their doctrine gives one of them the right to rule as emperor, but no single candidate is strong enough."

Peter listened as he ate (or dreamed he was eating). The man went back to his machines, but glanced, grinning, every few

Devils and Warrior-Scholars

The Searing Wind is a sect of the Devil Tigers, a Kuei-jin Dharma that survives to this day (see **Kindred of the East**). The Searing Wind still despises the Akashayana for what they see as self-righteous posturing, while the Brotherhood finds their wanton immorality inexcusable, regardless of whether it's Heaven's will. Still, both groups exercise some restraint when dealing with each other. Akashics destroy any Devil Tiger *wu* they catch tormenting virtuous Buddhist or Taoist clergy, and the Searing Wind likes nothing better than to supervise the slow torture of an Akashic who turns to the Yama Kings.

In the modern era, the Akashayana respect the Shih (see **Demon Hunter X**) from a distance. Most see these hunters as kindred spirits who have decided to pursue enlightenment by a different route. While no Shih would hesitate to punish an Akashic for harming people, this rarely happens. The Brotherhood takes Shih enmity as a sign of their failure, and usually solves the problem internally first.

minutes. *He must think I'm a famine victim*, he thought. Peter looked down to see an emaciated, yellow-skinned body, clothed in rags. *He's probably the only one for miles with enough food, but he shares it with everyone who passes.*

"Weary from the Himalayan and Dragon River Wars we turn from Drahma to simple survival. Do proliferates at this time. Hundreds of styles develop from the best methods of the warring Sleepers.

"In return for our fighting prowess, we are sheltered by some of the old Chou nobility. They are Legalists, but we persuade them that power must be used with compassion, and that ties of obligation affect the whole Tapestry as much as the simple business of ruling. They accept our practices and become the Shi-Ren.

"Likewise, many Vajrapani follow Mo-tzu, hoping to cleanse themselves of past sins by fighting alongside him for a pacifist state, free from the bondage of tradition. These Li-Hai bring their practices back to the Sangha with them. They burn one copy of the Stone Sutra a day until they are recognized as a sect. Then they deride the Kannagara for 'cowardice' and the other Vajrapani for 'bloodthirst!' Since then, they have ever served as a voice to remind us of the essential emptiness of tradition.

"The faiths of China and India inspire our ways. Master Lao teaches that harmony in the soul is the same as harmony in nature, and that both, in fact, stem from the same interaction of Yin and Yang. We learn to find a simple joy in the natural world.

"The Buddha's teachings convince those Brothers closest to Chakravanti territory to give up the fighting, and leave the death-priests the lands south of the Ganges. When Emperor Asoka adopts the Buddhadharma, the Chakravanti leave our Brothers in the Buddhist Sangha alone. We give them the same respect when they come to Tibet to worship. They adopt an ethical code called the Chodona as a result, but in the end, reject the religion itself."

"Why?"

"The Buddha says that the atman, the eternal soul, does not exist, and that human beings can liberate themselves from karma and suffering. This contradicts the Chakravanti's very way of life. Without atman, they cannot argue that they are doing someone justice in a future life by killing him in this one. Without inescapable karma, they can't guarantee that their victims wouldn't have become good people or even world-saving sages.

"Even the magic they use to judge whether a soul is ready for death relies on a great fallacy — that the soul is an unchangeable spark, separate from all else. We live in a world where men and women Awaken at the sight of a stone thrown in a pond. Tell me, does the 'Avatar' come from the person, the rock, or the water? All of these things made the Bodhicitta flare into being. When you ask a question, even a magical question, what you ask determines the answer. When the Chakravanti divine the fate of an immortal soul, they will never learn the whole truth. They ask the wrong question.

"Reincarnation doesn't occur because a soul moves from one body to another. Rather, we leave the imprint of our karma on the primordial Akasha, and when the Wheel turns, the Akashakarma reconstitutes us from the elements that we have influenced in our past lives. The Bodhicitta is not a soul, but a potential Awakening that uses the lessons of our previous incarnations to remind us of our true, formless nature. Across many lives it tries to cure our ignorance by reminding us of the habits that have chained us to birth and death. An atman would have nothing new to teach us, Peter. The Bodhicitta has everything."

The First Emperor

Around him, the house grew into a huge palace. He was sitting on an ornate bench. Men and women with long, braided hair walked past, the gilt trim of their robes gently brushing the tiled floor. He was dressed this way as well. Silk slithered over his shoulders.

"Now it is the Second Century BCE, and the Wu Lung have their emperor, Fu Xia, even as the Chinese bow to Qin Shihuang, the first emperor of all of China."

It was a woman's voice, but unmistakably Raging Eagle's. Peter peered around a stone lion, and there she was, sitting on the other side. "Sifu?"

"The Wu Lung and the Dalou'laoshi now have the influence to destroy the Akashayana Sangha in China. In this incarnation, I'm on my way to assassinate Fu Xia." She pulled a thin blade out of her hair and stood. "I'll fail, but it will distract his attention away from the army that is gathering under Luo Fu, that means to seize part of the Silk Road for the Brotherhood. It will be retaken in the Burning Tiger War, but the brief victory gives us the momentum we need to survive until the Yuan dynasty." Raging Eagle stretched her neck to the left and right and stood, her hair cascading over the green silk of her robe.

She's beautiful, Peter thought. *I never thought that Sifu could ever look this way.*

With a knife up her sleeve, the woman smiled and walked away.

The Shaolin and the Samurai

Peter stood up to follow, and passing through an archway he arrived in a somber stone courtyard, far different from the opulent room he had approached. A line of orange-robed monks squatted in ma bu, the horse stance, thrusting their fists forward in unison.

Raging Eagle's voice entered his mind. "It's eight hundred years later. Buddhism has spread throughout Asia, and with it have comes the Akashayana Sangha. This is the original Shaolin Temple in Honan, China.

"At first, the place was infested with Wan Xian and the spirits of the dead. One day, an Indian teacher named Bodhidharma arrives with the doctrine of Dhyana, which will become Ch'an and Zen Buddhism. At first, he retreats to a cave and mediates, facing a wall, for nine years. Soon, the Shaolin Wan Xian are afflicted with a terrible burning pain. Most flee, but a few burst into flames in this very courtyard. The ghosts vanish. Finally, a monk rouses Bodhidharma by cutting off his own arm as proof of his desire to learn."

"Was Bodhidharma one of us?"

"No. I don't know if he was anything other than what he claimed to be, so I'll believe his words: 'Emptiness, nothing holy.' These are, of course, the holiest things of all.

"Akashayana from all over China come to study at the Shaolin Temple; they learn from Bodhidharma, and then his successors, who begin the Zen lineage. By 550 CE, the temple is under our control, and by 590, we have a voice in Buddhist and Taoist monasteries throughout China. We are still strongest in Tibet, where the Kannagara keepers of the Stone Sutra guide the Brotherhood through the great mental mandala of Akashakarma.

"Some of the Wan Kuei return to Shaolin. We are moved by the Bodhisattva Vow: 'I will delay my final liberation to help all beings who suffer attain enlightenment.' We allow them to study alongside us. The shen learn that the Temple is the one place where they can live lives of peace with one another. Attacks by the jealous shen and Chi'n Ta fail to conquer the Shaolin. It is only when we turn against each other that it falls.

"Escaping the Wu Lung and Dalou'laoshi persecution, many of us settle in Japan, with the earliest Buddhist missions. We keep a respectful distance from their shamans, and they in turn allow us to prosper. Vajrapani families are influential members of the peasant militias that will eventually become samurai clans. Throughout Korea and Southeast Asia, the pattern repeats itself, until our families and monasteries range from Burma to The Ryukyu Islands."

BARBARIANS

A single step forwards, and Peter was walking along the Great Wall. He noted the fresh stones and the smell of charcoal from spent torches. It was the middle of the night, and he could see torches along the battlements. A line of fire and stone ran to the horizon.

Ahead, he heard excited voices issue from an adjacent tower. He entered, wrinkling his nose at the smell of rotting meat.

Inside, bodies were piled in the center of the room. A woman spun to face him, with two hooked swords ready. Seeing him, she lowered her weapons and gave him a quick bow. Her companion, a dark, greasy-skinned man in lamellar armor, whispered something to her and walked out to the parapet.

"I'm Jiu Ling," she said. "Akkila and I were just talking about the plague."

"The Mongols are here, aren't they?" Peter was sure he recognized the period. His eyes kept wandering to the corpses.

"They've won, of course. The disease is a remnant of the fighting. Yu Lung of the Shi-Ren created it to keep them at bay, but it has spread to everyone involved in the fighting."

"The Jade Dragon?"

THE KAMIKAZE WAR

The Akashayana who settled Japan quickly adapted their methods to the local culture, mixing Shinto beliefs and traditional values with their own understanding of Drahma. In turn, the Brotherhood influenced Japanese culture; their philosophies contributed to the Japanese aesthetic of simplicity and natural harmony, and the Vajrapani influenced the samurai ethic. Japanese Akashics quickly developed a love for their new home, and distinct traditions outside of the mainstream Sangha.

In 1274, a Mongol fleet attempted to invade Japan. Despite the mainland Brotherhood's alliance with their invaders, Japanese Akashics rallied to the defense of their people. The rightness of the cause was confirmed by the kamikaze, a typhoon that all but destroyed the first invasion force. By 1281, Japan — assisted by the Akashic Brotherhood — had expelled the last of the invaders.

Unfortunately, this created a schism between the mainland and Japanese Sangha. They would have no contact with each other until Nichiba, the Weaponless Defender, accompanied mainland Akashic delegates to the Grand Convocation. The Japanese Brotherhood still has a number of customs that serve to distinguish it from its counterparts in other nations, a distinction that was only aggravated by the Second World War.

"Yes." Jiu Ling's knuckles whitened against the hilts of her weapons. "Everyone in his Bodhimandala was killed by the Khan's saman sorcerers, so he offered himself to the Yama Kings. All for this." She sheathed a sword and gestured to the bodies. "Many of us are dead. In the end we helped the samani drive him away. They hate the Stone People, who use rockets and machines that tear up the earth to fight them. Akkila says he will tell the Kha-Khan to be merciful to us."

"I remember. The Wu Lung and Dalou'laoshi will hate us for helping the barbarians and start the Screaming Ghost Purge, but we survive long enough to back the Red Turbans, who overthrow the Mongols and establish the Ming dynasty."

Jiu Ling nodded. "The Ming emperor supports us. Come with me." Jiu Ling grabbed his hand and walked him out the door.

Now, it was day. They were exiting the Temple of Heaven in the Forbidden City. Dozens of men and women passed them, bearing food, clothes and furniture. *All this for one man*, Peter thought. *If we were so strong, why did we let him live like this while others starved?*

Hundreds were seated in Tiananmen Square. Some wore the orange robes of the Kannagara. The rest looked to be bored eunuchs and advisors. They listened to a muscular, bearded man with golden skin.

"That's Sh'zar," Jiu Ling said. "He has traveled to us from the Middle East, to ask us to join in a great undertaking: the Council of Nine. I'll go with him." She was a younger woman now, with longer hair. "Sigung Wu Jin, Cheng Sa of the Li-Hai, Battering Ram of the Vajrapani and Darumha of the Kannagara form our delegation. Before we leave, Nichiba, a Jnani from Japan, contacts us through the Record. Our Japanese Brothers shunned us while we were under the Mongols, and he is the first to visit the mainland Sangha in years. Other emissaries called the Walkers will follow."

"What about the Shi-Ren?"

"The Screaming Ghost Purge frightened them. Some left the Akashayana and went to the Convention of the White Tower. Others were content to solidify their holdings here."

"Those were foolish choices. The Dalou'laoshi will absorb them, and the Wu Lung will deprive them of their power here. The Dragon Wizards have already corrupted key bureaucrats in the Ming regime. Even though we stand in the capital of the Middle Kingdom, our power is already gone."

STRANGE BROTHERS

During the Grand Convocation, the Akashayana was approached by a small group of Hermetic and Verbena consors, warriors who found something familiar in the Brotherhood's teachings about Do and the unity of mind and body. Under Akashic tutelage, three of them Awakened, basing their magic around the fighting arts they had learned in service to the Western magi. They were accepted into the Li-Hai as a fellowship called the Gladius Argentum, over the strenuous objections of their former masters.

The Li-Hai began to recruit non-Asian martial artists, dancers and ascetics, especially from West Africa and Spain. By the early 18th century, Portuguese and Spanish-speaking members dominated, and the name of the group was changed to the Roda d'Oro, or the Circle of the Sun. They remain a little known but important influence on Akashic practices.

"At the Convocation, we are befriended by the Dreamspeakers, who remember how we helped the samani, and our old allies, the Batini. We clash with the Order of Hermes and the Celestial Chorus over theories of magic. Hermetic wizards misinterpret and steal elements of Drahma, and the Chorus despises us because the Buddhists in our ranks do not believe in God. The Euthanatoi avoid us, and we them. Seventeen years earlier, the Long Red Night nearly brought us to another war."

"I will die in the Great Betrayal, forgiving Heylel Teonim. Sometimes, our sins mask the greatest sacrifices, Peter. This is something all Akashayana know in their hearts."

THE LONG RED NIGHT

In 1438, Akashayana and Chakravanti cabals met while stalking a Dalou'laoshi warband that had been keeping other mystics from traveling the Silk Road. After the enemy's machines were dismantled, the two groups camped together — the first time that the two Traditions had peacefully gathered in almost two millennia.

It didn't last. Two of the mages in attendance had been dire enemies in several previous lives, and trouble started the moment they recognized each other. This in turn opened up a hundred old vendettas, leading to two years of hit-and-run warfare through Mongolia and Northern Burma until both sides decided to withdraw.

At least, that's how the Akashayana and Euthanatos tell it. Persistent rumors hold that both cabals abandoned their respective groups and began recruiting others to defect as well. It is said that the conflict ended with the assassination of both cabals by two suddenly cooperative Traditions.

Oddly enough, none have been able to recall the event through the Akashic Record, and no one has ever admitted to having been a participant in a previous incarnation.

SMOKE TIGER: THE WHEEL OF IRON

I've lived a lot of sinful lives; I'm surprised I'm still human.

When I Awakened in the Qing, my first memory was of Nu Ying's knife in my heart, the feeling of betrayal as my Sifu cut me down. Whenever I saw him at the Shaolin Temple, I kept my anger coiled tight, so that he couldn't sense it.

They call it the Long Red Night now, as if it was senseless violence boiled up from the ground, instead of the truth screaming to be told.

I would stalk the Forest of Stupas late at night, full of tense power. Like all of the Vajrapani, I hated being confined here. Behind the Qing invaders, the Wu Lung cut us off from the outside world.

We began to gather — and talk about fighting back — away from the Wan Kuei and the ghosts, and away from the Kannagara, who would no doubt tell us to train harder and abandon the world beyond the monastery. Every time Jou Shan, with Nu Ying by his side, said that to me, I felt the knife in my chest dig a little deeper.

When we grabbed staves and walked out the gate, no one moved to stop us. When we helped the peasants throw off a greedy Manchurian landlord, Jou Shan only turned his back. Even Nu

Ying fought at my side when the Tiger General's warriors sought to match Do with their magic and retake our hard-won territory.

No, the shen betrayed us. Wan Kuei consumed our sentries and ghosts showed the Wu Lung our secret defenses. They charged in with fire, killing and burning while vampire "Bodhisattvas" accused the Sangha of making the monastery a secret headquarters for an anti-Qing rebellion, betraying the peace that had held for over a thousand years.

They were right, of course.

My name was Hung at the time. While other Vajrapani fled to Japan or the Ryukyus, I stayed, helping anyone who would stand up to the Qing. I made myself live a long time, watching as China crumbled.

The Dalou'laoshi turned on the Wu Lung in the end, helping foreigners poison the people with heroin and blinding the Qing to the dangers posed by the Westerners. I even organized a rough alliance with the Dragon Wizards; that was the first time I'd ever seen a gun. The I Ho Chuan, used to magical invulnerability, often poked and prodded their bullet wounds in surprise, just before they died.

The secret societies I helped form turned to crime, and I turned to hating the Sangha again. Maybe this was another one of their schemes? After the Himalayan War, I knew that they would sacrifice everything for Drahma.

This time I was poisoned by the Lin Shen, or perhaps the Golden Dragons. It was 1920, and I was an old married man, cobbling together a book called *A Secret History of Asia*. I never found out what happened to my wife.

It doesn't matter. After all, Drahma is truth, and people are only empty, impermanent things.

PETER: TOUCHING THE EARTH

"Peter, wake up."

Peter opened his eyes and sat up in his seat. "I was asleep? I thought you were teaching me history."

"I was," Raging Eagle said. "You fell asleep after I talked to you about the Shaolin Temple."

"I dreamed of Fall Breeze."

"Did you? Your ability to listen to Akashakarma is growing. We've landed."

In Thai, French and English, the intercom told them it was time to disembark.

THE END OF THE ASCENSION WAR

At the luggage carousel, Peter said, "Tell me about the end of the Ascension War."

Raging Eagle kept looking at the ramp. "You have too many things, Peter. If you had only come with hand luggage, we'd be able to leave now."

"Sifu?"

"At first, we embraced the struggle with the Technocracy. After the Boxer Rebellion, we knew the damage they could do to humanity. We modernized our methods and accepted apprentices from outside of Asia. You may have heard terms like 'Orange Robe,' or 'Scale of the Dragon.' These were attempts to couch our teachings in concepts that the Traditions as a whole understood, such as the Sam Chien. The Golden Dragons claimed a place in Doissetep and gave us a voice in the place where the Council's policies were *really* decided.

"The Second World War tore the Sangha to pieces. Pacifist and militant, Chinese and Japanese would neither speak to nor assist one another. We squabbled like a noisy mind, until a bell of mindfulness brought us back to the war: Hiroshima. Years later, when Gentle Mountain came to Colorado to recognize me as a rinpoche in 1968, he was still bitter about the feud.

"The atom bomb showed us how far the Technocracy had come, and how far they were willing to go. Gentle Mountain led a campaign to increase the number of Brothers around the world. That is how he found me again, at a time when many Akashayana still believed that we would not reincarnate as anything but Asians.

"The Shi-Ren financed films and books about Eastern spirituality and the Li-Hai adapted the teachings to serve people from all walks of life. I was concerned that we were changing our ways too much; the Kannagara agreed. After the 80's, such innovations halted.

"In 1998, Master Hyemyŏong, our Primus on the Council of Nine, was killed in the invasion of Concordia. The year after that, the Wall shattered. Millions devoted to the beliefs that we share with the Euthanatoi were killed with nuclear strikes and potent magic. The Vajrapani urged a final, suicidal revenge, and elements of the Euthanatoi prepared for the same.

"The Kannagara and the surviving leaders of the Euthanatos saw the same trend that caused the Himalayan War building in these mages. Together, we urged the other Traditions to abandon the Ascension War.

"Endless war for a fractured peace. A hard choice, but I know I'm not prepared to be a warrior forever."

DRAGONS ENTWINED: THE WU LUNG AND THE AKASHIC BROTHERHOOD

Peter scrambled to get his bags as they tumbled down to him. "What about the Wu Lung?" he asked, as he hoisted a suitcase. "Why are we allied with them if they've treated us so badly in the past?"

"The Dragon Wizards have been… humbled by the events of the last few years. The Shi-Ren began the dialogue. There isn't enough room in a lot of Chinese communities for two groups of wizards to stay angry with one another. However, when they came to us offering a permanent alliance, we were genuinely surprised, although Jnani seers among us had hinted that it would come.

"They have a place at the table beside the other sects now, and through us the resources of the Traditions. There has been some tension between the Dragon School and the Kannagara — the nobles don't like the idea of having monks as leaders — but they work closely with our Shi-Ren in a number of projects. Sometimes, I think their viewpoints are too similar."

WHERE DRAGONS GATHER: GEOPOLITICS

They took the first cab in line from the airport. Raging Eagle paid him a hundred dollars, American. Responding to the puzzled look on Peter's face, Raging Eagle said, "The driver was going to rob us. He needs the money."

They walked into a dingy hotel, sandwiched between a shrine and a noodle shop. Raging Eagle walked straight up the stairs, two flights, and knocked on Room 309.

"Who is it?" It was a woman's voice, with a slight Spanish accent.

"Samo and Jackie."

The click of a lock, and the door opened. She had curly black hair, cauliflower ears and a thin scar on the side of her muscular neck. She smiled.

"Nu Ying. It's been a long time."

Raging Eagle nodded. "Five years. It's good to see you, Sataghni."

"That means 'Battering Ram,' doesn't it?" As Peter spoke, she reached to shake his hand.

"Or 'Hundred Killer.' I prefer it in Sanskrit. It sounds less violent." She held his hand in a firm grip and bowed slightly. "And you are?"

"Peter Lasky." He bowed a little lower.

"Well, come in!" She showed them into the room. There were two beds; on one of them, a woman sat frowning at a laptop. "That's Tanaka Masako." The woman waved without looking at them.

Raging Eagle sat on the floor and started talking to Masako in rapid Japanese. Peter sat on the other bed, working the kinks from the flight out of his body. A moment later, a wonderful, spicy smell assailed him.

Sataghni put a plastic bag on the bed beside him. "I figured you might be hungry, after eating nothing but rice and discipline in Lhasa."

He was.

THE AKASHAYANA IN THE EAST

They ate in silence. Raging Eagle picked the chicken out of his noodles with swift precision.

When they were finished, Raging Eagle stretched his hands out on the table and talked.

"Are you all that the Sangha could spare? For a mission like this, I'm used to having more people to work with."

"The Brotherhood has been trying to run operations more efficiently," Masako replied, startling Peter with her high voice. "We can't afford to send the Awakened into danger like we used to." Here she shot Peter an irritated glance.

"You've seen the mess in Garuda Valley. It will take us years to rebuild the Temple of Inner Truth. The Chinese presence isn't helping either. While it is our spiritual home and always will be, we can't rely on the Tibetan people to be as helpful as they've been in the past. It's dangerous to be seen supporting the lamas, and we can't have the Red Army following them to our oldest Bodhimandala!"

Peter saw Masako and Raging Eagle exchange mudra. As they talked, the hand signs became more rapid and complex. Even silent Sataghni wove her hands and fingers in response from time to time. He hated that. It meant that their speech only constituted about half of what they were saying.

It made him nervous, too. He had only just begun to learn the secret signs before he had been transferred to Raging Eagle, but he recognized the mudra for "danger," when it appeared several times in the conversation.

"In China, we still have a lot of support, but we need the Sangha there to stay put and guard our dragon nests against the Wan Kuei and the shifters. The Wu Lung have been a tremendous help here, but every day, the government orders one of our monasteries relocated or destroyed, to accommodate industrial projects or new housing. The Five Metal Dragons are using the population to their advantage there.

"The Shi-Ren are helping us slow some of the development down, but there's an ethical problem — the Chinese need many of these projects — and it doesn't please the Shi-Ren to work against what they could profit from.

"In India, our presence is a model one, but it couldn't be anything less or the Euthanatos would throw a fit. While relations have improved — we've worked together more than ever since the troubles there — things are still delicate enough that only Buddhist and Jain Kannagara ascetics stay for any length of time. And those wise and holy men would not serve our purposes here.

"In Japan, our problems are, if anything, the opposite of those in China. The Zaibatsu excels at diverting dragon lines away from our shrines and monasteries. The kami have fallen silent. Most of us are doing our best to minister to the people while materialism and stress take over their lives. The Vajrapani families there are fierce and competent, but are reluctant to leave the country. I can't blame them. There are a lot of Bodhimandalas on the mainland that wouldn't welcome them because of the war. A similar situation exists in Korea, except that there are few Vajrapani there besides the Sulsa, and they are needed to watch over the jade market, which stinks of Wan Kuei influence."

"Which brings us here," Raging Eagle said. "What local support do we have?"

"The Kannagara and Jnani will help the government here look the other way. Monks hold a lot of influence in Thai society; in that respect, they're a lot like the Shi-Ren. We'll be allowed to visit a local monastery to prepare ourselves and benefit from the Chi there, but we can't allow them to get directly involved. This mission is too sensitive.

"What about you, Nu Ying? Couldn't you find anyone else to come with you from the Mountain of Gold?"

THE BROTHERHOOD IN THE WEST

"You have to understand," he replied, " the Technocracy has a very tight reign in North America. We're losing a lot of recruiting to commercial martial arts schools, the kind of places where you buy your black belt up front. If it's the Syndicate, I'm impressed with their guile, but if it's the Sleepers, then I worry for our future there. There is a steady stream of students at meditation centers and martial arts schools, but the ones that teach the preliminaries to Do have trouble holding students. The old ways aren't exciting enough, I suppose.

"My own kwoon started losing students quickly. The handful that remained were no match for the Men in Black they sent for us. None of us were killed, but I've sent them to other Bodhimandalas to be on the safe side. Peter was Cheng Sa's student in Toronto. I was honored to continue his training where the Woodcutter left off.

"In Europe, we are a little more secure, but we are competing with the Hermetics, the Verbena and the Chorus for Chi and resources. In South America, you of course have the Roda d'Oro, but they are with us more out of a common practice then belief. Our work here will involve some of our oldest legacies. I couldn't bring anyone who won't take them seriously.

"I have relied on the Sangha's help to gather information. Both of our targets originally lived in North America." He pulled out two file folders from his bag. "Everything they've found out about Pratts and Wong is in here. We can look at them tomorrow, after we train."

MANDALAS OF POWER: AKASHIC STRONGHOLDS

The Akashayana lost several Bodhimandalas (Chantries) after the Reckoning. Many of them existed in Horizon Realms that have since been cut off from Earth. However, the Brotherhood still has strongholds and temples spread throughout a larger geographical area and population than any other Tradition, giving them a host of resources to draw from.

Tibet

The Brotherhood's ancestral Bodhimandala, the Temple of Inner Truth, has been lost to the Avatar Storm. An Earthly version of the monastery is being built over its dragon nest in the Garuda Valley. Nearby Mount Kailas is as sacred to the Akashayana as it is to Tibetan Sleepers. While it isn't a Node *per se*, it Resonates with the power of Correspondence and Spirit magic, both of which are easier near Meru's material remnant. Other Bodhimandalas exist throughout the country, but since the Chinese occupation they have become extremely secretive for fear of Technocratic attack or simple harassment by the Chinese government.

India and Sri Lanka

The Akashayana maintains a small collection of Kannagara settlements north of the Ganges. The Jain and Buddhist Brothers eschew external politics or travel, something which calms nearby Euthanatoi and provides a place for Akashics seeking peace and isolation to retreat to.

A sizable portion of the material anchor for the Akashic Record exists in Sri Lanka. The Brothers here are Kannagara and Jnani, with a small contingent of Vajrapani descended from the Kshatriya caste, who have been charged with defending the Record through all of their incarnations.

China

Chinese Brothers make up the majority of Akashayana, but they have less security than in other countries. The communist government scrutinizes religious leaders and jails members of any organization that might threaten the status quo. Groups such as Falun Gong, which served as a cover for Akashic recruitment, have been outlawed, and all monks are technically government employees.

Under the cover of the state, Kuei-jin and Technocrats often move against the Brotherhood. Alliance with the Wu Lung has helped relieved the burden, but for the most part, the Akashayana have been moving away from monasticism and integrating their practices with modern life. Many Brothers work as martial arts coaches or members of criminal conspiracies. Still, in a few remote mountains and forests, some of the mightiest members of the Tradition lead reclusive, peaceful lives.

Japan

Japanese Shi-Ren and Vajrapani tend to follow samurai traditions, supporting traditional martial arts practices and Japanese customs. However, the Zaibatsu has seized many of the country's Nodes. In the mountains, however, Jnani still benefit from the power of the kami. These mystics have access to several untainted dragon nests, hidden in Hokkaido and northern Honshu.

Okinawa has served as a refuge for the Vajrapani for hundreds of years. Shuri Castle, the home of the old Sho dynasty, serves as a meeting place and a Node for both the Brotherhood and the native Dreamspeakers. Many other potent spots have been lost to the construction of American military bases.

Korea

This divided country supports a balanced proportion of each sect, although they cultivate a more discrete presence in North Korea. The Akashics maintain Bodhimandalas in a number of monasteries, martial arts schools and private estates. The pride Koreans take in their heritage has served the Akashayana well, since it has spared a number of sacred sites from destruction and provides a steady base of acolytes who already understand the basics of Akashic philosophy.

Southeast Asia

Aside from the Kannagara's considerable influence in Thailand and Burma, war and turmoil have depleted the Brotherhood. Many Vietnamese Sangha fled to France or the United Sates.

The Sangha has reestablished itself in Cambodia in small numbers, after being nearly exterminated by the Khmer Rouge's murderous regime. Angkor Wat, once one of the most powerful dragon nests in the Brotherhood's care, is currently the subject of a three-way struggle between the Akashics, the mysterious Toc Faan cult and a mysterious force that kills or harasses anyone who tarries around the sacred ruins (see **Dragons of the East**). Other sites have been defiled by the genocide of Year Zero or lie in ruins from bombing and defoliation.

Europe

After the Walkers' first visits, the Brotherhood has slowly grown in numbers, though not in influence. The magical resources of Europe remain the tightly held property of the Order of Hermes, Celestial Chorus and (to a lesser extent) the Verbena. The only well-known Bodhimandala consists of a group of Kannagara Vietnamese expatriates. These monks live in Southern France where they operate a commune that attracts the spiritually needy from all walks of life. For the most part, European Akashics are attached to Chantries that belong to the Western Traditions.

Generally, the materialistic emphasis of Western Chantries keeps Akashic Brothers from getting too comfortable. Many of them serve as Heralds in the Chantries to which they're attached, to avoid any personality differences that may arise from a long stay in any one place.

The Americas

The Akashayana's numbers are growing here due to the popularity of martial arts, alternative spirituality and other practices. At the same time, North America has the largest proportion of failed acolytes, as students raised with modern comforts find the Brotherhood's methods harsh and lacking in immediate rewards. On the West Coast, the Akashayana prospers due to the prevalence of Asian communities. Toronto, with one of North America's largest Chinatowns, has a large Bodhimandala staffed by Brothers from all of the sects and a contingent of Wu Lung.

Chicago boasts an Akashic presence of a less benign variety. Yu Lung, the Jade Dragon, holds court over an array of corrupted Akashics, Orphans and stranger creatures. While he cannot return to Earth, he is still able to relay orders to his followers through some unknown means.

Finally, in Rio de Janeiro, the Roda d'Oro shares a Chantry with the Dreamspeakers and Celestial Chorus. When the sect meets, it is usually there.

The Way and Its Power: Akashic Philosophy

Training at the monastery began with a lot of bowing and greeting. All of the monks asked after Peter's health. A few of them chatted with him about soccer in French, and he was relieved to find that his language skills were no worse than theirs were.

After half an hour of this the monks filed into the main hall to begin meditation. The four of them changed and went out into the courtyard. Raging Eagle was wearing his robes again, but Sataghni and Masako chose ordinary sweats to practice in. Peter threw on a pair of gi pants and an old shirt, and spent the next two hours moving through the basics of Dharmamukti. Practicing the katas calmed him. There was only technique, with no past or future to worry about.

"Don't be so absorbed in it," Raging Eagle said. "Do is meant to be used as well as practiced."

"Spoken like a true Vajrapani." Sataghni spoke while working with a straight sword. "I still can't believe you became a monk." She let the Sanskrit-etched blade drop to one shoulder and marched over.

"Peter's spent enough time with the Kannagara," Raging Eagle replied. "It's time that he chose his own path."

"Peter?" She smiled and sat down on the steps to the main hall. "What do you think Drahma is? How would you go about cultivating yourself?"

Health and Materialism

Raging Eagle stopped stretching and rolled forward to hear Peter speak; that made Peter nervous. He took a breath and began.

"Well, I suppose the first step is to create a proper foundation for training. You need a healthy mind and body. That means exercise and meditation. You can't act in accord with Drahma unless you are prepared.

"The Buddha prescribed the 'Middle Way.' When he first attempted to solve the problem of suffering, he turned to extreme asceticism, to rid himself of a body that would tie him to suffering.

But he found that there was a trap there. First of all, his body screamed for attention, so the practice became less about liberation and more about defeating the body. The second problem was that an ascetic was in danger of seeing his ability to withstand starvation and self-torture as an accomplishment in and of itself, losing sight of the Wheel.

"The Jain members of the Brotherhood would disagree," said Sataghni.

"I know. Perhaps their faith trains them to see things differently, so that isn't a problem for them. There's still the problem of going too far in the other direction." He dropped into the splits. "I used to obsess over the ability to do this. I thought I'd be able to kick high, like a movie star." He chuckled and swung his legs together. "But it doesn't have anything to do with what kind of a person I am. A lot of people are stuck on the idea that what they own or what they can do will make them happy, but it just leaves an appetite for more. It doesn't matter whether it's the ability to win a fight or the keys to a new car. They're all forms of materialism.

"I guess what I'm saying is that I'd try to find a middle ground, where I can take use my body as a vehicle for understanding without centering my attention on it. I want a clear window to look though out to the universe."

"So?" she asked. "How would you find that middle ground?"

BALANCE AND ACTION

"You have to understand that I came into the Brotherhood through aikido and karate. Those arts still speak to me," Peter said. "We have to remember the soft as well as the hard, the external as well as the internal.

"In aikido, we talk about yielding to force and acting in harmony with it. When someone attacks or offends me, there's no use simply resisting and pushing back. What will that prove? If I fail, then the struggle was useless, and if I succeed, it only means that I was stronger, not that I was right.

"On the other hand, we can't be passive beings. We've Awakened for a reason. We can't just go through life accepting every assault and accident. Eventually, the combined force of the things not remedied will destroy your life. So drawing an analogy from karate, when we act, we do it with kime, or focus, and complete commitment.

"The combined principle is like the Tao. We have to live our lives in harmony with the things around us. When we are faced with an aggressive or unpleasant intrusion upon our lives, we have to redirect it into something worthwhile or just let it pass us by. At the same time, when we feel an absence in our lives, if we're hungry, or being treated unfairly, we have to go and get food or justice, and we have to do it with our best, most committed efforts. Yield when you can, use the minimum effort you must, and make that effort the best effort possible. To do that, you have to look beyond preconceptions, so that you know *what* to do.

"When I was in my late teens, I traveled all over the world, looking for answers to the important questions in life. I talked to holy men in China and India, and I spent a month in Jerusalem, where I thought that walking down those streets would give me some sort of inspiration. There was nothing. I lost all of the money my parents left me, and I didn't know how I was going to support myself when I got back to Toronto.

DIVERGING VIEWPOINTS

The opinions expressed in this section represent the Akashic Brotherhood's party line — the views that a new Sidai might share with the Tradition before she deepens her sectarian ties and turns her basic beliefs into more complex metaphysical claims. However, each sect has its own take on the best way to cultivate the mind and body.

The **Shi-Ren** believe that the body needs stern discipline, as it houses a mind prone to laziness and avarice. Rather than taking the path of asceticism, the Legalists stick to strict exercise regimens complemented by intense study and mnemonic drills. Memory skills are highly valued as a way to efficiently organize one's material affairs and mental states. The Superior Person masters his own life first to master others later.

The **Li-Hai** prefer an eclectic approach, drawn from ancient and modern sources. Li-Hai rarely deny their bodies or minds new experiences, but they try to approach them with a sense of moderation. Guided, goal-oriented meditation is a popular practice, since many of the Mohists want immediate, utilitarian benefits and prefer not to dwell on abstract concepts when they could be out fighting for a cause. The Li-Hai train to serve to their communities as much as any grand cosmological concept.

Asceticism is the chief method of body control employed by the **Kannagara**, but not the only one. Repetitive Do training is used to still the mind. The monks also focus on ridding themselves of extraneous thoughts through silent meditation and mantras. A Phoenix Robe uses these time-tested techniques to obliterate the distractions that stand between her and Ascension.

Jnani practice self-denial before a major working, but use trance states, dancing and the discipline of wilderness survival as well. Japanese members of the sect especially favor running and mountain climbing as ways to both improve their health and trace the paths of the spirits. Most training is designed to sensitize the adherent to the mystical forces of the Tapestry, so that the self can identify with the whole.

Duty is the focus of **Vajrapani** training. The Akashayana's warriors use meditation and devotional chanting to remove their fear of death; this frees them from distracting fears and doubts when they serve the Brotherhood. Physical exercise is geared toward combat prowess. Sparring and "Iron Body" conditioning drills are common. As a vessel for the Sangha, a Vajrapani attains moral virtue and replaces egocentrism with commitment to the Brotherhood.

Finally, the **Wu Lung** gear their practices to their specialties. A Tiger School warrior trains for strategic expertise, while a pupil of the Dragon School learns the Confucian classics and the postures that align his personal Chi with the Mandate of Heaven. In all cases, the Dragon Wizards discipline themselves to be the very image of the Celestial Bureaucracy on Earth. See **Dragons of the East** for further details.

"When I got back, the first person who talked to me was Cheng Sa. He said 'You have the look of a man who's given up on everything.' He was right, and I told him so.

RELIGION AND THE AKASHIC BROTHERHOOD

The Akashic Brotherhood doesn't require a specific religious practice from its members, although some faiths require radical reinterpretation in order to jibe with Akashic belief. One myth outsiders have about the Akashayana is that all members are Buddhists, or followers of Eastern religions in general. While this does describe a large number of Brothers, many subscribe to other faiths without fear of censure from the Sangha.

For more information about Eastern religion and magic, see **Dragons of the East.**

Buddhism

Many, but not all, Akashic Brothers are Buddhists, and most incorporate Buddhist elements into their practice. The Akashic paradigm is compatible with the Buddhist path, and many Akashic Masters couch virtually all of their teachings in Buddhist terminology.

Impermanence, subjective karma and the importance of a Middle Way between self-indulgence and self-denial are a few of the beliefs shared by both Buddhist and Akashic thinkers. The religion has a dedicated following throughout every sect, although the Wu Lung generally only make token gestures of piety.

Jainism

Almost all Jains in the Brotherhood are Indian Kannagara ascetics. These jina never leave their communities and have ironclad vows of poverty and chastity. Many eschew clothing or even food as an unnecessary tie to the world. Practically a sect unto themselves, these Brothers are revered for their wisdom, and are often consulted by the rest of the Sangha to answer moral and ontological questions. Even a few Euthanatoi and Ecstatics, who respect these renunciates for their own reasons, come to them for advice.

Taoism

Most Chinese have Taoist beliefs. Most celebrate Taoist or Confucian rites at some point in their lives. Akashayana are no exception. Akashayana believe in the forces of Yin and Yang, and thus study philosophical Taoism as well.

Magic is well integrated into Taoist beliefs. Many Akashics use Taoist internal and external alchemy, as well as other magics borrowed from the faith. The Jnani and the Shi-Ren are the most likely to do this, although every Akashic is influenced by Taoist philosophy.

Confucianism

While Master K'ung's writings are more political philosophy than religion, later writers added mystical beliefs to the Confucian canon, such as the theory of the dual soul (Hun and P'o) and the goal of refining li (propriety and harmony) out of base Chi. Most Asians have at least a passing familiarity with Confucianism, and many household customs draw from this tradition.

Except for some of the Kannagara and all of the Li-Hai (who have inherited Mo-tzu's anti-Confucian beliefs), most Asian Akashayana respect Confucian mores. Even the Shi-Ren, who disagree with Master K'ung's assessment of people as basically noble, accept the Confucian model of the household and state.

Shinto

Nearly all Akashayana of Japanese descent practice Japan's national religion. Most practice Dual Shinto, which combines Buddhist and Shinto beliefs into a metaphysical system that equates the Buddhas with powerful kami. Furthermore, Japan's supernatural communities are notorious for acknowledging only Shinto rites. A rote that may serve to entice a spirit in Burma often has no effect in Japan, while a devout follower of Shinto might get results even without magic. Thus, even foreign Brothers who come to live in Japan learn the Kami Way.

Christianity

A faith not usually associated with the Brotherhood, Christianity has become the fastest growing religion in its ranks, even if it is a brand of Christianity considered heretical by more conservative worshippers. For a long time, the only Christians in the Akashayana were Nestorians who combined Buddhist and Christian beliefs, and the Roda d'Oro, who were heretical Catholics, followers of Santeria or had other leanings derived from their home cultures.

Now that ecumenical movements in the Buddhist community and radical theology have expressed many Akashic beliefs in Christian terms, the religion has grown more popular. Western Brothers now see little contradiction between their religious choices and their magical lives now that concepts such as the Holy Spirit are equated with the impermanent nature of reality and Jesus' teachings are compared to the Buddha's.

Other Faiths

Hinduism is the civic faith for many Akashic Brothers from India or Southeast Asia. While Hindu theories of the soul are usually left to the Euthanatos, rites of passage and social customs are commonly practiced by Hindu Akashics.

Sufi Islam is practiced by a small number of Jnani and Li-Hai, but the Ahl-i-Batin (even hidden as they are) have usually been quick to absorb the Awakened among these practitioners.

Bon, Tibet's original religion, is still practiced by Jnani shamans. Like the Sleeper religion, it has been deeply influenced by Vajrayana Buddhism, and vice versa. Bonpo (Bon shamans) usually draw the distinction to separate the ceremonies to honor specifically Tibetan spirits from those used to contact Bodhisattvas, Buddhas and Indian sages. Many Akashayana practice Mongolian, Okinawan, and other brands of shamanism. Usually, they integrate these practices with a more mainstream religion such as Buddhism.

"He said he was a friend of my sensei, and that he didn't speak to me before because I looked like I already knew what I was doing. I told him, 'Well, I sure don't feel that way anymore.'

"Then, he told me that I was ready to learn."

ILLUSION AND EMPTINESS

"Yes," Masako said, joining Sataghni on the steps. "It's important to stop clinging to fixed concepts.

"Every second is new and different, and any experience might lead you to Samadhi. When you rely on old mental habits, you are always looking through a filter based on your own prejudices. To

live in harmony with the universe, you have to see things as they are. In Japanese, it's called mushin, or no-mind. You quiet your consciousness so that what you perceive isn't mediated by your opinions, dreams and fears. Otherwise, you'll live in a dream, while you get farther and farther out of balance with the real world. That's what Samsara is, Peter: willful blindness to the truth."

"That's correct," said Raging Eagle, "the world isn't made of fixed concepts. Things, people and ideas all have cycles. When we hold on to one of these things, we are creating a fiction, such as 'I'll never be able to master this technique,' or 'This is the happiest moment of my life.' So you never learn the technique and every moment after the happiest makes you miserable."

The Sam Chien, Karma and Reincarnation

"What does that mean for the Akashayana then?" said Peter. "Does that mean our ideas are no better than anyone else's?"

"Everyone has their own path, even in the Sangha," said Raging Eagle.

"That's right." Masako flexed her knees and jumped up onto the top stair. "The Li-Hai emphasize that. If a time-honored tradition is useless, throw it out! The difference is, we *know* that our ways aren't fixed, immutable keys to the universe. The one constant is that there are none."

"That isn't all." Raging Eagle walked up to join her. "We understand karma. Other mages misuse the word. The Verbena say that the Threefold Return is a magical law, and Euthanatoi say that it's the price levied on a soul for its journey along the Wheel. We know the truth — karma comes from our own willful blindness.

"We inflict the fruits of karma on ourselves by refusing to face reality as it is. We have regrets and grudges, and they influence our actions until they harm us."

"Isn't there good karma?" Peter asked.

"Karma is neither good nor bad, but it binds us to Samsara by confirming our beliefs about the world. If we fix on feelings of anger, the world becomes an angry place. We argue and fight all of the time. Even diseases and accidents happen this way.

"Our own internal struggle, the Sam Chien, is driven by the very forces that turn the Wheel of Ages. Our desire for order is where we intersect with Heaven. Phoenix, Heaven's messenger, exists in our hearts as much as it fixes the stars in the sky. Tiger, wild, unformed Yang, gives us the same energy and vitality that animates the spirits of nature. Dragon helps us let go of our desires by breaking down the world and taking our bodies from us with death. Too often, we reject the Dragon and hold on to our sense of self even after the body has passed on. That is how reincarnation occurs.

"We aren't 'souls' passing from body to body. We arise because the Tapestry obeys the karma that we have set into the Great Wheel. If our passions were simple things, we will be embodied as an animal. If they were refined, we may arise as gods. However, they are still passions. Even the gods are chained to suffering, because they exchange their freedom for power. This is a lesson many mages would do well to learn.

"The most wretched beings are ghosts and demons. They have bound themselves to craving or avarice. It takes the lessons of Hell to teach them the path to liberation."

Akashic Names

Unusual names, such as "Raging Eagle," or "Fall Breeze," populate the annals of Akashic history. There are a number of reasons for this, aside from the fact that many Asian names sound unusual when translated into English.

Upon entering monastic life, an Akashic Brother receives a new name that represents either an element of Drahma that she tries to exemplify or a personal flaw she strives to overcome. Often, a name represents a quality which, while initially negative, can be turned into a vehicle for greater understanding.

Take Sataghni ("Battering Ram, Hundred Killer"). In the short term, this name would be given to a woman with an explosive temper. As she progressed, her flaw became an asset, as she directed her drive toward taking the most direct route to solve a problem and ending confrontations quickly and mercifully.

Many Akashics, especially Vajrapani and Shi-Ren, prefer to go by their family name. Some give themselves entirely new names in order to sublimate egotism with a task or attribute. For example, Cheng Sa's moniker, "The Avenging Woodcutter," was given to him to signify his role as a protector of the Brotherhood on their journey to the Grand Convocation, able to hew a new path through strange lands — or enemies' bodies.

However, Akashic names are *not* used to strengthen ties to the mystic self, in the way that Hermetic Shadow Names or True Names are. If anything, their intention is the opposite — to dissociate an Akashayana from the idea of a special intrinsic identity. At the Storyteller's option, Akashics might be especially resistant to magic involving the use of True Names, since the concept is so foreign to their beliefs. However, a list of the character's karmic stains, or her place in the hierarchy of the Sangha, her family and her social life, may fulfil the same purpose.

Drahma and Samadhi

"But, with time, even Hell can be transcended," said Masako. "Samadhi. It's more than the conditioned reflex that comes from mastering Do, and more than mushin. It is when your own nature becomes no different from the universe's. You can't reject the world; you have to look and listen for the movement of the Wheel and act in accord. You have to *become* the Wheel, and accept that you are no different from its turning. When that happens, you are free — beyond all karma because your actions can never violate its flow.

"It is Drahma, 'the law of transcending the enemy.' When we reject duality and illusion, the Wheel turns with us rather than against us. We know how to act and when, so miracles arise and we feel a sense of peace.

"Samadhi is what the Traditions call Ascension. It isn't magical prowess; it isn't being a messiah or a god. It's the final understanding that all magic, and all gods, are no different from you. You have to reject the idea that you are a separate being, apart from the cycle that binds all together.

"When we approach the truth of our original nature, there is a gap in the Wheel. In this timeless interval, we are freed from it, and visions arise about the truth of our existence. We call these Bardo. Most people are only familiar with the Bardo of death and rebirth, when every being is given a chance to attain Samadhi. When you Awaken, Bardo occurs in this very body. We are given the chance to escape the Wheel in a single lifetime, or to prepare ourselves for the next.

"It's a moral struggle as well as a metaphysical one. Violence is nothing but disharmony. Forces rise in opposition and cause the Wheel to shudder. Conventional social mores often lure us to Samsara by telling us that some people deserve to be attacked or oppressed. The Drahma Sutra tells that the cycle of the All should be ruled by balance, not disaster."

Peter frowned. *Then why did we fight the Euthanatos? What purpose did it serve if we were risking the integrity of the Wheel?*

From the Drahma Sutra

Oh Nobly born! Heed the Drahma; follow the Way, do not do evil! Nothing is hidden to the Wheel. All actions flow along the great body of Akashakarma like blood through the veins. Foolishness, selfishness, hatred — all pass through the heart of the world.

Learn the way of righteousness, the way of peace. Do not be fooled by Samsara. Look deeply, and see the eternal law.

Trican

The Wheel of life and death turns, always created, always preserved, always destroyed, spinning on the sacred axis of Meru. This is the Threefold Struggle, through which all beings in the Six Realms of existence arise, each part illusion, but Truth in the whole.

Know that your own original nature is no different from the entire Wheel, governed by the Threefold Struggle: that Tiger spawns the inner light, Phoenix disciplines it, and Dragon judges it, returning to the All. Listen to the Triple Law of your true being.

Vyahgradharma

Listen to the Law of the Tiger. Passion arises, activity arises, suffering arises. Do not indulge passion blindly! Let Drahma be your passion; desire peace. When the Tiger arises in you and around you, use it like a tempered blade, cutting away at illusion. Accept the passions that destroy hatred, grief and selfishness. Cultivate them with the Way. O Jnani, desire wisdom above ecstasy.

Garudadharma

Listen to the Law of the Phoenix. Heaven's mandates fix the stars in the sky and bless the mind with reason, but entangled in order, the sky cannot turn and the mind cannot grow. Enamored with fixed concepts, the self becomes blind to change. Entranced by its own cleverness, the mind contemplates evil, for how can a lie be defended except through violence? Order the All to understand it, but never ignore what arises outside of fixed concepts. O Kannagara, do not confuse ritual for truth.

Nagadharma

Listen to the Law of the Dragon. All things pass away. To deny this throws the self and the Wheel out of balance. But do not become obsessed with emptiness. The Dragon suffers; afraid of dissolution, its servants ignore the Wheel, destroying what is healthy, preserving what is sick, because they have turned Oblivion into what is instead of what passes. Do not take this path! To make your goal the Void is to descend into the Pit of Harmony, and turn the Wheel with the screams of demons. O Vajrapani, do not be tempted by destruction.

Haridharma

Listen, at last, to the Law of the Windhorse. Tiger is not a separate being. Phoenix is not a separate being. Dragon is not a separate being. All spring, divided, from dreams, Samsara. Remember the mind alone; it creates, preserves, destroys. Use the dream of the Wheel to oppose your own selfishness and find harmony with the All. Let Samsara teach the Drahma. Let it point the way to Akasha, beyond concepts, beyond all laws. Follower of the unknowable Way, abandon truth for Drahma.

"The Li-Hai believe in accomplishing this by getting rid of fixed ideas," said Raging Eagle, "but there are other ways. In the Kannagara, we divest ourselves of the things that cause egotism and selfish habits, such as wealth and sensual pleasure. We use an ordered path to realize our individual emptiness and our fundamental connection to the All. The Shi-Ren use the invisible ties of obligation and law to cement a relationship with something greater than themselves. The Jnani observe spirits and gods, and the forces of nature, and find the similarities between themselves and the universe, and the Vajrapani— "

"We serve the others," interrupted Sataghni. "We let the desires of the whole Brotherhood become our own, and hone our abilities until we are merely vehicles for the Drahma. That's the hardest path. Nu Ying knows; that's why he left."

Raging Eagle's eyes widened. "We each have our own path to tread. They say that there are 84,000 Dharma Doors, ways to become a Buddha, or an Akasha. I have my own karma to contend with, and so does Peter.

"We all have our sins, Sataghni."

STRANGE SUTRAS: EXTERNAL RELATIONS

They trained for five more hours: two hours of meditation and three more hours of combat practice. Peter was amazed by the diversity of Do. Sataghni's simple, brutal techniques were nothing like Masako's eclectic style, from which he recognized elements of boxing, Filipino stick fighting and Western gymnastics. Peter sparred with both of them. Fighting Sataghni was like attacking an iron bar. The black imprint of where her callused knuckles had bruised his arms caused Raging Eagle to stop the session and treat him with a herbal remedy. Masako would constantly surprise him, drawing him through false guards and lightly tapping him on points that would have been fatal had they been struck. Throughout, Raging Eagle simply practiced the same basic movements as Peter had at the beginning of the day.

They showered at the hotel. Peter felt alert and invigorated. *My Chi must have been replenished at the monastery*, he thought. He had only ever felt this way before in Lhasa, when the monks had raised flags around a stupa to welcome them.

Raging Eagle moved a table into the middle of the room and laid the two dossiers on top of it. Masako was back on her laptop. A staccato, modular whine started to issue forth, climbing in pitch until it passed beyond their ability to hear. Masako let out a long exhalation, pressing her hand forward in a mudra.

"It's the Heart Sutra. I've sped it up and altered it so it won't distract us, and should keep out unwanted listeners." Raging Eagle gave her a long look. "Listen," she said, "I wrote it mindfully. Just because a tool isn't six thousand years old doesn't mean it can't be used to touch a Dharma."

A NINE-SPOKED WHEEL: THE TRADITIONS

"All right," said Raging Eagle, pulling up a chair. "Here's some information about our targets.

"Mitchell Pratts. He's a Euthanatos Adept in his early forties. He's had several teachers, including Senex."

"The Old Man." Sataghni let out a long sigh. "So he's one of their problem children."

"In 1990, the Celestial Chorus asked the Euthanatos to provide a Knight of Radamanthys for the Saint Peter in Chains Chantry in Nome, Alaska. Pratts took the position and comported himself well, minimizing losses when the Technocracy took over their Node."

Peter spoke up. "Why didn't they ask us? I thought that was the sort of work we did for the Traditions."

"Ever since the Grand Convocation, we have disagreed about the direction of the Council. Many of us remember the Technocracy and the Chorus entering Asia hand in hand, and are reluctant to trust them again. On their side, they blame us for failing to support belief in God as a basis of unity for the Council. We believe that you must discipline yourself to serve anything greater, and not the other way around.

"In 1996, Hong Endi, an Ecstatic from the K'an Lu sect, came to Sigung Jou Shan with several visions about a 'tattooed man' coming to 'open a dusty bottle of poison, for us to drink and remember.' The Cult of Ecstasy has always helped us. While our paths have parted over time, we recognize the same primordial source, as the creation of the Ahl-i-Batin attests to.

"The next year, Pratts looked like this."

Raging Eagle passed a photo around. On it was an emaciated man with a shaved head, in loose, dark, clothing. Convoluted shapes marked his temples, ears, neck and the backs of his hands; some flowed into twisted Sanskrit characters. Peter recognized Yama — Death — over his jugular.

"We don't know how he received these marks. The next year, we sent a Vajrapani, Marie Rowlands, to watch him. By this time, he had joined a mixed-Tradition cabal, the Divine Stone. Pratts and a Dreamspeaker by the name of Rosa Valdez assumed joint leadership.

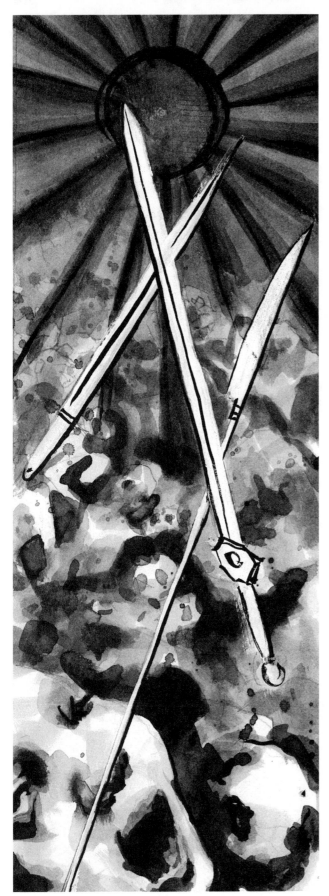

"Rowlands joined the cabal herself, but couldn't gain Valdez's confidence. That was our mistake. Some Brothers, such as the Jnani, have enjoyed a strong alliance with the Dreamspeakers. "

"The Mongols. We helped the samani." Peter's felt strange saying a word he had only heard in dreams.

"That's right. That's where the word 'shaman' comes from." Raging Eagle nodded to Peter. "However, like many of us, Rowlands believed that spirits were a reflection of the mind alone. This didn't endear her to Valdez. The Dreamspeakers have a very limited tolerance for that sort of thing.

"The Divine Stone volunteered to track down renegades from the Consanguinity of Eternal Joy that year. They sighted the House of Helekar, Voormas's fortress, in northern Poland. Accounts become confused at this point, but we do know that Rowlands and two others were killed in an ambush after being separated from the rest of the cabal. Pratts and Valdez came to New York with the head of Serge Payjak, a member of the Consanguinity.

"Valdez refused to speak about what had happened and retired a month later. Attempts to question Pratts were fruitless. He would only speak to other Euthanatoi. The Knights of Radamanthys made it clear that we were to mind our own business."

Peter noticed mudras flashing between Raging Eagle and the others again. *What is it this time? Damn! I'm the one who's most likely to get killed here. Jesus, why am I even…*

Raging Eagle made a final gesture and took Peter's gaze in his own. "Despite our past enmity, we have always been fascinated with the Euthanatos. Our beliefs are so similar and we have consistently supported the same policies for the Traditions. I think we must keep this in mind when we interrogate Ming Wong. She volunteered to follow him."

"What happened to her?" Peter returned Raging Eagle's gaze, his voice harsher than he wanted it to be.

"All we know is that Pratts left two acolytes dead in New York. Wong witnessed it, but rather than report to us, she followed him here.

"She's Vajrapani as well. She worked with a cabal in Liverpool. For a mage, her life was remarkably uneventful, so our information is sketchy. Few of us stay in the British Isles or Europe for any length of time. The magic there isn't attuned to our ways."

"You mean the mages," said Masako. "The Verbena think they have us all figured out. Every time I've met one I've been treated to a polemic about how I'm 'denying the flesh.' They tend to believe all of the stereotypes about us. After all, they're descended from the mighty Wyck! I find their emphasis on the physical amusing, considering that they take so little effort to master their own bodies.

"Anyway, it says here that her cabal were scientists," she said, flipping through a folder. "Hermetics, a Virtual Adept and a Son of Ether. Did she have any leanings in that direction?"

"Usually, Li-Hai such as yourself explore these things. According to their Deacon, Louis Eades *bani* Bonisagus, she was the odd one out. In any event, I doubt that he was too interested in her. Hermetics view power as an end in itself, while we consider it a side effect of greater understanding. They tend to exclude us when they're working on anything they consider to be truly important.

"The Virtual Adept and the Etherite expressed similar opinions, although the latter wanted to involve her in a number of experiments to 'prove' that Chi is Ether. Both Traditions are very materialistic, so our ties to them lack a common ground. My contact was too limited to discover much that would be of use.

"Let's get some sleep. We'll start looking for them tomorrow morning."

NIGHT

As Peter arranged a sleeping bag on the dingy floor or their room, Sataghni came to him, dropping into a half lotus and lightly touching his shoulder.

"Peter, I'm sorry that we've been keeping you in the dark about so many things."

He whispered, "Why have you? How can I be a part of the team when I don't even know what to do?"

"Gentle Mountain wanted it to be this way."

"What?"

"He knew that he would never survive crossing the Wall. He did it to plan this mission, and he asked Nu Ying to take you, without telling you why."

"Who am I, Sataghni? I saw you in the Record. You called me 'General.' What does it mean?"

"I can't tell you, Peter. Don't you know that it would harm your development?" She frowned, and spoke softly. "It takes maturity to encounter your past lives. I know this from personal experience."

"Dammit, I know that!" Peter pressed his hands together to release the tension. "All Raging Eagle has been doing is telling me about how I have to work harder, concentrate, own less, even keep my hands out of my damn pockets — there are all sorts of little things he's letting me know I'm doing wrong, every day."

She grabbed his shoulder, and Peter was, for a second, afraid of her fingers digging in, hurting him, but there was nothing. She looked into his eyes.

"Nu Ying's done more for the Brotherhood than anyone still living," she said. "He saved my life on the first day I met him, and has *never, ever* failed us, even when it cost him greatly. He still bears the scars for his service. You left Lhasa what, six days ago?"

"Yes."

"Don't you know? He carries a heavy karmic burden. The Akashic Record says that he will die if he leaves the Bodhimandala for more than a week.

"I'll tell you this. You're a vital part of this mission, so vital that he's willing to risk his life to bring you here. Your previous incarnation knew one of the targets."

"Pratts or Wong?" Peter forced the words out, to keep his composure.

"I can't tell you, Peter. Sleep now."

Peter couldn't.

MERU'S OTHER CHILDREN

The Akashic Brotherhood believes that all beings have their place on the Wheel, but that true wisdom is easiest to cultivate in a human body. Of the mass of humanity, those who reject materialism and follow Akashic teachings (whether or not they practice the same forms and rituals) have a chance to reach Samadhi in this life. This is related to the Akashic view of the Tellurian, which holds that there are six realms of existence, through which beings take on the role of humans, spirits, ghosts and a host of other forms.

The Technocracy

Materialism at its most extreme, the Technocracy is looked upon more with pity than hatred by the Brotherhood. Their vision, while it has produced some clever tools, is ultimately foolish, because they try to entice Sleepers into a world of trinkets and pleasures that will ultimately pass away. The Akashayana do have some respect for the achievements they have made in the field of psychology and physical performance, but Technocratic theory ultimately limits both.

Orphans

The Akashic Brotherhood is an ancient and powerful Tradition. As such, they don't like having their hard-won beliefs ripped off for the casual amusement of someone drawing mandalas in their parents' basement. While some of these mages show promise, most seem to see magic as simply another tool to satisfy their egos. Since Orphan magic relies on individual creativity, many Brothers see this as a more seductive trap, as one convinces himself that he can create magic without the Wheel. The worst of these are quickly punished by Samsara, but a few can be pawns for the Yama Kings.

Kuei-jin and Other Vampires

The Akashayana hold little love for the undead. From the slopes of Kailas to the halls of the Shaolin Temple, the Brotherhood and the Kuei-jin have fought over dragon nests, territory and ideology. Finally, ancient legends accuse the Kuei-jin of causing the destruction of Meru. Although it isn't important to most Akashics, a few of the oldest members of the Brotherhood see the karmic burden from that event as a sign that the Demon People are unclean things that are dangerous just to be around.

At the same time, the Sangha recognizes the right of these beings to seek salvation. Akashic metaphysics see the Kuei-jin as beings who have fallen from the realm of the asuras, the lower Heaven of Celestial demons and godlings. An Akashic might help an earnest vampire who searches for inner peace and harmony, provided that she exercises compassion for others.

The Brotherhood has very little experience with the West's vampires. Although the Shi-Ren have sometimes found their businesses subverted by mysterious, blood-drinking adversaries, their Mind Arts usually set things to right. Westerner Brothers are only slightly more interested in the western undead. Akashics are not morbid people.

Hengeyokai — The Shapeshifters

Guardians of the Yang Realm, the Hengeyokai are respected but rarely seen by Akashic Brothers. They fulfil their mandate perfectly. Rather than searching for wisdom, they protect the natural world from being defiled. Akashayana don't typically raid the dragon nests of Hengeyokai, but arguments over abandoned or newly discovered dragon nests do occur. In such cases, both parties negotiate an arrangement where they have rotating access to the site — so they can promptly ignore one another for the duration of the bargain.

The one exception to this is the Stargazers. These werewolves are the only shapeshifters who seem to understand Drahma. Encounters with the Stargazers are usually brief but unusually open and friendly considering their normally insular natures. The Stone Sutra claims that the Brotherhood shared their secrets with the Stargazers in exchange for being spared some mysterious disaster; in return, all Brothers avoid angering them, and assist them when they can.

Ghosts

The Akashayana rarely contact the denizens of the Yin Realm. Only the Wu Lung speak to the ancestors on a regular basis. Of late, they have been disturbed by what they're hearing.

Akashics do not believe that ghosts are emanations of a living soul. Instead, a ghost is an entirely new incarnation, ruled by craving for its former life. Thus, even a ghost has a place on the Great Wheel. Although their salvation comes from passing through their existence as quickly as possible, and seeking a good human birth, it should never be hastened except through compassionate advice. For this reason, Akashic Brothers rarely practice necromancy.

Hsien and Changelings

To Akashics, the hsien are gods in exile. Few would take an encounter with one trivially, and most Akashayana and all Wu Lung work to keep the traditions that please these beings, just as most of them did before Awakening. While the hsien are revered as living signs of Heaven's will, they are seen as ultimately limited. After all, a god cannot reach Samadhi. Still, hsien are the living embodiment of the Wheel's design; even observing them can be a rewarding, if dangerous experience. hsien alchemy, based on Heaven's mandate, is as powerful as the Dharmas themselves.

Western Changelings, on the other hand, are creatures of illusion and deception. While the Technocracy promotes Samsara by fixing the world in static forms, these beings do the opposite, wrapping up the world in selfish fancy. While a few

do so to point to a greater truth, whimsy and avarice rule the majority. In either case, Maya's children are best avoided; a tranquil Brother is unlikely to attract their attention anyway.

Imbued Hunters

Although only a few younger Akashayana, mostly Shi-Ren, realize that these people exist, resistance to Mind magic makes any Brother defensive and curious. Those few who have gathered more information have been surprised to find that the Imbued appear in every corner of the world, as if overnight, and that they don't appear to gain their powers after any sort of training or act of Awakening. In a way, a hunter is a walking koan, a question without any rational answer.

Other Beings

Many Asian Brothers believe that all other supernatural beings belong to the Celestial Bureaucracy, a divine order that delineates every being's duty in the Great Wheel. The Awakened are the exception, for they have the ability to change that structure, but few would do so without an excellent reason.

The Jnani often work with spirits; these Akashics treat the spirits either as officials of Heaven or as external reflections of their own internal qualities. When used clumsily, many spirits find the latter method demeaning.

On the other hand, Akashayana also believe that many spirits, including demons, were human in other lives or have the potential to become human in their next life. This often inspires Akashics to look at spirits as beings in need of salvation in their own right, instead of being merely representatives of greater cosmological forces. Spirits who are swayed by this (either through being forcefully bound or occasionally genuinely converted) become known as Dharma Protectors, and guard Bodhimandalas.

Finally, the Akashic Brotherhood is fascinated by the beings Westerners call mummies. While the Brotherhood knows nothing of the Egyptian Spell of Life or its recipients, Brothers tell tales of beings who have used Taoist alchemy to turn themselves into true immortals. While the Euthanatos study them for their immunity to the vicissitudes of the Wheel, Akashayana are more interested in the mental and physical discipline that allows a human being to become an immortal.

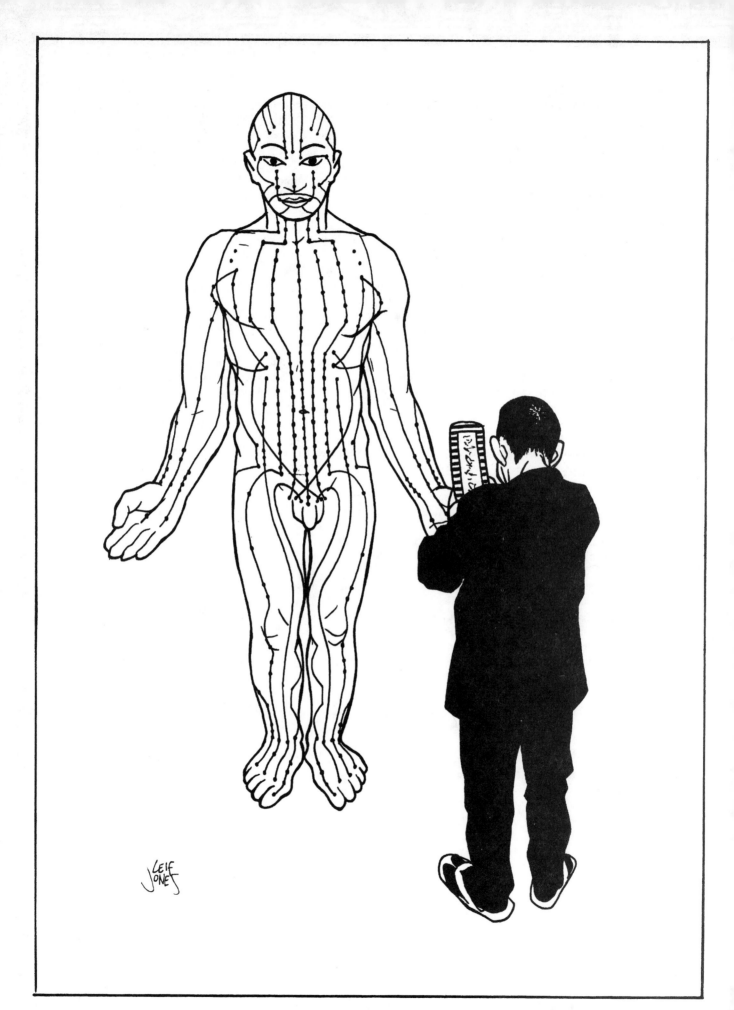

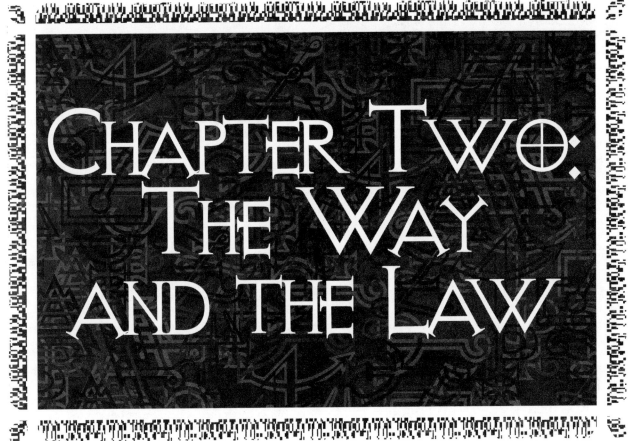

Chapter Two: The Way and the Law

All in the world recognizes beautiful as beautiful.
Herein lies ugliness.
— The Tao Te Ching

Smoke Tiger: The Hidden Corpse

I find the third body at the foot of the Sathorn Bridge, a woman stuffed between a Dumpster and a concrete pillar. A crowd gathers; tourists, laden with bags and phrase books, point at the body's pale hands. They take pictures as the police approach on scooters, pushing through under the glare of camera flashes.

"Out of the way, miss," says one, in thickly accented English. They repeat it in French and Thai.

"This one's diseased." I stand still. "You have to tell these people to leave." My hand makes the mudras for trust and peace, and I growl out a hard exhalation to shape the Chi around me.

One of the cops starts shouting at the crowd. The other's eyes open wide, and his head falls slack. His hands shake, rapping against the handlebars of his bike.

"Yes, miss," he says in a distracted tone. "Will there be anything else?"

"No. Nothing occurred here. Do you understand? You'll get on your bike and leave. Now."

The officers leave and I kneel down to her. The body is still warm. Ranjit must be only a few blocks away.

A rumbling in the sky and the rain falls again. I'm so tired, as if my spirit is bleeding. My feet stagger forward of their own accord, building into a run by the time I hit the next block.

You're a warrior, Lou Fu. Not a monk or a mystic or a master of anything but your duty. When you have a purpose, Drahma runs through you and around you. You are more than yourself. Tiger guides my steps through the brilliance of Indra's Net. There are a thousand secret ways between places, and he knows them all.

The wind and water in my hair, I turn an invisible corner, and there he is. There's a bone in his hand.

We run.

Peter: Discipline and Obedience

"Focus, Peter. Do as I've taught you."

Raging Eagle stood straight and still. He watched while Peter practiced the slow movements of the kata. With his hands and feet, he described the Lokhadhatu, the world as it unfolds from Meru. Every finger traced the primordial flow of Akashakarma. Ming Wong's face, memorized from a photograph, hovered like a distant star, the streams of power reaching for her. In an instant, an image burned into his mind: the woman, bloody-handed, running, a bridge in the background.

Peter was pale. Wheezing breaths issued from his trembling chest. "She's—"

"Yes, I know. Let's go. You all know your jobs." Raging Eagle took a deep breath and went out to the car.

Masako adjusted the hilt of her wakizashi in a PVC coat and threw it on. Sataghni opened a gym bag. In quick, economical movements, metal and plastic pieces snapped together under her fingers.

Peter turned to her, an astonished look on his face: "Is that a *gun?*"

"You're very observant," she replied, never looking up.

"It isn't our way! It isn't Do!"

"It isn't *your* way. I'm a soldier for the Sangha, Peter, not a philosopher. My way means getting the job done so we can go home and work off our karma in peace."

"We were never here to apprehend them, were we?" he said. "They're supposed to die."

"Are you so surprised?" She was on her feet now, pushing the last few bullets into the magazine in a steady rhythm. "The Kannagara can afford to be pacifists, because people like us do terrible things, things that could damn us for a hundred lifetimes. The Traditions scowl at us for what they see as hypocrisy and warmongering, but they never would have existed if it weren't for our work and our sacrifices.

"Know your place, Peter. You're Sidai. If you don't toe the line now, I can't be responsible for what happens."

AKASHIC ORGANIZATION AND TRAINING

Contrary to popular assumption, the Akashayana *does* have a hierarchy beyond the simple student-master relationship. Unlike other Traditions, it isn't enforced with vows or initiation rituals, but Brothers are expected to live and work together in harmony. Anything else is seen as a sign of immaturity. Outside of the Li-Hai, a rebellious Brother can expect to be shunned and refused magical and martial instruction.

RECRUITMENT AND APPRENTICESHIP

Apprentices, or Sidai, are typically selected from institutions that the Akashayana has influenced for millennia. Yoga ashrams, martial arts schools, monasteries and secret societies are all recruiting grounds from which to select students. In the case of physical disciplines, the Brotherhood runs many traditional schools, where the martial arts they teach relay watered down versions of Do techniques. The Akashayana using this principle developed several well-known forms of kung fu, jujutsu and other arts. Called "gate arts," they attract students who are tulku (Brothers in previous incarnations), and weed out impatient and undisciplined students.

After being selected by their masters for "special training," and being told the nature of the Brotherhood, a Sidai typically spends some time in a Kannagara monastic community. Here they receive new names and learn the history and traditions of the Brotherhood. From then on, a student is expected to find the sect that appeals to her in a noncoercive, serene environment.

At least, that's the way it's supposed to be. In reality, a Sidai's first teacher has a powerful influence on the sect the student will select. For example, Vajrapani and Shi-Ren families rarely have members who spend their productive lives as monks, shamans or rebels. Still, monastic life allows the student to absorb the roots of Akashic teachings.

After this period of training, which may last for a few months to several years (or forever, in the case of the Kannagara), the student is reassigned to her first teacher's Bodhimandala. A teacher from her sect (her first teacher, if possible) supervises her training.

Each teacher has only one student. The Akashic way is too intensive to be taught in any other fashion.

At this stage, some Akashayana take to the road as itinerant warriors and scholars. Called Ryugakusei ("exchange students") or Shugyosha ("student warriors"), these Brothers serve in multi-Tradition cabals, gather intelligence and maintain teaching standards throughout Bodhimandalas by competing with their residents. These sparring matches began as lethal contests between medieval Japanese Vajrapani. Since then, the custom has softened. Now, many Jnani and Li-Hai also take the opportunity to test their skills in a relatively safe fashion.

OLDER BROTHERS

In the past, Masters trained all Sidai. Now that mages this skilled are few and far between, a "master" is more often a Sihing, an "older Brother" who guides the Sidai's magic and Do training. In Tradition nomenclature, Sihing (called Shidoshi by Japanese Brothers) are Adepts of one Sphere and at least Disciples of Mind. A Sihing should also be a competent Tao-shih (have attained the fourth level of one of Do's limbs) and must possess unquestionable dedication and moral character. These Brothers are responsible for the day to day business of a Bodhimandala, from making sure that a visiting Kannagara monk receives a vegetarian lunch to coordinating the building's defenses.

Not every Sihing relishes the added responsibilities that come with the title. Many remain Sidai, although this is considered irresponsible behavior when a Bodhimandala is short on teachers and caretakers. A Vajrapani has the greatest freedom in this regard, since her martial duties often preclude the stability that a Sihing's life requires.

MASTERS

While the Akashayana discourage ranking based on power, there must be a minimum level of magical competence required to guide others along the path of Drahma, which is why Sihing rank has such stringent standards. This is even truer for a Sifu, one of the Tradition's Masters. Aside from the requisite magical prowess, Sifu are only recognized after an opening in the Kannagara appears due to death or retirement (this makes recognition particularly hard to attain in Kannagara monasteries!). A Bodhimandala typically supports no more than one Sifu of each sect. In the present day, having more than one Sifu at all is almost unheard of.

His predecessor usually designates a new Sifu ahead of time. When there is no one to select a new Sifu, the entire Bodhimandala decides on an interim leader and contacts the Sangha for advice. When there are multiple candidates, a test is devised to select the most able of them. They may be asked to compose poetry about the principles of Drahma, hold a debate, or face off in nonlethal combat.

GRANDFATHER-SAGES

Rarely seen, the Sigung are the Tradition's Archmasters. Most vanished in the Avatar Storm, but a few relay messages from time to time. These living incarnations of the Dharmas are said to watch over the Tradition from afar, to ensure that all Brothers keep to the path of Drahma. Sigung are revered for their knowledge, but most Brothers come to understand that, as powerful as a Sigung is, he will never reach Samadhi.

The only Sigung known to have regular contact with Earth is the sinister Yu Lung. The Jade Dragon attracts ambitious students who long for power instead of wisdom. The luckiest die under his tutelage. The survivors become fearsome, tragic foes for the rest of the Brotherhood.

BODHISATTVAS

Although the Wan Kuei have defiled the term, the Akashayana know who the true Bodhisattvas are. When a Brother forgoes Samadhi out of compassion for the suffering beings of the world, she is transformed into a living manifestation of enlightenment itself. Legends speak of such beings intervening in the Akashayana's darkest hours, dictating the Drahma Sutra and appearing to lead the worthy to Ascension.

While the Akashi, who have completed the journey of Dharma and have become one with the Wheel, are loved and admired, Bodhisattvas receive special attention because they have forsaken the ultimate enlightenment of an Akasha to guide others along the path. Veneration of the Bodhisattvas is thus an important part of Akashic tradition. Brothers sometimes believe that figures such as the Buddha and the Eight Immortals of Taoism are the earthly masks of these beings. It is also believed that they appear in disguise during Bardo states to gently guide Brothers to greater understanding and that they even come to Earth to set key events in motion for global salvation.

PETER REMEMBERS

The car was a rental. Peter's nose wrinkled at the sharp disinfectant smell of the upholstery as he got in the back seat. He held the door open for Sataghni but she shook her head, slung her bag over her shoulder and walked across the street. From the other side, she exchanged a nod and a mudra with Raging Eagle, who sat in the front, curled up in a seat too small for him.

Masako drove. The rain came down minutes later, hammering at the windshield. Raging Eagle turned to him.

"Peter, do you remember the plan?"

"Yes, Sifu. After we're done here tonight, we take separate routes back to the monastery. We'll meet our Shi-Ren contact,

Chan Chin-Fu, and Yen Ping of the Wu Lung. Chan will procure Visas for us over the next two weeks and Yen will alter our features. I'll take the first flight out with Yen, and you two will go with Chan three days later."

"Good. You see? We work together. Everyone has their place in the body of the Sangha." He flashed a weak smile. Peter could see Raging Eagle's neck muscles tensing, like cords ready to snap.

He's afraid of dying. It's been seven days. He thinks he's going to die. Peter suddenly felt breathless, disoriented. He whispered a mantra in his mind to make it stop. The world was folding in, circling him.

"Sure," said Masako. "We're a great human pyramid dedicated to lifting the Kannagara closer to Heaven."

Raging Eagle turned to answer her, and suddenly Peter was there, behind the eyes swinging to face her.

"Don't play the Li-Hai now." He felt Raging Eagle's lips move. "Not so close to the end." There was fear there. Peter followed the jagged line of it, like the shape of moonlight on the water.

And now he was floating on it, flying through intricate patterns. *I'm in his mind. I'm seeing his thoughts.* Faster and faster, through the smooth efficient lines of his trained soul, twitching at the muscle memories burned into his being by Do. The sound of Babel: English, Chinese, Sanskrit, ancient tongues that collided in a storm of whispers. And always fear, buffering his thoughts like a Tibetan breeze.

Ahead, a pale star, the gray light of the Bardo Thodol beckoned. He rushed to the light of his original nature, his Bodhicitta. It was a door.

In the field of blood and broken spears beyond it, Peter discovered who he was.

The Faces of Drahma: Akashic Sects and Factions

The Akashic stereotype — martial artists and bald monks — conceals a large and diverse Tradition. In the past, it was thought that the Akashayana was homogenous and small, as warriors and leaders (Vajrapani and Kannagara) made up the bulk of the Brotherhood's contact with outsiders. Many Akashics remained relatively uninvolved in the Ascension War as it was being fought in the West. Screaming raids on Technocratic Constructs seemed foolish compared to subtle economic tactics of the Golden Dragons.

Now that the Ascension War has turned into the same shadowy affair that most Akashayana have practiced all along, the other Traditions have had a chance to discover that their small collection of humble allies was neither so small nor so humble as they had thought. With the largest single base of Sleepers to draw upon in the world, only the rigorous discipline required to join has kept Brotherhood membership so low compared to the populations they recruit from.

Pai and Jati

In some ways, the Brotherhood is an Eastern counterpart to the Order of Hermes; both are a collection of diverse groups that function according to a shared set of beliefs. However, the similarity ends with the Akashayana's basic cohesiveness, which springs from the legend of Meru and expresses itself in the organization of its sects.

The jati ("birth groups") are sects that trace their ancestry directly to the Garuda Valley and Meru. Often thought of as castes, jati tend to attract the same Brothers for several incarnations. It is possible to change jat, but isn't done often, as the familiarity a Brother feels when she returns to her old sect is a powerful lure. The three jati are the Kannagara, Jnani and Vajrapani. Each has a specific set of obligations to the others and to the Brotherhood as a whole.

Pai ("schools"), on the other hand, are sects that do not originate with the Meru'ai. The Shi-Ren, Li-Hai and Wu Lung have joined the Brotherhood or gained Akashic converts, and are thus accepted into the fold. Pai are required to accept the Stone Sutra as the revealed truth of the Bodhisattvas and follow the Drahma, but they don't enter into the same interdependent relationship as the jati.

Within each sect, factions develop based on nationality and varied practices. Not all Akashayana are members of a specific faction, and all acknowledge that a faction is part of a larger jat or pai. That is the greatest difference between the Brotherhood and its fellow Traditions. All members, regardless of practice, see themselves as part of a unified whole, rather than a mishmash collection of houses or cults.

Leadership and Internal Politics

In theory, the Kannagara are the undisputed leaders of the Akashayana Sangha. The Stone Sutra says that "above even world-conquering rulers is an ascetic who gives himself over to the Akasha." Kannagara leadership is meant to keep the Brotherhood from becoming self-serving and straying from its principles.

In truth, the Kannagara is often accused of being ignorant of the facts of 21st-century life. Adamant in this view are the Shi-Ren, who have served as the Sangha's advocate and purse for two millennia. Many Vajrapani, who fight and die to keep Kannagara retreats intact, have begun to share this view, although they are currently the exception rather than the rule. The Wu Lung, humiliated by its current association with the Brotherhood, has consistently sided with the Shi-Ren. With similar goals and viewpoints, they are natural allies.

The Li-Hai are content to oppose the monks' decisions rather than the structure itself. They would fight a Shi-Ren or Wu Lung takeover more strenuously than they ever would a Kannagara dictate. Only the Jnani are uniformly loyal to the Kannagara. The two have shared a symbiotic relationship in every culture the Brotherhood has touched. The wandering hermit and cloistered ascetic each explore physical and mystical territory that the other misses.

Thus, the Akashayana must resolve a paradox in their policies. While the Kannagara block modernization, to reject their guidance would cripple the ethical backbone of the Sangha. Though they interfere with the Brotherhood's progress, the Phoenix Robes keep the Brothers from straying from the path of Drahma.

Administration and Cultural Issues

The Akashayana's loose structure accepts a large amount of cultural and personal differences. For more traditional Brothers, the jat and pai system is a little *too* loose. These Akashayana form cabals based on a common cultural practice, function or mystical specialty. The Karmachakra exists because *someone* needs to keep track of the incarnations of Brothers. However, this doesn't prevent the handful of Karmachakra that exist at any given time from being involved with the Shaolin. Larger organizations such as the Banners of the Ebon Dragon and the Ping Fa Academy claim all Brothers as members. These organizations consist of a majority of Sleepers directed by a core cabal. A Brother who makes the correct mudra at a Heilong Athletic Association school can get a meal or a place to crash, but is unlikely to meet the ten or so full-time Ebon Dragons that serve at any given period.

A Brother can belong to several groups or drift from group to group based on her personal inclinations. Exceptions exist: the Kaizankai insists on Japanese ancestry, and the Wu Shan consider all Jnani who safeguard lu ledgers to be members, no matter what else they do with their lives.

SHI-REN

Names: Benevolent Aristocrats, Jade Robes, Legalists, Eunuchs (derogatory)

History: The first Shi-Ren were of the Western Chou nobility. During the Warring States Period, these princes lost power and influence, as warlords and petty nobles refused to recognize a law greater than military power or feudal propriety. Many embraced the budding philosophy of Legalism — since human nature is essentially evil, it must be controlled with severe, strictly delineated punishments and sparse rewards. These despots brought order to their lands, making them attractive patrons for mystics, philosophers and proto-scientists.

While the Wu Lung and Dalou'laoshi provided some of these lords with strategists and advisors, the Akashayana took a different path. They challenged their masters to look for a greater meaning in the laws they enforced and the punishments they meted out. Explaining the Drahma in Legalistic terms, the Brotherhood soon attracted a small alliance of older nobles who were tired of the incessant strife caused by their contemporaries' ambitions.

The Shi-Ren schemed in earnest. They supported Buddhist monasteries for their brethren and patronized martial artists and mystics. However, the Wu Lung's pervasive influence of the Han and Tang dynasties provided few opportunities for them. As their influence waned in the 7th century, many immigrated to Japan, insinuating themselves into the local nobility.

After the Mongols invaded China in the 13th century, the Shi-Ren were devastated, as hereditary lands were placed into the hands of Confucian administrators. They also drew the enmity of Genghis Khan's shamans, as the corrupt Yu Lung sowed the invaders' ranks with plague.

In desperation, many of the Benevolent Aristocrats joined the Dragon Wizards and Dalou'laoshi. In 1325, a few of these attended the Convention of the White Tower. In less than a century, they were absorbed into the Stone People. The rest supported secret societies, dedicated to overthrowing the conquerors. The protests of the rest of the Sangha, who by and large enjoyed good relations with the Mongols, were ignored, as the Shi-Ren supported bandits and rebels who were willing to fight the Mongol-imposed bureaucracy.

Their ambition was finally rewarded in 1368, when the Shi-Ren-backed Ming emperor took the throne. The entire Brotherhood enjoyed a brief period of unparalleled peace and prestige in Chinese society. Unfortunately, the Ming dynasty was rotten on the inside; the Shi-Ren, proud of their achievements, ignored or covered up Wu Lung subversion and the presence of corrupt officials. Such willful ignorance afflicted the Akashayana as a whole, until the illusion of a cohesive Middle Kingdom blinded them to the rising threat of invasion and defeat.

In Japan, the Shi-Ren turned from being supporters of an ineffectual emperor into battle-hardened feudal lords. Shi-Ren daimyo encouraged the transition from feudal warfare to a unified nation by supporting Neo-Confucian initiatives and the ethos of bunbu ichi — "pen and sword in accord."

The rise of the Qing dynasty forced the last of the Shi-Ren nobility from power. As the Shaolin Temple burned, the Legalists returned to the tactics that they had used against the Mongols. Hundreds of secret societies soon fell under the coordinated influence of the Golden Dragons, an ambitious organization that united the interests of Shi-Ren throughout Asia. Their efforts were so successful that they became the political face of the Akashayana, with a reach extending from the halls of Doissetep to Asia's economy. Under the leadership of the venerable Kunio Ashida, the Golden Dragons dedicated themselves to thwarting Technocratic influence, especially that of the Syndicate.

When Asian currencies and businesses faltered in the late 1990s, Shi-Ren-backed institutions were among the hardest hit. Ashida's demise in the fall of Doissetep crippled the Shi-Ren's legitimate power base. While the Legalists are beginning to recover, they have concentrated more of their activities on criminal acts such as smuggling and the drug trade. Although they finance the whole Brotherhood, the Shi-Ren have become more and more secretive about the origins of their wealth. Many Brothers worry that power has become an end, rather than a means, for the Jade Robes.

Philosophy: The Shi-Ren combine Legalism with Akashic mysticism. The material world is an illusion that masks the ties of obligation and desire that all beings share. Attuned to these invisible connections, the Superior Person uses reward and punishment as tools to influence the turn of the Wheel. The karma of earthly beings forces them to accept such influence while spirits and gods in the Celestial Bureaucracy must obey the Mandate of Heaven, which, like all contracts, has its loopholes and penalties. Legalist doctrine holds that all beings are essentially selfish and can be influenced by actions that work upon their desires.

Style: Shi-Ren prefer long rituals, the use of writing, and the exercise of law and tradition. A Legalist must also exercise social discipline; close friends and excessive generosity impair the karmic ties that put the world at her mercy. Contracts, oaths, courts of law and debts provide foci by which a Jade Robe can influence the world. Shi-Ren magic is subtle — victims of their Mind Arts often excuse their actions as stipulated by the very oath or agreement that was used to bind them. Photographs and emblems of authority can serve as a way to sense and change the forces associated with them. The Shi-Ren approach to Do emphasizes self-empowerment and psychological advantage.

Initiation: The Shi-Ren train members of their own family when they can. The ethic of reward and punishment permeates the lives of children destined for the Benevolent Aristocracy. Outside of blood relations, business figures, dictators and politicians are carefully watched for potential. Successful candidates are offered membership in a secret society that can be anything from a college fraternity to a tong. If the prospect is loyal and takes to Shi-Ren methods, then she is accepted. All others have their memories altered or fall prey to "accidents" that ensure that they never share what they've seen.

Organization: Shi-Ren are strictly hierarchical. Nothing else is worth having, because nothing else guarantees that a Legalist's efforts will be rewarded. A Jade Robe's prestige among his peers is as important as his relationship to the rest of the Brotherhood.

The Han Fei Tzu Academy serves as the Shi-Ren's administrative arm. Members coordinate the pai's dealings with the rest of the Brotherhood. The Academy also attracts students from all over the world through front companies that teach "personal power through the ancient Chinese principles of leadership." The cabal's members come from all nationalities and walks of life, but they are uniformly clever and ambitious. The Han Fei Tzu Academy acts as a think tank for Akashic initiatives and a source of tutelage. Members are encouraged to use their skills for the Brotherhood first, themselves second. Those Brothers who hope to become influential Shi-Ren often attend the Academy just after finishing their initial stint with the Kannagara.

Membership is not exclusive. Kaizankai and Golden Dragons study and teach at the Academy regularly. In fact, the organization serves as an informal "sparring ground," where Shi-Ren can confound each other with games of influence and debates.

The Kaizankai are a cabal of Japanese Shi-Ren who trace their ancestry to the 7th-century court of the Emperor Shotoku. In one form or another, the Kaizankai have acted as landed nobles, samurai overlords and wealthy monks. The Meiji Restoration was a disaster for them, but the reinvention of Japan as an economic power has allowed them to move into business and politics. Many of their practices have been spun to the press as "corruption" by the Zaibatsu, but as patriots, the Kaizankai are loathe to oppose the Elemental Dragons for fear of damaging the prosperity that their rivals helped create. The Kaizankai do not accept non-Japanese members.

Finally, the Gam Lung, or Golden Dragons, is a secret society that was founded by a Vajrapani refugee from Shaolin and a Japanese Shi-Ren. The group had one mission: to use any means necessary to crush the Akashayana's enemies. The two Akashics quickly established a network of secret societies throughout Asia, using them as a foundation to build an empire that encompassed legitimate businesses and the underworld. During World War Two, they resisted the infighting that plagued the Brotherhood, coordinating the black market and gaining enough capital to create a business empire that prospered into the late 90s. When Kunio Ashida began to direct their efforts against the Syndicate and Pentex, economic and magical disaster struck. Although this effort crippled their legitimate holdings, they remain one of the strongest criminal conspiracies in Asia, manipulating Triads, Yakuza gumi and other groups. What purpose the conspiracy is serving after the Ascension War's end remains to be seen.

The Gam Lung accept members outside the Shi-Ren and the Akashic Brotherhood. For more information, see **Dragons of the East.**

LEIF JONES

Li-Hai

Names: Mohists, Empty Vessels, the Mongrel Dharma (an insult that many Li-Hai find flattering)

History: Mo-tzu was a student of Confucius, but broke with Master K'ung's teachings by refusing to accept the necessity of tradition and the concept of graduated love. Master Mo was an ardent pacifist but was versed in the arts of war. He led his disciples to defend small states that were threatened by larger, more aggressive rivals and railed against customs that asserted that some lives were worth more than others in the eyes of Heaven.

Weary from the Himalayan War, many Akashics embraced Mo-tzu's teachings as a way to live virtuous lives while making a difference to the common people. While the Kannagara courted the Shi-Ren, they refused to recognize Mohist Brothers as a distinct sect. Iconoclasm and pacifism didn't sit well with the Legalists, upon whom the Akashayana pinned its hopes for survival in China.

In response, Mohist Akashics gathered outside of the Kannagara stronghold of Omei Shan. During the "108 Burning Days," the Mohists went without food or water, burning one copy of the Stone Sutra a day. Finally, the Kannagara opened the gates and recognized Mohism as a legitimate door to the Drahma.

A day later, their leader Te Kwan decried the Kannagara's hidebound traditionalism. Aghast, several Vajrapani challenged him to single combat. Te Kwan laughed and claimed that this was yet more proof of their "dedication to Samsara." The Phoenix Robes might have reconsidered their decision then and there, had not a surprise attack by the Dalou'laoshi and allied soldiers been thwarted by Te Kwan's band of tired, outnumbered followers. When over half of the first Li-Hai died in battle, the very Vajrapani who threatened Te Kwan became his students.

With their utilitarian mores, the Li-Hai didn't just limit themselves to Mohist teachings. With the ideals of Master Mo in mind, the Li-Hai studied teachings from Tibet, India and even the West, where trickles of Greek and Roman philosophy reached across the Silk Road to influence their practices. The Li-Hai postulated the existence of a fourth Celestial Minister to complement Tiger, Dragon and Phoenix. The Lung-ta, or Windhorse, represented Drahma as it manifests in Samsara, symbolizing the Li-Hai belief that enlightenment can be found even in the most profane things.

When the Mongols invaded most of Asia, the Li-Hai made use of the Golden Horde's far-flung territory to explore the world. Christian and Muslim beliefs were melded with Drahma, and travelers renewed contact with the elusive Ahl-i-Batin. As a result of these experiences, the Li-Hai strongly supported Akashic participation in the Grand Convocation. At that event, the Akashayana encountered Westerners who used physical discipline as a focus for their arts. The Li-Hai accepted them into the fold, and in return, sent the first Walkers to explore the West and share ideas with the Council of Nine.

During the Boxer Rebellion, the Li-Hai saw brutal examples of the West's technology at work. The Empty Vessels adapted Taoist alchemy and rediscovered the old theories of the Dalou'laoshi. They pioneered the first attempts to merge Akashic methods with scientific principles. As industrialization swept through Asia, they attempted to find ways in which machines could be used to liberate as well as oppress. In Japan, the Meiji Restoration and the development of judo, a martial art adapted to Western principles, encouraged them to experiment with new approaches to Do. In the political sphere, many accepted Communist theories as a way to adapt to a technological world.

However, the Li-Hai never predicted the results of Mao's victory. Because they hoped that a peaceful, egalitarian society would rise out of the chaos of revolution, they were alarmed to watch the old tyranny reassert itself with red stars instead of golden dragons. The sect's rebellious pacifism made it an easy target for the Red Guard. Supporters of the Mohists vanished or were exiled in disgrace. From time to time, the Technocracy contributed to their decline, but for the most part, the Sleepers were willing to do the job themselves.

Many Li-Hai joined with pro-Democracy protestors in Tiananmen Square. When the Red Army massacred the demonstrators, it touched off a new wave of fervor throughout the sect. The Mohists are returning to their old ways, bolstering just regimes against aggression and backing revolutions against the unjust. With the Ascension War's end, little has changed for them. While they once attacked Technocratic elements first, now they simply defend their charges against the most dangerous oppressors, no matter their origins. Being Li-Hai may be risky, but the pai has more than two thousand years of heroism to inspire them.

Philosophy: Whatever works. Li-Hai practices are based on a moral foundation more than a metaphysical one. One principle is that of chien-ai, "equal love." In contrast to Confucian morality, which holds that love belongs to the family first and then to others in lesser degrees, the Li-Hai believe in an ethic of universal caring and respect. The Li-Hai also hold that arbitrary customs cause chien-ai to be tainted with propriety and envy. While they believe in Drahma and Akashakarma, they hold that these principles can be accessed in a theoretically infinite number of ways. Mohists follow the paths that allow them to realize their potential and care for others.

Style: The Li-Hai take the basic elements of Akashic magic and modify them according to personal taste and the needs of their community. If a Mind effect needs to be couched in Western psychoanalysis, so be it, as long as it essentially follows Drahma. The Li-Hai also gain power from breaking taboos and turning assumptions upside down, to emphasize the inherent emptiness of subjective experience. The 108 Burning Days was a magical as well as political act. For the Li-Hai, the two are inseparable. A Li-Hai may use computers, anarchist theory and Western fencing to explicate Drahma and Do. However, they are *not* Orphans; every valid focus *must* obey Akashic theory and chien-ai.

Initiation: The Li-Hai take Sidai who are passionate about their ideals and walk the straightest path to fulfil them. A Sihing

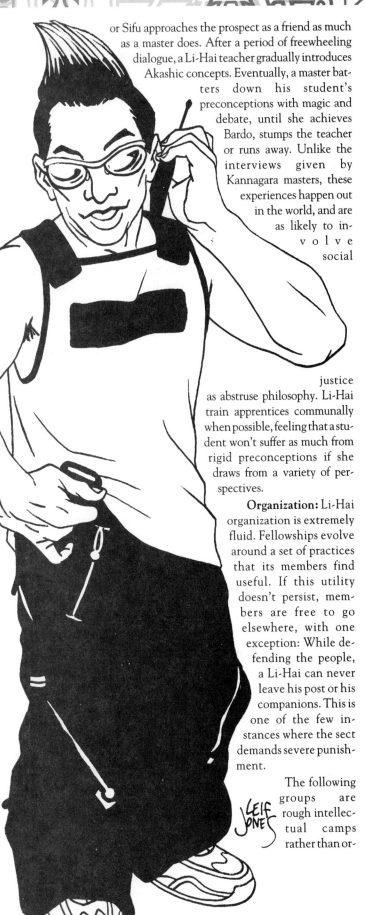

or Sifu approaches the prospect as a friend as much as a master does. After a period of freewheeling dialogue, a Li-Hai teacher gradually introduces Akashic concepts. Eventually, a master batters down his student's preconceptions with magic and debate, until she achieves Bardo, stumps the teacher or runs away. Unlike the interviews given by Kannagara masters, these experiences happen out in the world, and are as likely to involve social justice as abstruse philosophy. Li-Hai train apprentices communally when possible, feeling that a student won't suffer as much from rigid preconceptions if she draws from a variety of perspectives.

Organization: Li-Hai organization is extremely fluid. Fellowships evolve around a set of practices that its members find useful. If this utility doesn't persist, members are free to go elsewhere, with one exception: While defending the people, a Li-Hai can never leave his post or his companions. This is one of the few instances where the sect demands severe punishment.

The following groups are rough intellectual camps rather than or-

ganizations. Each philosophical stream is supported by the whole of the Li-Hai. Names are used when one Empty Vessel wants to explain her magical or intellectual work to the sect or the Brotherhood as a whole. It's possible, of course, for a Mohist to pursue multiple directions in the sect: These simply personify some of the prevalent beliefs among the Li-Hai.

The oldest school of the sect, the Mo-tzu Fa carry on the traditions of folk heroism and universal love begun by Master Mo himself. Members vow to use any means necessary to promote chien-ai; anarchists, utopian thinkers, philanthropists and vigilantes all over the world coordinate efforts to assist areas torn apart by poverty, violence and disaster. These Li-Hai also maintain the original Mohist position on the spirit worlds, which holds that under one supreme being, a chaotic array of spirits must be placated through animal sacrifices and consulted through divination rituals. The invisible world does not divide itself into offices, but must be placated by offerings of friendship and love. Currently, the sect is divided on the issue of authority. Traditional Mohists want strong rulers, while the modern activists distrust powerful leaders and want to see the Drahma taught in less authoritarian terms.

The Blue Skins were once the best-known element of the sect. Derived from a synthesis of Tibetan mysticism and Mohist doctrine, the Blue Skins take their name from Indian and Tibetan legends in which blue-skinned divine beings point the way to Samadhi. The Li-Hai created this school to better induct Westerners, but since the Akashayana's return to more traditional practices, fewer Li-Hai use the Blue Skin's approach. The school espouses "Crazy Wisdom." These teachings hold that Samadhi is in the heart of Samsara, and that even intense, "sinful" feelings point the way to enlightenment. Fear is the feeling of impermanence disguised and lust is the passion for wisdom inarticulately expressed. While these Akashayana engage in Tantric practices and dress in fine clothes, in their own way they are as controlled as the Kannagara. In their view, fashion exists to discipline the body with the mind, and pleasure is a living mantra to aid concentration.

Specializing in non-Asian traditions, the Roda d'Oro, or the Circle of Gold, accepts students from outside the Akashayana's traditional framework. Formed in the wake of the Grand Convocation, the Roda d'Oro took its present shape in the wake of Portuguese and Spanish colonization. In the Philippines, West Africa and Brazil, indigenous peoples developed fighting arts every bit as potent and connected to spirituality as their Asian counterparts. Upon Awakening, many found that the Akashic Brotherhood provided the only framework with which to magically express their training. Capoeiristas, escrimadors, fencers, boxers, dancers, renegade theologians and others fuse their perspectives with the Drahma. One might use Catholicism, the other Jungian analysis, but all interpret these systems as frameworks with which to understand Akashic teachings. The group consists of a core cabal of martial artists and academics. These scholars share their insights with the rest of the Brotherhood.

KANNAGARA

Names: Phoenix Robes, Monks, the Elder Path, and (less complementary) the Lesser Path

History: The Kannagara trace their origins back to Mount Meru itself. It is said that the first Akasha's sermon Awakened the Garuda Valley people to their heritage as Meru'ai. The first Phoenix Robes took charge of the teachings and called upon the Garuda people to wander the earth, passing on the teachings of the Stone Sutra.

The early Kannagara searched for other children of Meru. Their Western journey put them in contact with the predecessors of the Euthanatos. An earlier alliance based on their similarities soon turned to conflict. Through the chaos of the Himalayan War, the followers of the Elder Path embraced the asceticism of Indian communities, largely avoiding the brunt of the violence. Weary Akashic warriors joined them when they could no longer fight, and young, bloodthirsty tulkus, eager to avenge their previous incarnations, were sent to these retreats to end the cycle of hatred. Subsequently the Akashayana began inducting all Brothers into the Kannagara during their apprenticeships.

Indeed, when Buddhism flowered on Indian soil, the Chakravanti allowed Kannagara monks to follow the teachings wherever they led them — even into the heart of Chakravanti territory. This wasn't a perfect agreement — spies and killers wore yellow robes in the hopes of striking at their enemies — but the overriding faith of the communities they hid in, as well as the disapproval of both Traditions' leaders, made this a difficult prospect. No one wanted to taint the Buddhadharma with the affairs of wizards.

Soon, Kannagara settlements existed throughout India, in secret associations of Buddhist monks. The teachings of the Jain saints attracted a small but devoted sect of extreme ascetics who rejected clothing, speech and even food. In China, Lao-tzu's teachings were adapted to the needs of those Kannagara who used Taoist internal alchemy as a focus for the arts of self-mastery. In Tibet, the Kannagara's power allowed it to influence temporal affairs and disseminate the secrets of the Stone Sutra into popular religion. Japanese Kannagara participated in the evolving monastic community, and in Southeast Asia, the Phoenix Robes influenced the design of mandala cities in Cambodia, Thailand and Laos.

After the Kannagara followed Bodhidharma to the Shaolin Temple, they began to do more than lead the Brotherhood and practice in isolation. Monasteries became community institutions. The precepts of Mahayana Buddhism compelled the monks to guide others toward Awakening and final enlightenment. To earthly rulers and scheming shen alike, their guidance was tantamount to interference. While the Wu Lung were certainly jealous of the sway the Kannagara had over the people, more often than not, Sleeping bureaucrats and nobles directed the resulting persecution. Holders of powerful offices were suspicious of Kannagara teachings, which seemed to offer happiness and peace without resorting to violence and conquest. The fact that the Phoenix Robes were forced to refine the martial aspect of their Do in response was unfortunate, but provided another avenue of practice for the burgeoning sect.

After the rise of Western colonialism, the Phoenix Robes withdrew from Sleeper affairs, and pressured the rest of the Akashayana to do the same. During World War Two, the directionless sect acted along national lines, crippling the Brotherhood as a whole. The efforts of Sigung Jou Shan reunified the monks and expanded the Sangha to include more Westerners. With the end of the Ascension War, the Elder Path has shifted its activism to encompass Sleeper concerns. This "Engaged Drahma" follows the trends set by Buddhists in opening up their philosophy to different interpretations. It emphasizes that community service can be an enlightened practice.

Philosophy: Kannagara embrace core Akashic teachings with an emphasis on disavowing materialism and promoting asceticism. Suffering comes from relying on pleasure, fearing pain and feeling dissatisfied with one's basic nature. Thus, a Phoenix Robe rejects the fleeting, illusory pleasures of Samsara for a life of self-discipline and quiet study. This not only serves to purify the spirit but also provides an example to the rest of the community. Unhindered by material concerns, the Kannagara can dispense advice and guide others to the Drahma. Phoenix, the Minister of Stasis, balances the monks' renunciation of the world by giving their simple lives order and a clear purpose.

Style: Ascetic practices and the rejection of sensation as an end in itself allows a Kannagara to look past Samsara and touch a cosmos of emptiness and change. Awareness is cultivated through prolonged meditation, yoga, Do training, chanting and the use of language, which divides the eternal Drahma into perceivable events and forms. Art and song have similar functions as the microcosmic emanations of a larger whole. Even mundane manual labor can be used as a focus, so long as it is performed with the same concentration as a chanted mantra or Do movement. The act is as important as its product. Everything is performed with sincere effort and the recognition that it will pass away in time. After all, even the most ornate sand mandala must scatter to the winds.

Initiation: Every member of the Akashic Brotherhood spends part of their Sidai years as a Kannagara, but those who stay with the sect were usually monks before Awakening and simply decide to remain so. Akashics of other sects often retire into Kannagara communities. Sleepers abound in a Kannagara Bodhimandala. Awakened monks usually form a special group within a monastery, but claim no more influence than the Buddhist, Christian and other clergy that live with them. By contrast, the Kannagara's control of the Sangha, as stipulated by the teachings of the Stone Sutra, give them a quiet authority among the Awakened. The teachings are of the essence, and a monastic Sifu concerns himself with these over temporal matters.

Organization: Kannagara gather in fixed groups, centered on ascetic communities. Wandering Phoenix Robes are rare, but not unheard of. Their associations usually mirror the religious communities of nearby Sleepers. Most Kannagara are simply monks; some place emphasis on certain teachings, while others simply hold to the core of the Stone Sutra.

The Jina are Jain ascetics who follow the most stringent restrictions of any of the Sangha. All Jina are celibate ascetics. The Jain Brothers renounce all material possessions, practice an ethic of strict nonviolence and do not travel or otherwise involve themselves in worldly affairs. Some even forgo clothing, and all take special precautions to ensure that they do not even harm invisible or microscopic organisms. By using filters to drink water and brooms to sweep aside insects that might be trampled underfoot, they attempt to practice nonviolence for the benefit of all living beings. Thus, Jina have never been involved in the Ascension War. Their magic is mostly used to prevent them from harming any being. These pacifists are greatly respected in the Sangha for their wisdom and the strength of their convictions. While the Jina are but a single cabal, they hold a great deal of moral authority within the Brotherhood. Many Brothers visit their community in Benares when an ethical dilemma or moral failing troubles them.

The Shaolin are the best-known members of the Kannagara, if not the entire Tradition. While they no longer inhabit their eponymous monastery, they maintain several others in China, Taiwan, Korea, Japan and the West. The Shaolin use an acrobatic variety of Do and practice Zen Buddhism to focus their Arts. The level of asceticism varies from monastery to monastery but is always observed to some extent. In Japan, a Shaolin Brother may be married, but a vegan and strict pacifist, while a Chinese Phoenix Robe may be allowed to defend herself but must exercise chastity and poverty.

Scholars of the Great Wheel, the Karmachakra school maintains the most ancient traditions of the Akashayana. The elder Brothers of the cabal are the most respected members of the Brotherhood. Drawn from the Shaolin and other Phoenix Robe lineages, the Karmachakra tend the reconstruction of the Tradition's ancestral Bodhimandala in the Garuda Valley. These historians and linguists also tend the Akashic Record, recognize rinpoche and are the final arbiters of Tradition policy. Although it is not specifically required, custom has long demanded that Brothers who have been with the Sangha for several incarnations staff the Karmachakra. This creates a strong sense of continuity — and of stasis. Many Akashics see these Phoenix Robes as too fixed in the past and unaware of the realities of the modern world.

Before the Reckoning, the Karmachakra consisted of the Brotherhood's Primus and several Akashayana of at least Sifu rank. In the aftermath of the Council's fall, the school is content to appoint outside representatives when circumstances dictate it. There simply aren't enough competent Brothers to tend the Akashic Record and represent the Tradition at the same time.

LEIF JONES

Names: Rishi ("sages"), Yogis, Lamas, Vagabonds (a slur used in reference to the Lin Shen)

History: The Jnani were one of the three original sects of the Akashayana to spring from the Garuda Valley. Jnani were hermits, shamans and wanderers, traveling throughout Asia and absorbing the influences of local cultures. This remains a distinguishing mark of the sect as a whole, as its practices vary widely from place to place.

During the Himalayan War, the Jnani learned to put their skills to violent use. Jnani used their divination and spirit binding skills to counter Chakravanti necromancy. In the process, both groups influenced one another. The Jnani developed a facility for the ways of karma and their effects upon the spirit as it passes through the Great Wheel. In Tibet, this merged with Bon shamanism and gave rise to a conflict between Jnani Bonpo and the Kannagara, who promoted the introduction of Buddhism as "a more perfect representation of the Drahma."

After the war, Akashic expansion in the East continued. While the Vajrapani mingled with warrior families, the Kannagara established monasteries, and the Shi-Ren and Li-Hai stayed close to their Chinese roots, the Jnani took the mountains for their homes and the stars for their ceilings. Jnani hermitages flourished in places where the people needed an alternative to the orthodox religions of their area. Jnani spoke to the spirits, warded off evil forces and enchanted simple charms for their benefactors. This often made them the targets of Dalou'laoshi and Wu Lung purges, who saw Jnani ways as a threat to the secular Confucian hegemony that held sway in China.

Chinese Jnani often came from Taoist or shamanistic backgrounds and spurned social conventions. Still, they abstained from the decadent practices that led to the formation of the K'an Lu of the Cult of Ecstasy. To the Jnani, Taoism expressed an unhindered route to Samadhi, and not a license to indulge the senses. Similarly, Tantric practices still permeate Jnani mysticism but emphasizes the symbolic elements of Vajrayana occultism rather than drugs and sexuality to achieve higher states of consciousness. In Japan, Jnani took the Drahma to the mountains and forests, and learned to reconcile it with the Way of the Kami.

During the Mongol invasions of the 13th century, the Rishi averted disaster for the Akashayana by making contact with the samani, nomadic shamans who supported the Mongol cause. After the crimes of the Jade Dragon were uncovered, the Jnani and Mongol mystics worked together to end the plague he had conjured and drive him from his defiled Bodhimandala. That cooperation allowed the Akashayana to survive and flourish through the period that Vajrayana Buddhism spread to the Mongols.

By this time, the Japanese branch of the Jnani had abandoned their lives as hermits to protect Akashic interests throughout the war-torn country. Jnani Bodhimandalas became havens for rebels and insurgents. In time, these assassins and mystic were called shinobi, or "stealers-in." Unlike the ninja, these Jnani didn't act as mercenaries. For the most part, they protected the Sangha against warlords such as the infamous Oda Nobunaga, who instituted a pogrom against Tendai Buddhists. After Japan's unification by Tokugawa Ieyasu, these yogis returned to peaceful pursuits but retained a more martial outlook than their mainland cousins

Jnani also participated in the great experiment of the Shaolin Temple, adding esoteric doctrines to the teachings offered by the Kannagara Shaolin. The Lamas contributed few permanent residents, but disseminated intelligence about the temple's enemies and carried messages that couldn't be transmitted through the Akashic Record. When the Qing and the Wu Lung devastated the monastery, the Jnani disappeared into the wilderness. The only signs they left were the deaths of Qing officials, Wu Lung and other enemies. Combining the ancient skills of the Yamabushi with refined use of the Sunyakaya teachings of Do, they had transformed themselves into the Lin Shen, a secretive faction of assassins and spies.

As the Ascension War intensified throughout the 20th century, the Wu Shan used their Spirit prowess to harass the Five Metal Dragons while the Lin Shen quietly disposed of Technocrats and Traditionalists who directly threatened the Akashayana. The Vagabonds were also responsible for increased animosity between the Brotherhood and Euthanatoi mages in the early 90s, as Jnani and Thanatoic knives crossed over their respective targets. In the halls of Doissetep and Concordia these secret factions played out their struggles, while Akashayana and Euthanatoi on Earth struggled to comprehend the confusing directives that resulted.

In the 21st century, the Jnani have started to embrace the cities as they once did the wilderness. Technoshamanism and Tibetan mysticism have become allies in the struggle to transmit Drahma's values to the people. Many Jnani find this only natural, as New Age mystics of all stripes appropriate their methods without crediting the source. When Wiccan books discuss the chakras or Technocratic postmodernists talk about the emptiness of Self, the Yogis smile and use it as fuel to light the fire of Awakening.

Philosophy: Jnani believe that their bodies, minds and sprits are essentially identical with the whole of the Tapestry. Further, spirits and gods are not clearly outside of the self. Jnani Sprit magic identifies the individual with the supernatural world and affects one by altering the other. A gesture to the universe is also a gesture to the self. Drahma is the final realization that Self and other, natural and supernatural, profane and divine, are but arbitrary divisions. The sage stands at the center. Listening to Meru's song, he is like the first mountain itself, the center of a lotus from which the cosmos unfolds. Meru is the symbol for the Absolute, the Buddha nature and the eternal principle of Drahma that underlies the world of illusion. Their patron, Tiger, smashes down barriers and illuminates the universe of possibilities, while tearing away the "truths" that hide an even more profound vision of the Absolute.

Style: The Yogis use elaborate mandalas, lists of celestial beings and internal martial arts in their quest to identify themselves with the All. Visualization exercises are used to merge the Yogi's being with a spirit, and internal alchemy gives her the power to invest her mind and body with cosmic forces. Jnani skilled in Prime and Spirit often house spirits in their own bodies. Aside from providing the spirits power, such magic also serves as an exercise in discipline, as the Jnani attempts to yoke his will to it, destroying the barrier of identity.

Initiation: Jnani don't seek out students. Their apprentices have to find them. A Yogi doesn't make this easy to do, as many live in remote or dangerous areas by choice. A Jnani Sifu will be as discouraging as she can without being downright abusive, but will "grudgingly" teach the Way to a persistent follower, vanishing after each lesson to begin the chase anew. Eventually, the routine reverses itself, as the Sifu starts to intrude on her student's daily life at unpredictable moments. Sidai are expected to be respectful and disciplined when their mentor appears. Since a Rishi's pupil is never quite sure when that's going to be, this form of training quickly cultivates a student's self-discipline. After a stint in the Kannagara, the Sidai returns to his master's side, taking up the same eccentric lifestyle.

Organization: Jnani usually meet around sacred sites such as dragon nests and temples. Travel and hermitage make Jnani associations a lot like communes. On the road or in the mountains, everyone is expected to do their part.

The Jnani classify themselves by cultural affiliation. Jnani are loners by circumstance (and often by nature) but retain a sense of identity from their formative early training. A Yamabushi might very well be considered one of Wu Shan as well if he traveled to China and incorporated their magical lore into his practices. The exception is the Chabnagpa, who preserve controversial parts of Akashic lore; their low numbers mean that their secrets may die with them unless they accept new members.

Yamabushi is a term that refers to Japanese ascetics who follow Shinto and esoteric Buddhist practices. Jnani Yamabushi follow the same traditions as their Sleeper counterparts, and like them, return from the mountains to perform cures and exorcisms when they feel it's warranted. In the mountains, they perform superhuman physical feats to focus their minds, such as running long distances faster than the greatest Olympians or honing their Do skills by training with the wind, the trees and the earth. In modern times, the Yamabushi also train in the cities. Their distinctive robes can be seen on street corners and on Japanese television, as they use wilderness metaphors to describe urban life.

The Chabnagpa, or "Black Water Sect," combines Tibetan Bon spirituality and Vajrayana rites. Members are either lamas who have taken strict monastic vows, or yogis, lay teachers who perform practical rites such as weather divination and exorcisms. Spirit possession and binding are common acts for these Jnani. Meru plays a central role in their teachings as the immovable point from which the Drahma springs. The Chabnagpa is the oldest branch of the Jnani; they use a number of secret rites, preserved from the Brotherhood's earliest days. The Black Water Sect keep secrets that were stolen from the Chakravanti during the Himalayan Wars. They keep sutras and chronicles from the Akashic Record that detail the secrets of necromancy and cursing, and many of their strange powers derive from this forbidden study. These monks keep a reclusive Tibetan monastery, under which lies a series of deep cellars said to hold physical transcriptions of the whole of the Record. Some whisper that other things reside there as well....

The Wu Shan are Taoist mystics who specialize in internal alchemy. Taking their names from mountain hermitages, the core of Wu Shan practice is the lu, a ledger passed from teacher to student that catalogues a group of spirits, their properties and the rituals to summon, placate and bind them. Wu Shan use Do to balance their physical energies to cultivate a serenity that resonates in the invisible world. To these mages, the body is more than a veil of flesh. It contains a spiritual universe, with its own gods and rites, every bit as important as the lands beyond the Wall. Sympathetic principles connect the two — purifying the self can heal the world.

The Lin Shen don't exist. According to Akashic policy, the Vagabonds are but a paranoid rumor cultivated by the Brotherhood's enemies. In any event, the legends attached to them are similar to those associated with the ninja. Stealth, hidden weapons, survival skills and the power to alter the land to their advantage supposedly make up the bulk of Lin Shen training. Said to have evolved from Shaolin refugees and forest recluses, the "forest spirits" are a whisper in the wilderness, or a fluttering shadow on the ceiling at night.

That is, of course, if they were to exist at all.

In fact, the Lin Shen *don't* exist as an organization per se. Instead, they serve as a convenient moniker for those Brothers who spy and murder on the Sangha's behalf. Jnani teachings provide the core mystical principles that these Akashics use. This common collection of spells and techniques creates the illusion of a group of assassins. The only concrete aspect of the Lin Shen is the Forest Classic, a book that describes the strategies, spells and ethical justifications for espionage and killing. A copy of the Forest Classic is typically passed to the Brother who has been designated to do the deed, and she, in turn, wears the mantle of the Lin Shen for as long as it takes to get the job done.

VAJRAPANI

Names: Scales of the Dragon, Warriors (bushi, wu-shih), Warring Fist (incredibly common, but insulting).

History: The Vajrapani began as Meru'ai who practiced the Drahma through hard physical labor and devotional exercises. These men and women revered the Bodhisattvas and hoped that their devout lifestyles would lead to a "transfer of merit" from those enlightened ones.

Traveling throughout Asia, the Vajrapani found their physical prowess to be a useful tool to repel bandits and hostile armies. Do transformed from a way to perfect the activities of everyday life to a war art. By the time the Brotherhood reached India, the Scales of the Dragon were hardened soldiers. Their leader, the Sigung Chan Ng, was charged with protecting the Sangha against possible threats. He used Akashakarma to coordinate India's scattered Akashic groups.

When the Himalayan War began, Chan the Protector became General Chan. The Vajrapani united under his leadership. As one, they fought against the death cults that would eventually unite to form the Euthanatos. Not even death would repel the Warring Fist, as warriors were propelled by their beliefs into new bodies almost as soon as they were slain. Toward the end of the conflict this became a serious problem, as attempts to end the strife would be ruined by rogue Brothers who were obsessed with avenging their former incarnations. As the phenomenon consumed the Sangha and the Chakravanti alike, Chan Ng turned to a grim task: hunting down his wayward comrades.

After the war, the Brotherhood retreated to its traditional territory, only to find itself embroiled in China's Warring Sates conflict. The Vajrapani, fresh with regret for the Himalayan War, joined the battle in earnest, searching for just causes to support and relieve them of the karmic debt they carried. One group of crusaders followed Mo-tzu's ideals, transforming into the Li-Hai. The rest settled into smaller communities and served as a lay auxiliary to the Jnani and Vajrapani. A large number of them settled in Korea and Japan, where their Arts and ethos became enshrined in their hosts' cultures.

During the Kamikaze War, Japanese Vajrapani ignored the pleas of the mainland Kannagara and fought the invaders with patriotic ferocity. With the subsequent rise of the samurai class, the Warriors became increasingly independent of their cloistered superiors. Only the Grand Convocation provided a suitable enticement back into the fold, and even then, the Warring Fist demanded more say in Brotherhood affairs.

In Korea, the Vajrapani became attached to the Hwarang warriors, a military fellowship that received the blessing of Buddhist clergy. Unlike their Japanese counterparts, they worked closely with the Kannagara, acting as loyal supporters of the kingdom of Silla and their successors. The Sulsa, a Vajrapani faction of Hwarang, combined the Buddhist mysticism of their Kannagara patrons with their own martial arts.

During the decline of the Mongol Yuan dynasty, the Vajrapani threw their weight behind Shi-Ren independence efforts. When the Ming dynasty arose, many retired to Akashic monasteries with the honest belief that their work was finished. The Manchus and their Wu Lung allies caused even more Warring Fists to choose the monastic life, albeit for less innocent reasons — Buddhist monasteries provided an ideal place to plan another rebellion. When the Wu Lung finally broke the Shaolin Temple, the Warring Fists insinuated themselves into a host of anti-Qing movements, often accompanied by the Shi-Ren.

Eventually, even these plans fell by the wayside, as their Sleeper allies devolved into mere criminals and an even greater threat arose: the West. The Wu Lung and the Brotherhood united in a struggle to fight off Western imperialism and the Technocrats that followed, but Sleeper and Awakened alike fell to bullets and opium. Some warriors joined with the Shi-Ren to form the Golden Dragons, while others left for the Americas or simply went into hiding. Similarly, the Meiji Restoration overthrew the samurai, and the Vajrapani had to fight to hold on to their ancestral traditions.

World War Two and the annexation of Korea saw the Warring Fists turn against one another. Japanese Vajrapani are still widely shunned by their Chinese and Korean cousins. After the war, North American Warriors were the first to heal the rift, as they made tenuous contact through the nascent martial arts community. Today, Vajrapani use traditional martial arts schools to attract new members more than any other sect. While the training they offer is unusually harsh, few would have it any other way.

Initiation: Like the Shi-Ren, the Vajrapani have a strong family tradition and prefer to teach Awakened family members if at all possible. In the past 500 years, the attitude has softened to include sincere members of the gate arts they support and ethical woman and men of action who Awaken and search for guidance. Martial Do is the cornerstone of training. Most Vajrapani see their monastic period as a necessary evil to endure before they get back to *really* learning. Regardless of lineage, Warring Fists think of themselves as members of a family where their mentors are parents and their comrades are siblings. This solidarity makes the Vajrapani dangerous to cross. An interloper rarely offends just one of them.

Philosophy: Vajrapani believe that sincere effort is the path to the Drahma. The truths to be found in action are ultimately more important than moral minutiae, although right effort can never be achieved without a clear conscience. Their Celestial Minster, the Dragon, reveals their weaknesses and challenges their notions of order by destroying ideals that have become corrupt. To gain mental clarity, a Warrior must be utterly devoted, be it to the Sangha, her family or a sworn oath. Violence is a metaphor for inner turmoil and must be confronted instead of denied. Faced with the savage truths of her own heart, a Vajrapani can use them for the greater good. Sometimes, one must come to the shrine with bloody hands.

Style: More than any other sect, these Vajrapani focus their magic through Do. Weapons, athletic techniques and the like must all serve to make the Brother a more keenly honed blade to put in the Sangha's hands. Ritual magic involves the use of oaths, chanting mantras of devotion, and ascetic exercises to synchronize the mind, body, and spirit. In every case, the Vajrapani reduce these rituals to their core essentials. Kata lack flowery movements and Mind Arts take the direct path, using the power of the Warrior's spirit to terrify and immobilize enemies.

Organization: Vajrapani societies are divided along nationalistic and familial lines. Technically, there are 36 Vajrapani clans, but less then half of them have Awakened Brothers at any given time. To preserve methods that might otherwise be lost, the Warriors developed out into schools that teach the combined methods of the 36 families. Most students are Sleepers who study or teach a gate art associated with the school. Awakened Vajrapani coordinate several schools or travel from school to school to complement the efforts of Sleeper instructors. Consequently, the schools prosper despite the rarity of Awakened members.

The Tenshin Arashi Ryu is a Japanese martial arts fellowship that was founded shortly after the Kamikaze War. Originally restricted to members of the Tanaka clan, it was opened up to outsiders shortly after the Meiji Restoration. The Ryu teaches its gate art publicly under the same name and selects Vajrapani to become uchideshi, live-in students who learn the Way while caring for the Tanaka Bodhimandala. They express Drahma using the terminology of Shinto and Tendai Buddhism. Swordsmanship, mounted combat and archery are all parts of the Tenshin Arashi interpretation of Do, and many katana-wielding Brothers come from this sect. The school trains Brothers from around the world. With the exception of the Sulsa, most Vajrapani have studied at a Tenshin Arashi dojo at one time or another.

In Chinese communities, the Banner of the Ebon Dragon teaches kung fu and wushu as gate arts to anyone willing to learn. These Warriors have been extremely successful in both mainland China and Taiwan, integrating their teachings with state-sanctioned martial arts training and subtly returning the old methods to modified arts such as competitive wushu. The Banner is a secret society of Vajrapani clans that care for their own and guard Chinese Kannagara and Jnani. In North America, the Heilong Athletic Society teaches their gate arts from gyms and storefronts wherever a Chinese population has settled.

The Sulsa is a secretive cabal of Korean warriors and spies. Theirs is among the most complex Vajrapani magical styles, as Kannagara and Jnani practices heavily influence it. Like the Tenshin Arashi Ryu, the Sulsa specialize in swordsmanship. Their blade, the gum, comes in many shapes and sizes but is always forged by the warrior who uses it. The Sulsa also learn a unique style of sword dancing that can entrance enemies and hide violence under a veneer of graceful steps. Sulsa combine martial prowess with the arts of invisibility and mind control, making them more than just Awakened spear-carriers. Any Vajrapani may train with them, but they demand complete obedience during the training period. Unlike the other schools, the Sulsa consists exclusively of Awakened members and sorcerers.

WU LUNG: THE DRAGON WIZARDS.

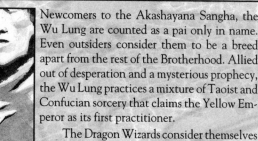

Newcomers to the Akashayana Sangha, the Wu Lung are counted as a pai only in name. Even outsiders consider them to be a breed apart from the rest of the Brotherhood. Allied out of desperation and a mysterious prophecy, the Wu Lung practices a mixture of Taoist and Confucian sorcery that claims the Yellow Emperor as its first practitioner.

The Dragon Wizards consider themselves to be the mortal representatives of the Celestial Bureaucracy. As such, they relentlessly persecuted the Akashic Brotherhood for hundreds of years. This culminated in the fall of the Shaolin Temple, when the warriors of the Tiger General fought the monks in vicious hand to hand combat. A temporary alliance during the Boxer Rebellion soon fell apart, and it wasn't until Chinese members of both groups were forced to share territory abroad that the old vendettas faded. During the Reckoning, the Wu Lung was severely crippled by the Avatar Storm and came to their former enemies to offer an alliance.

The Shi-Ren and Wu Lung now work together extensively, as their philosophies and goals are quite similar. One trend that has worried the rest of the Brotherhood has been extensive intermarriage between Shi-Ren and Wu Lung families. Will this cement a lasting peace, or turn the Heavenly Aristocrats against them? Only time will tell.

The Dragon Wizards use a strict hierarchy of magical offices. The Dragon Emperor Wizard, his Phoenix Empress Wizard and the Tiger Lord General head this Magical Bureaucracy. They in turn direct the Dragon School (rulership and Spirit magic), the Phoenix School (healing, mercy, and Life magic), and the Tiger School (strategy, tactics, martial arts). Only the most skilled Wu Lung rise to leadership positions. The lazy and faint of heart are weeded out through grueling Magical Service Exams.

The Wu Lung paradigm combines Taoist mysticism with Confucian rites of propriety and ancestor worship. Magical rites are designed to appeal to the Celestial Bureaucracy or the ancestors, or alter the elemental properties of a person, place, or thing. Wu Lung are guided by their Avatars, or shih. According to Dragon Wizard doctrine, the shih is a deified ancestor who guides a Chi'n Ta along the path of propriety and enlightenment. While the Wu Lung pay lip service to the Akashic sutras, most would rather turn their back on the Brotherhood's philosophy completely. Inner peace is all well and good, but compared to the splendor of Heaven, it's a dull reward!

Most eschew Do. Martially inclined Dragon Wizards practice Kuei Lung Chuan, a martial art developed by the Tiger School to defend the Magical Bureaucracy. Tiger School Wu Lung develop a small array of magical techniques to improve their fighting capabilities and strategic skills.

For more information on the Wu Lung, see the **Mage Storytellers Companion** and **Dragons of the East**.

SMOKE TIGER: THE WORDS OF THE DEAD

A begging bowl shatters under my running feet and I see the monks scattering out of the way. Their muddy saffron robes whirl aside like dancing flames in the rain. I'm close enough to hear Ranjit choking on the air with every inefficient breath, making a strange rattling with every clumsy swift step in flight — and feel, beneath the shroud of flesh, the roiling fire of a god.

Ranjit sends a piece of Shiva into the wall beside us. It collapses into a thousand sharp fragments. I leap and spin, a lotus petal caught in the wind, and the clay knives of the brickwork sever only my braid. When I land in a bow stance, a strand of hair drifts before my eyes, and when I focus on the street beyond he has vanished.

He's above me. The roof. I inhale, hold the power in my navel until it burns for release, then exhale. I leap ten, then twenty feet, with Samsara rippling in my wake. I roll to a stand.

Ranjit gestures with his bone. I can feel the years slip away and my skin wither. Dragon is eating away at my life. My arms cross and my palms press forward, the Chi flaring. In my mind, I see Tiger, strangled in the dark coils of the Ebon Judge. I inhale and take in the power, feeding it to him. He grows and rips the coils, breaking the yantra of death that Dragon's body was trapping me in.

The ache in my bones ceases. I throw my knife.

The air screams with its passing. Ranjit shifts to one side to escape, but that's where I want him. The blade pins his shoulder to the chimney. He howls and writhes, fixed in place. Soon, the ragged breathing calms, and, trembling, he raises his good arm in surrender.

"The water was killing them already, Vajrapani," he says. "They would have suffered over months instead of days. All of them lived near a factory that poisoned them." When his coat flutters open, I see the rattling bone apron, like the one Jou Shan sometimes wore for rituals. Could we really be halves of the same truth?

"No," I say. "Now they can never choose to wash away the stains of karma. Where you see mercy, I see another lifetime of torture. Where you see destiny, I see freedom. How do you know that the next moment of the life you stole wasn't the one that might have liberated them?"

He looks up at me and smiles. "How many times have you told me this before, Smoke Tiger? But the killing serves another purpose: How else would you know that it was me?"

"Yes." A second blade comes into my hand, unbidden by conscious thought.

"We both know the truth about the war. That's why our lives are so brief. Our masters fear the things we might say or do to bring it into the light. Just like you, I spent my apprenticeship at the knee of a master who hid it from me. Then Voormas showed me the terrible reality.

"All our souls cursed, Vajrapani, for the liberation of a few others. And what has it brought us? The Stone People tread the earth until it weeps. Death walks among the Chakravanti, clothed in our very bodies. Sometimes, I think it would have been better if we had lost."

A sliding step closer and my knife is ready. "You're still a killer, Handura."

"You could live a thousand more lives and never know why, Smoke Tiger. Was my blade drawn across every throat with mercy in my heart, or judgment? You have what you came for. You know I'm real, and that your visions of the past are real. I levy this price: As long as you live, you'll never know if you were right to kill me in your dreams, and you'll never know if you're right to kill me here, under the clouds."

He looks up to the storm-dark sky.

"Now take up the blade, and take the truth to our wounded families."

It will be painless. Yin burns in my hand and the numbing frost takes to the knife's edge. And this old tattooed man I've never seen before widens the same young eyes he's had forever. The gesture horribly familiar, I raise my arm to strike.

Suddenly, there is the sound of a thunderclap. Ranjit's face bursts into a red flower. Blood showers my arm.

With the Dharmas burning so strongly in me, I can see the bullet spin, tumbling from the top of his head. There's a smell of smoke and cordite.

There are feet scraping against the rust of a metal ladder. I pivot to face the three of them.

I will not turn my back to my people.

PETER: A SWIFTLY ROLLING MIRROR

"Peter?" Raging Eagle's voice. "Are you feeling ill?"

"Shit." Masako. "We're here, Eagle. Samsara hit him pretty bad. Leave him." Rain on the windshield thudded like a thousand angry footsteps.

"No. He has to come with us. Wake up, Peter."

"What?" Her voice was angry and loud. "So he can distract Smoke Tiger with his past life? Christ! We're gonna get killed, you goddamn crazy koitsu!" The door opened. "I'm leaving now, Sifu. I can die with you or without you."

"Wait," said Peter. His eyes opened, and he slid to the door in one easy motion. Everything was swift and fluid, and he could feel the Chi crackling in him. "I'm all right. Give me a sword, Nu Ying. I know you have an extra one with you."

He swung his legs out of the car and stood. A flash of lightning backlit the tasseled hilt that his Sifu passed to him. The weight of the blade was familiar.

Raging Eagle wiped the water from his eyes. "You're ready to come with us, Peter? This will all be finished soon. You can return to Cheng Sa to finish your training."

"I've always been ready, Nu Ying. It was just a matter of remembering." His hands formed mudra: *I know, Sifu. You were right to take me with you.*

Raging Eagle nodded. They turned and ran together, leaping over the rubble of a broken wall in their path.

At the foot of a rusty ladder, they heard a loud crack ring through the night: Sataghni's rifle. In that instant, Peter knew that Pratts was dead, and, with his sword slung over his shoulder,

The Akashayana doesn't usually insist on the same level of formality as Traditions such as the Order of Hermes and the Celestial Chorus. Since members are expected to be self-disciplined, the only set of strictures is a loose code called the Sanghakarma.

The root of the Sanghakarma is a series of proscriptions that are rooted in the Akashic sutras. These rules consist of a number of precedents set by various Sifus when a situation demanded them. The resulting regulations now cover apprenticeships, Bodhimandala etiquette and punishments for crimes against the Sangha.

One tradition the Sanghakarma emphasizes is obedience to one's teachers. Different jat and pai enforce these to varying degrees. A Li-Hai master rarely demands complete obedience. A Shi-Ren almost always does. Inattention to instruction is never tolerated and is usually punished with ostracism. The Brotherhood simply refuses to recognize the existence of a failed student. It is possible to redeem oneself in the eyes of a Sihing or Sifu, but it requires a gesture so impressive (many point to the example of Hui-ke cutting his own arm off to prove his commitment to Bodhidharma) that it rarely occurs.

Other crimes are treated as variations on failure. The Brother was simply too undisciplined to conduct herself in an ethical fashion. Typically, a group of experienced Sangha attempt to rehabilitate the offender with intensive training. If this fails, the Brother's Bodhicitta (Avatar) is branded with a list of her crimes, and she is either ostracized (often with Mind magic used to prevent her from endangering the Akashayana) or killed. Gilgul is rarely advocated by the Brotherhood. Most Brothers see the act as tantamount to killing a Buddha or enlightened sage.

Serious cases are traditionally judged by one of the Kannagara, although a well-respected Shi-Ren has served from time to time. The judge prosecutes the case, and the accused is permitted one advocate, but it is not an adversarial system. The judge is trusted to reach a fair verdict rather than attempting to punish the accused regardless of the truth of the matter. The judges, and no others, are allowed to use magic as part of the proceedings.

While many outsiders decry the apparent imbalance of power in the Akashic system, it typically works. As ascetics, Kannagara aren't distracted by material lures, while Shi-Ren are required by their own beliefs to impose fair, if harsh, penalties.

he began to climb. He ascended, hand over hand, overcoming the weight of incarnations.

Peter Lasky. Nichiba. Chan Ng. He'd seen the brightness and the blood of those lives, but they were not his. They were just names, no heavier than a breeze on his back.

The last of the three, he leapt to the roof to take the burden of Smoke Tiger from Ming Wong's shoulders.

HARMONY AND RIGHTEOUSNESS: THE AKASHIC PARADIGM

Akashic magic is not an end to be pursued in of itself, but a side effect of Awakening. Spiritual understanding is the key to advancement. The ability to perform miracles is a secondary concern that can distract an Akashayana from the true path.

Magic comes from knowledge of the Dharmas, the primordial principles of creation, form and destruction. These powers are set in motion by the Sam Chien and are invisible to Sleepers, who prefer the materialistic dream of Samsara, the Consensus.

DRAHMA

To transcend Samsara, the Akashayana practice the Drahma. Drahma is a contraction of two concepts. Drala, a Tibetan term meaning "above the enemy," is a special state where dualities are reconciled and illusions are pierced. To meet Drala is to reject the divisiveness of concepts such as self and other, matter and spirit. Without opposition, a Brother is above the enemy because all enemies are no different from his own intrinsic nature.

Dharma is a Sanskrit word with a number of meanings. In Hinduism, a Dharma is a duty to family, caste and society. Doing Dharma helps a man or woman attain higher incarnations and eventually a union with the Godhead itself. In the Buddha's teachings, the term was transformed into a description of the principles of reality. While this is the definition that the Brotherhood embraces, do not think that it has no implications on personal responsibility. The underlying truths of the Wheel integrate one's moral awareness into mystical understanding. To the Akashayana, there is no difference between the two.

Drahma is thus an approach to the universe that advocates living in harmony with nature and performing only those deeds that bring one closer to realizing the great truth of existence: that the Ten Thousand Things of reality are no different and not separate from the individual's true nature. All act as part of a greater whole. Creation, preservation and destruction break the barriers that isolate people from the flow of the Great Wheel.

THE SAM CHIEN

When an Akashic Brother lives according to the principles of Drahma, she naturally invokes the power of the All, as she always acts in accord with the dynamic forces that surround and permeate her. Based on her jat, pai, or personal temperament, she aligns herself with one of the Three Ministers of the Sam Chien: Tiger, Dragon, or Phoenix. She doesn't become a vehicle for her chosen patron, such as one finds in the twisted Nephandi or the impulsive hengeyokai. Instead, the personifications of Dynamism, Stasis, or Entropy balance out the Brother's tendencies to reject or ignore those forces in her daily life.

The Sam Chien, like other aspects of Drahma, is not just external phenomena. The Triple Struggle is an internal one. Thus, a Kannagara who focuses on destroying his ties to the material world invokes the Phoenix to impose order on his practice so that it doesn't become an exercise in nihilism. Magically, it means that he becomes an empty vessel through which to manifest that Minister's powers, moderating it with his contrasting temperament.

The Li-Hai speak of a fourth Minster, Lung-ta, who serves to balance all of the others. The Windhorse represents the power of Drahma in the phenomenal world, even in the midst of chaos, destruction, or stultifying law. Lung-ta's great lesson is to find enlightenment even in flawed, ordinary things. The Li-Hai act in its name, seeking to keep the Sangha from becoming isolated from the modern world.

BODHICITTA: THE HEART OF ENLIGHTENMENT

In the midst of the Triple Struggle is the Bodhicitta, known to other mages as the Avatar, manifests. Akashics don't believe this is a Quintessence battery, a god or the soul. The first smacks of irreverence. For all its power, the second is inferior to an Awakened human, and the third isolates the Brother from the Wheel.

Rather, the Bodhicitta is the spark of Akasha, the primal wisdom called Buddha Nature, the Tao and a host of other names. All beings have a Bodhicitta — enlightenment is inherent, not a function of lineage or luck. But for most, Samsara's easy answers drown it out in the materialism and noise of the selfish mind. All beings may see their true nature after death, but too many fear the light and flee into a new incarnation. Even the Awakened have trouble coping with the true nature of the Bodhicitta, which escapes all attempts to define or conceptualize it, so they often conceal it with a divine form or a mystic symbol. To most, this represents their Awakened light. The Bodhicitta will even provide guidance in this form, wearing Dynamic, Static, Primordial or Questing masks to teach the Drahma. Many call upon an aspect of the Sam Chien to fill this role, so that the illusion will, at least, lead them to balance. More tragically, servants of the Yama Kings often transform their inner light into grotesque form with the force of their delusions. Yet even this is the Bodhicitta at work, as it tries to terrify a Fallen mage back onto the righteous path.

SAMSARA: THE CONSENSUS OF ILLUSION

Awakened gifts aren't always easy to use. Too often, the Superior Person falls prey to illusion. Samsara isn't just the product of runaway dreams or baseless beliefs. It's a whole attitude to the world, where one sees oneself as a separate, unchangeable being, immune to the forces that surround her. Such ideas only serve to force the will against the turn of the Wheel and reject the truth of impermanence. Changing a universe of fixed entities with the force of will isn't just arrogant; it's deluded. An Akashic Brother who tries to do so may find that the forces she seeks to command have already left her fixed notions behind. They may have twisted into something altogether undesirable.

Samsara isn't entirely bad — we need a fixed conception of the universe in order to live in it — but it isn't a true picture of the Tapestry. Ironically, Sleepers caught up in isolation and permanence strengthen the power of illusion because of an interdependence that they will not recognize. As part of the body of humanity, the Akashayana is just as much a part of that whole and is prone to fall to Samsara in the presence of Sleepers. Indeed, the real danger is that a Brother thinks of himself as separate from Samsara and constructs a duality between Awakened and Sleeping life. But Samsara isn't a place, or a synonym for reality. It holds the keys to Samadhi within it.

AKASHAKARMA

Aside from simply being a magical resource, the Akashic Record is a paradigmatic phenomenon in its own right. Akashakarma is the sublime imprint of actions upon the Wheel itself. Every act is set in motion by a thought and leaves a trace on all other actions and thoughts. Akashic Brothers use the idea of the Record to study the consequences of their actions, and to work magic that transcends the principles of karma itself. For example, a Brother could sense the emotional states or thoughts that occurred on an ancient battlefield by attuning himself to the imprint that its history has left on the Record. Deep breathing and the recitation of a mantra might free him from material distractions. Then, he can sense the Akashic flow that existed prior to any cycle of creation or destruction, and can use the karmic echoes that appear to learn the name of the losing side's general, or perhaps the temperament of a Vajrapani who fought in that ancient conflict.

Calligraphy, creating mandalas with sand, paint or movement, and the reciting holy writings also opens the mind to Akashakarma. Methods that use a sympathetic tie to the object being studied or influenced (such as if the Akashic in the above example recites the history of the place as he learned it from an ancient document) favor that magical working at the expense of overall flexibility.

DO

To follow the Drahma, Akashayana must act with focus, determination, and with a sense of the effect their actions will have upon the whole. Do is the study and practice of focused, correct action, and as such is integral to Akashic belief and magic.

For example, a Vajrapani might use a sweeping, clawing gesture to focus his rage into a block that not only wards off an attack but also inspires terror in his enemy. Faced with an illness, the same Brother could move through a kata designed to rectify the energetic imbalance in his body. Combined with proper breathing, the Chi flow through the stimulated meridians leads to improved health.

SAMADHI

Sat-Chit-Ananda. Unity with the Tao. Nirvana. Ascension. It has many names, but to the Brotherhood, it all stands for Samadhi, the state of undifferentiated being. The Bodhicitta reveals itself in its true form, and the wisdom of the Akasha permeates all things. She is one with the Wheel and free from it. The fetters of delusion are gone, and, as Confucius observed, she can do as she pleases, for what she pleases is no different from Heaven's will.

The Akashayana have many stories about the Akasha, Ascended beings who have mastered the Wheel of Birth and Death. These koans, parables, poems and songs are the most treasured part of Akashic lore, for they point the way to attaining all that the Brotherhood trains, studies, and sacrifices for.

PETER AND SMOKE TIGER

Pratts's —Ranjit's— body sat hideously upright, affixed to the wall by a long knife. The remnants of his skull lolled on his shoulders, a jagged cup that bled over his tattoos like a hideous libation. To Peter's right, Ming Wong settled into a shallow, combat-ready stance, another knife pointing from her rear hand. The blade and the arms carrying it were spattered in blood. The rain turned it into a rivulet of pink water that flowed across the tarred roof.

To his left, Masako drew her sword, covering the distance with sliding staccato steps. Raging Eagle motioned for her to stop, and spoke.

"Ming." *Peace,* his hands said. *Calm your heart.* "We can help you. The Drahma won't depart you, even in these times. We can teach you, and we can learn from you, but you have to come with us." Chi rippled as he tried to take the Santana, the stream of her thoughts.

Her hand slapped her fist in response, the salute hardening the energies around her. When she spoke, Peter was surprised at the gentleness of her voice. "I think you know my real name, Nu Ying. In the turn of the Wheel, it hasn't been so long since you killed me last. Or would you rather forget about Luo Fu?"

"You want me to call you Smoke Tiger? Your past lives don't bind you, Ming. You can change, and work towards Samadhi with the rest of us."

"Is that really true?" she asked. "Every time I've tried to tell the truth, each life has come crashing down on me. The 'Brotherhood' takes in a lie with every breath. We've done— you've done terrible things. Have you ever incarnated in the Pit of Harmony, Brother?"

Raging Eagle's face suddenly twisted in pain, but his words were stone calm. "Yes."

"Then you know you're cursed, just as I was. I can see the karma tearing through you, ready to punish you. I *will* end the cycle. I *will* let the truth be known!"

And there was Sataghni, hand held in a claw, emerging from an invisible curtain of wind and water. Kaja characters were painted on her wiry brown arms.

In the rain, there was a blur and a sudden stream of red. Peter reached across the glittering lattice of Indra's Net and saw violence.

NINE DHARMAS, TEN THOUSAND TOOLS

The powers of the Akashayana don't come from something so forced as "True Will." Instead, by aspiring to Samadhi and practicing Do, they open themselves to eternal truths that manifest as a side effect of enlightened practice.

This is not to say that such powers are not deliberately invoked. The Drahma needs its defenders, and it's is an auspicious thing to use your magic to guide others on the path. At the same time, this approach — in which magic is a truth to be realized instead of an impersonal force to conquer — means that Akashics rarely fall to the trap of valuing magical accomplishment over personal Ascension.

Because of the influence of the Council, the Brotherhood recognizes nine mystic Dharmas. Older and more traditional members of the Akashayana sometimes measure the laws of reality differently (see **Dragons of the East**), but most accept this standard.

CORRESPONDENCE — INDRA'S NET, THE LOKHADHATU

Because of the principle of impermanence, all things are connected, part of the same Cosmic All. Indra's Net is a lattice that covers the world. Where the cords of the net cross, there is a mirror, so that each point on the net reflects every other. Thus, the separation of objects is an illusion, one of the comforting lies of Samsara. The Lokhadhatu is the entirety of the universe, where Meru is the sole immovable point, the axis around which turns the Wheel. All of the Ten Thousand Things are ultimately joined by the immovable mountain — which is no different from the truth of one's own being.

Mandalas show the karmic connections between objects across space, and Meru, as the Brotherhood's conception of the Correspondence Point (among other things) is depicted at the center of it all. Do forms with spinning movements and the quiet contemplation of far off places all use the idea that an ever-moving Wheel is nonetheless governed by an immovable center.

ENTROPY — KARMA, SUNYATA

The Great Wheel is kept in motion by karma. The thoughts and actions of sentient beings set all events in motion. The results of those actions reflect upon the causes. Sunyata, the principle of impermanence, teaches that all things pass. Objects, people and ideas wither away, and their elements reconfigure themselves in new and wondrous ways. Even karma depends on our attachment to the structures of cause and effect. The Awakened One cuts through the illusion that we are bound to karma; with her understanding of sunyata, she can dispel karma's attachment and alter its course.

Manipulating weak points with Do strikes allows a Brother to damage targets with frightening ease. Chanting portions of a sutra and making the correct mudras can transfer "good" or "bad" karma to another person or thing and allows an Akashic to temporarily defy the Wheel of causation and consequence.

FORCES — THE FIVE AGENTS

Chinese mystics assert that the primordial Yin and Yang expresses itself through five elements: Earth, Metal, Water, Wood, and Fire. Metal arises from Earth, diffuses into Water, as Water nourishes Wood that becomes fuel for Fire and, as ashes, returns to Earth. This creative cycle is balanced by a destructive cycle where Earth captures Water, Water extinguishes Fire, Fire melts Metal, and Metal cleaves Wood, whose growth chokes the Earth. The Five Agents are more than the gross physical elements. They represent the interaction of cosmic and individual forces. Thus, an aggressive Do maneuver in the spirit of Fire can overcome a languid, precise attack akin to Metal. In the holistic spirit of Akashic magic, this concept can be used for more than physical forces, but it is here that it finds its chief application. For more information on the Five Agents, see **Dragons of the East** and the **Changeling** supplement **Land of Eight Million Dreams**.

While Do techniques can channel Forces with supernatural efficiency, it isn't the only method the Akashayana use to touch the Dharma of Forces. The creative and destructive cycles of the Five Agents can also be manipulated by drawing the characters for the appropriate element, appealing to an agent of the Celestial Bureaucracy for intervention with offerings or taking on a physical posture that symbolizes the appropriate force.

Matter — External Alchemy

Matter is the most difficult Sphere for the Akashayana to practice. Akashic alchemy involves impressing the Five Agents on a material object, using rituals that involve astrology, moving the object to a special location (such as a mountaintop to absorb Earth), and the skills of an expert artisan. The nonmaterialistic outlook of most Akashic Brothers requires them to use intense concentration to focus on the process rather than the outcome. Still, some weaponsmiths can forge blades as sharp as the Technocracy's monomolecular-edged Wonders, and Shi-Ren who guard their strongholds with animated stone lions. With their superlative skill in this field, the Wu Lung have begun to overshadow these accomplishments with mechanical and alchemical wonders preserved from the court of the Yellow Emperor.

Crafting objects in a state of meditative absorption is the chief manner by which Akashic Brothers harness this Dharma. For example, a diligent swordsmith can control the composition and sharpness of her creations with supernatural skill. Machines based on or enhanced by the principles of Chinese alchemy also see use within the Brotherhood. Materials such as mercury oxide and minium (rust) are used as the inorganic counterparts to the elemental energies of Life Patterns and can be used to invest objects with motion or alter them to interact selectively with living beings.

Mind — Mushin, Santana

Paradoxically, the Sphere of Mind is described by many Akashics using the Japanese concept of mushin, or "no-mind." Mushin is a state where the mind is not cluttered by egotism or conscious "noise," able to perceive, act and react without hindrance. By quieting the mind, one opens up to other minds. When the illusion of self disappears, one *is* other minds. This is not telepathy as Western mages understand it but a spontaneous understanding that arises in a group of minds that are exposed to the truth that lies past Samsara and selfishness. Without reference to the self, the mind is a santana, a "stream" of consciousness that can flow into others.

More pragmatically, Shi-Ren Legalists see the selfish thoughts that clutter the mind as tools to change a subject's behavior. Selfish motivations dictate a person's reactions to discipline and reward, and can be effective tools to manipulate them.

Meditation is the fundamental tool of Akashic Mind Arts. Do can also be used to alter the mind by altering the body, as can acupuncture and massage. Mantras, mudras, calligraphy, trance states, asceticism and severe exercise also allow a Brother to rid themselves of distractions and alter their own and others' mental states. In many cases, an Akashic also makes use of the Akashic Record to sense and alter the stream of pure consciousness before it manifests as a physical event.

A pacifist monk in quiet meditation can contact other minds by eliminating the barriers of the ego, and a Li-Hai can chant relevant portions of the Stone Sutra in such a way as to fill a greedy politician with shame.

Life — Internal Alchemy

Called neigong (internal achievement), the Akashic study of Life centers around training the individual to master his own body rather than making the body a static, physical subject. Chi flows through the body in meridians that correspond to Yin, Yang and the Five Agents. Thus, the human body is a microcosm of the Tapestry, with its own dragon lines and elemental balance. Chi balance can be harmonized, unbalanced or disrupted through herbs, pressure point manipulation and acts of Do.

The environment can affect the body as well. The Tapestry affects its human microcosm. All beings follow the primordial template, being energies manifested as plant and animal tissue. Only the exact interaction of the primordial elements differ.

An Akashic Brother might use pressure-point manipulation to dispel pain and stop the bleeding from a wound. Shouts and chants may also be "tuned" to the vibrations of specific organs, meridians, muscles and bones. One Akashic Life rote called the Mahasuklaja ("Great White Shattering") consists of a specific mudra and chants designed to destroy particular tissues. While it's based on a technique used to remove infections and destroy malignant growths, it can, like any medicine, be turned to less merciful purposes.

Prime — Chi

Chi began as the breath of Pangu, the Cosmic Person. The basic energy of existence, Chi coalesces into Yin and Yang, and orders itself according to the Divine Mandate. The Sam Chien and its ministers Tiger, Dragon and Phoenix, regulates Chi flow. It is the Absolute manifest, where karma and the interaction of the Five Agents break down all phenomena before it is given new existence. Chi is identified with Akasha, the primal revelation of existence. Human beings regulate Chi through breathing. The act by which Pangu brought it forth into the universe. All beings and objects possess Chi, but only a few beings can consciously gather and harvest it. Beings such as the Kuei-jin steal it from mortals, accumulating dark Resonance. The Awakened may tap the energy of the All with penalties that vary according to their intent and the source of the power. Yin (Entropy), Yang (Dynamic) and Li (Static) Resonance must be balanced and purified, or an Akashayana risks losing touch with her own Awakened nature.

Yoga aligns an Akashic Brother's meridians to the ambient Chi of an area. His body and mind become very receptive to changes in the Resonance of a place or thing, and he can store and discharge this power by practicing Do techniques where his body mimics the alignment of the Cosmic Furies. Asceticism removes self-centeredness, keeping his Chi from freely interacting with the Tapestry's, and vice versa. An enlightened mystic can make use of his austerities to manifest miracles such as the spontaneous creation of jewels, flowers or even fire, and the aura that surrounds him is painful for malignant spirits to be near.

SPIRIT — SHEN

Akashic Brothers are of two minds about the realm of Spirit. One school, supported by the Jnani and Kannagara, believe that spirits are the reflections of sentient beings upon the All. Spirits are no different from aspects of one's nature. Therefore, the Awakened mind contains the spirit realms themselves. While this leads some to believe that the Akashic Brotherhood has little respect for the shen, the truth is that Akashic shamans and summoners believe that they are just as much aspects of the spirits as the other way around.

The other school holds that all shen, from the filthiest Kuei-jin hustler to the Dragon itself, belong to a Celestial bureaucracy that administers the affairs of the Ten Thousand Things. Spirits and gods are separate beings with their own agendas, but they are ultimately bound to the portfolios given to them by the August Personage of Jade. This is the adamant belief of the Shi-Ren and Wu Lung.

Both schools accept that there are of six realms of existence, through which all beings travel on their journey through the Wheel. Tien (Heaven), known in the West as the Astral Umbra, is the abode of the gods. At its summit, it reaches into the remnants of Meru. Below that, Maya, the Dreaming, is where godlings scheme for mastery over one another and the mortal world. The Yang World is the Realm of Beasts, where the spirits of nature descend and the struggle of the Sam Chien begins. The Yin World, much in disarray, is where all things dissolve into the Dragon's coils, save those with a passion for their previous lives. The Ten Thousand Hells, often called Yomi, or Tu Yi, is where those consumed with sin are reborn to eternal torture. One hell, the Pit of Harmony, is said to specialize in fallen Akashayana.

But the most important realm is the Human Realm. Without divine pleasures or infernal tortures, the Awakened can reach towards Samadhi. Only mortal men and women Awaken — and only they can find true salvation.

Taoist Jnani use records of the offices of important sprits and then trek to the places they might be found. More metaphysically inclined Brothers meditate upon thought forms and render them in movement, drawing or writing. Do the spirits that arise from such practices arise from the Brother's consciousness? Only the spirits and Bodhisattvas know for sure.

TIME — THE WHEEL OF AGES

Time is not a straight line, but a cycle. The Wheel of Ages is a continuous circle of creation and destruction by which karma resolves itself. The great mahakalpas of thousands of aeons breaks down into yugas of mere thousands of years, decades, years, days, hours and seconds, all reflecting the primal Wheel. But time itself is not an objective phenomenon. It is seen through the eyes of the limited self. With training, Akashayana can see beyond the time they measure with mortal breaths. With this insight, a millennium can pass in a single breath, and an hour can expand to a lifetime.

Meditation and trance states can free a Brother's mind from an attachment to a particular place. Since the Brotherhood's theory of karma holds that is reducible to mental events, Akashics can manipulate time in the physical sphere by beginning with the mind. Akashayana can appear in several moments simultaneously — or none, vanishing from the Wheel completely, if they discipline their minds and bodies to the point where the Great Cycle no longer acts upon them.

DRAHMA — RIGHT EXISTENCE

The Akashics hold the tenth Sphere to be the Drahma. The Law of Transcending the Enemy is the principle from which all Dharmas emanate. To touch the essence of the universe, you must live according to its rules. To achieve harmony with the All, act with sincerity and let go of desires is all that the Bodhisattvas expect of a mage — or anyone, for that matter.

SORCERY

The Akashic Brotherhood has other miracle-workers in its ranks. While sorcery is potent, it is not a sign of greater enlightenment. Sorcery does not challenge Samsara but works inside its confines.

Static sorcerers who join the Brotherhood do so in the hope of gaining sufficient merit to attain Samadhi after death, or to gain the merit to Awaken later in life or in their next incarnation. Akashic sorcerers gravitate towards the Jnani and Shi-Ren, where their careful, ritualistic style is appreciated. Most Akashics know that being Awakened confers the possibility of true enlightenment at any moment, but have little idea of the functional difference between practicing Awakened and sorcerous magic. They merely believe that sorcerers aren't yet ready to see what lies beyond the world of illusion and attempt to help them make that breakthrough.

THE END OF VIOLENCE

The blade struck her in the eye, but violent, smiling Sataghni still twisted with the claw hand. Ming, Smoke Tiger, dropped to one knee as her shoulder wrenched out of its socket. She slid forward, leaving a wake of rainwater for Battering Ram to fall to, dead.

As she fell, Peter saw that her hands still twitched, eager to strike another blow.

Masako rolled under a kick to slash at Ming's supporting foot with her wakizashi, but her target took to the air. Smoke Tiger's spinning body cut through the rainy sky in a maneuver that kept all of them in her line of sight. Peters drew his sword,

and Raging Eagle swept his feet through the water, weaving space through the conduit of Meru with his steps.

Indra's Net rippled, and there were two of him. One appeared at Smoke Tiger's flank, checking her arm and striking with his fingers, while another still stood in front of Peter, hands raised to guard his Sidai.

Smoke Tiger reversed Raging Eagle's trapping arm, twisting his wrist away, while his spear-hand cut her across the temple. She sunk and stamped the roof. A wave of water flew along it, washing past Masako's knees. Peter saw the Li-Hai slide off of the roof, her sword spinning out of her hand. She clung by an gutter with one hand.

Smoke Tiger wrenched Raging Eagle's wrist, but he shifted, catching her own hand to reverse the hold. She turned her hips into the big man, forcing him to step back, a palm extended to defend the motion. Leaping away from him, she gestured with her injured arm. Two fingers wrapped with prayer beads thrust towards Masako. The gutter snapped and Masako fell.

Peter lowered his stance, raised his sword to join the fight, but Raging Eagle, standing in front of him, held up a hand to keep him at bay. *Not yet*, it said to him.

One of his Sifu's bodies closed in on Ming, and the two lashed at each other so quickly that only dark trails and flying droplets of water could be seen. Then Raging Eagle was staggered by a fist, and in front of Peter, his double flinched, as ribs broke, piercing the skin, from the blow delivered to his counterpart. The ragged bones shone in the neon light that reflected off the wet roof tiles.

Smoke Tiger roared. The animal sound issued from a face streaked with red from Raging Eagle's blow. Both of her feet lifted and pointed toes drove into his torso, but he shifted back with the strike, rolling forward again with a slow forearm that seemed to just brush her chest.

She was lifted off her feet. She backflipped to regain her footing, but skidded a dozen feet away along the wet tile, finally stopping on one knee.

While one of his bodies advanced on her, Peter heard pained, quick breathing from the man beside him. Raging Eagle's skin was mottled from bruising, and he shivered.

"Please, Ming," the one walking towards her said. "You have to come to the Garuda Valley with me. The Kannagara will make you see that this is the best way."

She grinned and shrugged, her shoulder sinking back into its socket. "It all falls apart, Nu Ying. That's what the Chakravanti knew. Our best plans. The doors we barricade our secrets behind. Even our bodies." She turned to the one guarding Peter. "Even your real body, over here."

Her right arm lashed out again, and the prayer beads whipped forward. The string of her rosary broke, and there was a cracking noise like the sound of Sataghni's gun.

The man advancing towards her vanished and Peter saw Raging Eagle tumble backwards with three crimson holes in his midriff, each the shape of prayer beads. He saw the rest of the beads float down to the water from her throwing hand, falling slowly as his Sifu crumpled. Peter caught him as he fell, and Raging Eagle's dark, tired eyes looked up to him.

Smoke Tiger stood and walked toward him. She wasn't smiling any more.

THE THOUSAND PETALED LOTUS: AKASHIC SYSTEMS

I declare to you that within this fathom long body lies the origin and ending of the whole universe.
— attributed to the Buddha Sakyamuni

Mastery of Do, hidden advantages, and secret flaws make members of the Sangha distinctive among their colleagues in the Tradition.

NEW TALENT: DO

Xiao Mengli parried the saber, barely feeling the bite of the steel on her conditioned forearms. Crimson Thunder curved his weapon around her blocking arm, showing his skill by refusing to lean closer and provide an opening.

As she clasped the blade between two callused palms, Xiao Mengli's mind began to overlay the battle with a swirl of elements. Her opponent's blade was like a rushing stream, trying to find a way to flow around her unyielding defense. Like stone, her swift blocks would eventually be worn down or bypassed.

She changed tactics. When the swordsman spun a backhanded strike around the anticipated guard, he left an opening for her hand to strike straight for the throat, like a metal spear piercing the eye of a typhoon.

As the swordsman's death rattle rang at his fingertips, Xiao Mengli was seized by a sudden sense of futility. Life was a fleeting thing.

The Do skill represents a character's all-around dedication to Akashic training methods, with an emphasis on the Dharmamukti, or unarmed combat arts. Do is the "secret art" whose many names are whispered of in martial arts legends, the progenitor of more modern forms and the most efficient, effective style of unarmed combat in existence. As a vital part of the Akashic paradigm, it serves as the focus for much of the Brotherhood's magic. So much so that the magical and mundane aspects of the art are considered inseparable.

Strictly speaking, Do is far more than the talent presented below. Other Abilities must be purchased to learn it, and it is restricted to Akashic Brothers and very close allies. For more information, see page 61.

Do is a Talent because, to Akashic thinking, it's a way of removing excess baggage and returning to pure, unfettered human existence. Although it's practiced, it is not a formal Skill.

- • Novice: Sometimes, the right movements come naturally, but usually you just respond by reflex.
- •• Practiced: Your mind and body work efficiently together, but remain separated by a lack of understanding.
- ••• Competent: You can call yourself a Tao-shih without your master raising an eyebrow in amusement.
- •••• Expert: Reflex and perception are one. Junior Akashics call you Sihing.
- ••••• Master: You never plan your movements in advance, or use a particular technique. You *are* movement and technique, and your actions flow with the Wheel.

Possessed by: Akashic Brothers, their most trusted allies and their best Sleeper students. Enlightened martial artists have been known to develop it independently as well, but most of them are inducted into the Brotherhood posthaste.

Specialties: Restraining without harming, Pressure point attacks, Noncombative performance, a specific style

NEW KNOWLEDGE: BODY CONTROL

Xiao Mengli could feel every spasm of her heart as it pumped blood and Chi through her body. It was unsteady, racing like a tripping sprinter. Her leg had broken in the fall and her head had bounced off a windowsill. She was in shock.

She saw her heart in her mind and visualized it slowing, returning to a steady pace. She pulled the pain from her leg and stood up.

"There's still work to do," she said to herself. "It's not time to die."

Practice for a few days and one can master the simple movements of a limb in combat. Practice for years, and even the muscles and systems of the body that function naturally come under control. With sufficient discipline and study, a focused student can learn to moderate breathing, block out pain, even take charge over heartbeat, digestion and other bodily functions.

Body Control is *usually* a nonmagical, though rigorous, feat. Like Do, it's a skill that requires dedicated study and focus, but in theory anyone with enough discipline could learn it. However, it often functions best when augmented with a little Life magic, which in turn allows the practitioner to perform truly extraordinary feats — metabolizing poisons, rapidly healing wounds and resisting burns.

Under stress situations, use Wits + Body Control (difficulty 8) to exert one facet of this Knowledge. In calm situations, use Intelligence + Body Control (difficulty 7). Usually, an extended roll is possible, representing a character taking several minutes of concentration to adjust his bodily functions.

Successes	Feat
1	**Withdraw Testicles:** The character does not suffer debilitating pain from a strike to the groin.
1	**Hold Breath:** The character holds his breath for one minute per dot of Stamina. Each additional success adds another minute. Extended successes don't add to this duration, though.
1	**Moderated Sleep:** With a moment's relaxation the character can fall asleep under any circumstances.
2	**Tolerate Temperature:** The character manages to mitigate the effects of extreme heat or cold. Reduce the damage dice pool for fire, heat or frost by one die. The character doesn't suffer any fatigue or inconvenience due to temperature.
2	**Transcend Pain:** Reduce dice-pool penalties due to wounds by one for the remainder of the scene.
3	**Slow Bleeding and Breathing:** Regulation of breath, heart rate and body repair allows the character to mitigate the effects of shock and severe injury. A character reduced to the Wounded health level or worse can stabilize injuries without risk

of further bleeding or other complications (aside from being hit again, of course).

3   Digestive Control: The character can exert control over the muscles that aid digestion in the stomach and intestines. This can slow the rate of absorption, in case the character has ingested poisoned or diseased substances. Although the character eventually absorbs the substance, this delays the onset of toxicity by a full hour per success scored.

4   Death Trance: The character enters a coma-like state. Only advanced medical technology (or magic) can determine that the character still lives. In this state, the character consumes little oxygen but the body maintains itself. Bleeding halts, the body delays the effects of poison and the individual essentially remains in a state much like suspended animation with all bodily functions at a crawl.

You may only use one of these effects at a time, though with concentration (and multiple successful rolls) you might be able to combine them. You don't automatically stack them if you roll multiple successes, nor do you automatically take the effects of the highest roll (that is, just because you scored five successes on your character's attempt to hold his breath doesn't mean that the character enters a coma). You can't score a level of success greater than your number of dots in the Knowledge — having a high associated Attribute simply makes you better at achieving certain levels of effect.

- •   Student: You've learned to feel your breathing.
- ••   College: With concentration you can ignore needles, shrug off heat and soothe your breath, just like a yogi.
- •••   Masters: Even normally autonomic functions fall under your sway when you pause to pay attention to your body's rhythms.
- ••••   Doctorate: You can bring your body near death or incapacitation and still recover due to your startling control of muscles, blood and the healing process.
- •••••   Scholar: You've learned to *feel* your breathing.

Possessed By: Shamans, Yogis, Jnani, Freakshow Performers

Specialties: Any of the above-listed feats

New Knowledge: Strategy

Gar-Quen closed his laptop and looked up to the other Sihing who anxiously watched from across the heavy oak table.

"The Metal Dragons are planning a major offensive, to seize the dragon nest from a local temple. Their 'gift,' a new shrine, will include surveillance devices.

"They've started by surrounding the local clergy with their security. Patrols regularly sweep the area to catch any of our scouts. However, they didn't count on one thing."

A Kannagara raised his eyebrows in curiosity.

"We won't go for the shrine, we'll go for them. With all of their people busy, they've left their headquarters dangerously unmanned.

"Kill the brain, Brothers, and the body dies."

You are skilled at organizing people and resources to overcome an enemy, be it an army, a tong, or an up-and-coming law firm. You can give effective orders, although making people

believe they're the right orders is the purview of the Leadership Ability. Similarly, you must have a basic grasp of the organization you are working with, which may require other Abilities. However, only you know how to pick out an opponent's weak spots and exploit them with the assets at hand.

- •   Student: Miniatures gamer.
- ••   College: Armchair general. You've read the *Art of War*.
- •••   Masters: A commissioned officer. You actually understand the *Art of War*.
- ••••   Doctorate: Oda Nobunaga
- •••••   Scholar: Sun Tzu

Possessed by: Shi-Ren, Vajrapani, Wu Lung from the Tiger School, Crime bosses, Soldiers, Business figures

Specialties: Military, Business, Crime, Ancient, Modern, Nuclear, Espionage, Games

The Seeds of Karma: New Merits and Flaws

The following Merits and Flaws provide new ways to make Akashic characters distinctive. Some of these arise from Akashic philosophy of peace and mental discipline, while others relate to the cultural traditions that the Brotherhood has embraced throughout its history.

Folk Hero (3-pt. Social Merit)

Your people love you. You stood up to a corrupt official, ended a drought, got a new hospital built, or did any number of things that endeared you to the people in your community. When you're there, they'll do almost anything to help you, as long as you maintain your previous upstanding behavior.

A signature merit for Li-Hai, *Folk Hero* gives you a blanket -2 difficulty on Social rolls with people from the community you helped. Furthermore, your character can always get basic food and shelter there, and if he's in trouble with the law or just needs a place to hide, they'll find him a garage or back room to lay his head. Just keep two things in mind: First, these are ordinary working class or agrarian people; your character isn't going to be borrowing a jet or a laptop from them (though he might get a bicycle). Second, while they don't expect him to rescue every cat and till every rocky field for his sick neighbor, they do expect him to stand up for his community when times are tough. If he turns his back on them, they'll turn their backs on him.

MET: You gain two Traits on the resolution of Social Challenges with members of your community. On a successful Social Challenge, "your people" will hide you from the law or make sure you have the basic necessities of life, providing you help them periodically and don't abuse the privilege, as noted above.

Drahma's Voice (4- to 6-pt. Social Merit)

Whether you're a child, a drunk or a monk, you speak with more wisdom than you possess. Perhaps you are a reincarnated sage, or you simply have an intuitive connection with the Absolute that expresses itself in your voice and actions.

In game terms, your character is a *Mentor* for Akashic mages (and, at the Storyteller's discretion, others who might understand her words), despite the fact that she isn't particularly wise herself. The four-point version of this Merit turns your character into a one-dot *Mentor* — you may add more dots at a cost of one point per dot. For six points, your character serves as a three-dot *Mentor* to other people, even if she lacks the usual knowledge to teach in such fashion. She can't benefit from this herself. She doesn't know why the other Sidai light up with sudden understanding when she tells them a joke or a bar story!

MET: Though you aren't particularly knowledgeable or enlightened you can act as a *Mentor*. The four-point version gives you one Trait of the *Mentor* Background, and additional levels add *Mentor* Traits on a one-for-one basis that your allies (though not you) can use to justify the purchase of Spheres and Abilities normally teachable by a *Mentor* of the appropriate Trait value. To do this, they have to discuss the knowledge they're trying to gain with you.

Judge's Wisdom (4-pt. Mental Merit)

You aren't swayed by emotion. Ever. Perhaps you're a strict Legalist who follows Han Fei Tzu's advice to keep emotion out of the business of living, or your heart has been calmed by years of meditation. In any event, even magical attempts to alter your emotional state almost always fail.

Your character is immune to all Mind effects that work on the emotions, the power of vampiric Presence and similar effects. He can still be swayed by attempts at direct mind control, such as possession, mental illusions, vampiric Dominate and the like, and extremely potent powers (with six or more dots) may overwhelm his defenses. Your character can be calm but weak willed, after all. Note that you cannot take both this Merit and the Merit *Iron Will*. That would result in a quick ticket to Clarity!

MET: Short of the use of Archspheres, Superior Disciplines and similarly potent powers, you're immune to any attempt to sway your emotions. No test is required.

Ontological Pacifist (3- or 5-pt. Mental Flaw)

You literally believe that peace is the way of the Drahma. Violence is an offense against the Dharmas themselves, and they would never manifest in someone who had stained himself with it.

For three points, your character immediately loses all benefits from use of foci if he ever commits an act of violence that isn't direct self-defense (i.e. striking preemptively or without cause). You will probably have to use the Surpassing Foci rules (**Mage: The Ascension**, p. 203) to cast effects. The foci won't work for your character until he makes some sort of restitution to the victim or purifies himself in a suitably arduous fashion (the restitution should generally be the easier option). For five points, you suffer this penalty if your character directly or indirectly commits a violent act against any sentient creature for any reason. In both cases, magical compulsion makes no difference. And yes, the problem becomes less severe as you discard foci.

MET: If you trigger the conditions listed above, any attempt to cast magic is treated as if you have no foci for any sort of effect, even if you have the focus right in front of you or have more than enough Ability Traits to normally proceed with the task. This lasts until you compensate your victim or genuinely repent for your actions. The Storyteller determines what counts as adequate compensation or sincere repentance.

In the Field of Corpses

Smoke Tiger studied Peter, and for a moment old Chan Ng came out, adjusting his sword to prepare for the fight. Peter fought the urge off and dropped the weapon. It landed with a splash.

Smoke Tiger raised her fists in a Wu Chuan guard, the killing knuckles extended and raised to cover the navel and throat. Settling into a deep stance, she spoke. "So, why was he protecting you?"

Peter's voice fell deep and steady as he replied. "I'm no threat to you, Lou Fu. I'm here to help you." He glanced down. Raging Eagle was still alive, though he bled from three wounds. "I— I'm not like him. I'm no killer." In the corner of his eyes, he saw his Sifu's pale fingers spasm.

"So you're here to learn the trade, eh? They must have something important lined up for you."

Peter? It was Masako. He felt her thoughts wash into his mind. *Keep her talking. I'll be up soon.*

"I remember, Lou Fu. I was there. I want to help the Brotherhood remember." He could feel Masako silently sliding up between this building and another, her muscles straining.

Smoke Tiger frowned. "Too obvious, Sidai. Your eyes move too much when you're being spoken to. It gives her away. I'll deal with it." She pivoted, making a crescent from the rainwater. Her waist twisted, storing power, as she faced the direction where Peter knew Masako would come.

"No, Luo Fu. Come into the Record with me. I'll open my mind and then you can do as you wish." He swept through his mind, the great mandala of his thoughts. He turned the lines of power guarding it into sand, and the wind in his soul blew it away. He dropped the mental defenses he'd learned from Cheng Sa so long ago. "If you look deeply, you know I mean it." He choked on his fear, knowing that the woman in front of him could order him to kill himself or Masako, to do *anything* she desired. And he would see those desires as his own.

With his mental guard down, Masako's voice seemed to scream in his skull. *What are you doing, Sidai? She'll kill you!*

He winced. *Stay away. You're too hurt to fight. I think I know what to do now.*

"So, it just means you're willing to die," said Smoke Tiger.

"No. Look deeper, Smoke Tiger. Don't you recognize your general?"

Do

Do is a mysterious practice. It is virtually never taught outside the Sangha and any outside knowledge of the Way consists of a set of educated guesses gleaned from the thousands of mind/body disciplines that the Brotherhood has influenced. In the past, Do's formidable techniques were taught to non-Brothers who simply fought alongside the Tradition. Now that the Akashayana are returning to their roots, Do's methods have become closely guarded secrets, shared only with those mages who can understand and accept Akashic magic and ethics alongside their own.

Origins

The ancient sects of the Akashics have always practiced holistic disciplines that cultivate the mind, body and spirit. These trace their history to Meru, whose sages performed every act with focus and sincerity. Gardening, war and song were all approached this way. To discriminate between "important" and "unimportant" acts could only blind an Akashi from the truth of Drahma.

After Meru's fall, these arts were used to ensure the Brotherhood's survival through persecutions and political upheavals. The Vajrapani pioneered Wu Chuan, to protect the Jnani and Kannagara from harm. The ancient techniques of Indian, Chinese and Korean ascetics and warriors influenced and were influenced by the peoples that the early Akashi encountered. In response, the Brotherhood began teaching gate arts to the people. These were intentionally watered-down or distorted varieties of Do that served their practitioners well enough but prevented the truly dangerous methods of the art from falling into the wrong hands. Furthermore, a gifted student of these arts grew beyond the limitations of the practice, and showed herself to be ready for the Brotherhood and its undiluted mysteries.

Do divided into hundreds of styles to serve the needs of a particular Brother or group. Drala Yoga, Akashamukti and Jou Chuan were just three of the many arts that formed out of expediency, egotism or both.

The Warring States Period and the Himalayan Wars provided a brutal testing ground for Do's ethics and methods. Impractical techniques died with their users, and corrupt warriors revealed themselves when they quickly reincarnated, thirsty for revenge.

In response, the Akashayana accepted groups such as the Li-Hai and Buddhist magi into the fold. These new sects emphasized ethical duty and pacifism, reigning in the worst excesses of the Warring Fist. Finally, in 300 B.C., the Jnani composed the Drahma Sutra from the recollections of the Akashic Record and the bitter experiences of Himalayan warriors and pacifist sages. The styles of Do, as well as its name, were codified for the first time.

This structure has been used for the past 2300 years with little change. The Li-Hai and associated schools such as the Roda d'Oro take the loosest approach to the teachings. The Kannagara, the strictest. Few students master the strictest form of Do as laid out in the Drahma Sutra. The techniques are often taught with no individual adaptation and little guidance beyond the traditional forms. In the past, this was done to prevent selfish or lazy students from progressing, but in the 21st century, the oldest forms of Do have succumbed to both the Technocratic view of the body (which has made some traditional Do skills, such as body hardening, more dangerous than useful). Fewer people are willing to give up their freedom without asking some serious questions of their "masters."

The Art

The Drahma Sutra divides Do into eight "limbs," or areas of study. While it emphasizes certain practices to cure physical, mental and moral ailments, no limb is considered more important than the others.

The Eight Limbs are:

Dhyana: The limb of meditation is used to calm the excitable mind and relax the grip of the ego upon the Akashic's consciousness. Tiger, Dragon, Phoenix, the Five Elements and mandalas of movement and design are only a few of the techniques used to liberate the mind.

Abilities: Awareness, Enigmas, Meditation

Prajna: The study of ethics and philosophy, this limb is emphasized for students with impulsive or violent tendencies. From Mo-tzu's pacifistic iconoclasm to the Buddha's sermons, the Akashayana learns to reflexively treat others with compassion and respect by learning the origins of suffering and their solutions, and how they are mirrored in the Tapestry and the laws of karma.

Abilities: Academics (Philosophy), Cosmology, Law (Akashic codes)

Karma: Hard work, aside from its sheer utility, focuses a Brother's attention on the here and now and emphasizes the importance of everyday life over the spectacular, dangerous pursuits of a magician. The limb of Karma teaches a student to treat cooking and cleaning with the same devotion and aesthetic care as occult diagrams or swordplay.

Abilities: Crafts (Artistic or professional skills), Etiquette

Sunyakaya: The limb of the Empty Body contains the techniques of stealth, illusion and espionage. While these are often cultivated to teach humility through anonymity, their practical use is not necessarily so innocent. The Lin Shen and Sulsa often devote their lives to mastering the sunyakaya arts.

Abilities: Performance, Stealth, Subterfuge

Dharmamukti: Do's unarmed combat techniques are taught to every member of the Brotherhood. The violent years of the Ascension War made this the most popular facet of Do. Katas, sparring and thousands of drills comprise the methods of the "Dharma Clasped Hand." As Sleeper martial arts have developed new innovations, unarmed Do has been adapted to accommodate them, particularly by the Li-Hai and Vajrapani. While the art's techniques comprise practically every effective combative movement ever developed, different styles and teachers often diverge in their methods.

Abilities: Alertness, Do, Dodge

Shastamarga: The Way of Weapons extends Do beyond the body, teaching the disciple to become one with the tool. A specialty of the Vajrapani, shastamarga is also used by Brothers who wish to perfect the use of an object rather than become better killers. These Akashics often construct complex or extra-heavy weapons to challenge their abilities to the limit.

Abilities: Crafts (Weapons), Melee, Strategy

Tricanmarga: The Way of the Triple Struggle includes the secrets of internal alchemy, breath control, athletics and asceticism as the student resolves the struggle of the Tiger, Dragon and Phoenix in his mind, body and emotions. By taming the microcosm, an Akashic can perform amazing physical feats and act in harmony with the cosmological forces outside himself.

Abilities: Acrobatics, Athletics, Body Control

Jivahasta: The Hand of Life comprises Do's therapeutic and medical arts. These include herbalism, acupuncture, massage, body movement and more mystical methods involving the use of chanting, written charms and even tattooing.

Abilities: Academics (Tibetan, Chinese medical theory, Herbalism), Medicine, Survival

Ten Thousand Fists: The Styles of Do

The Himalayan War and China's Spring and Autumn Period forced Do's rapid evolution from the relatively simple, efficient skills that the Akashi brought with them from Meru to a host of methods to deal with specific problems. Many of these have fallen into disuse. A technique to fell a mounted warrior with a spear rarely comes into play in the 21st century.

The Brotherhood used watered-down versions of these techniques to teach its ideals to the common people and to recruit new Initiates. At the same time, mortal innovations in the martial arts influenced Do's methods. Today, many Tao-shih teach a gate art, such as aikido, wing chun, or karate, to draw followers and test new ideas.

By the time of the First Convocation, the Brotherhood had instituted a standardized training scheme that trained each sect in the skills they needed to serve the Tradition and the Council as a whole. Nevertheless, some Tao-shih stuck by their personal methods and continued to teach ancient arts in concert with the official styles.

Today, the following styles see frequent use among the Akashayana. Others exist, but their teachers are hard to find and require the utmost loyalty from prospective students.

Lohan Chuan: Monk Fist was the art of the famous Shaolin monks. Kannagara use it to test the limits of the physical form through arduous exercise, acrobatics and complex postures. While it is an "external" art in terms of its techniques, it is rarely used for combat. Some of Lohan Chuan's postures are so complicated and athletically demanding that only a martial artist as well trained as an Akashic

could use them effectively in combat. Yogic postures, ritual chanting and a strict diet are part of the regimen as well.

Hsien Chuan: Immortal's Fist is an internal style that focuses on cultivating Chi, misdirecting the enemy and manipulating emotions. The Shi-Ren practice this art as much for the boardroom as the battlefield. They learn how to use body language to frighten or charm, and they can call upon their internal power to radiate calm and confidence. Legalist classics and medicine are studied alongside gentle, languorous postures.

Wu Chuan: Warring Fist is a brutal and practical style whose name has been used to define the Brotherhood as whole. Developed during the Himalayan War, the style combines internal and external movements with a variety of weapons. A student learns strategy and tactics and how to exploit the weaknesses of the mind and body. Direct and martial, the Vajrapani's method is criticized by other sects for being *too* combative and bereft of spiritual qualities.

Shen Chuan: The Jnani teach their students an internal method that explains the body as a microcosm of the whole Tapestry. Medicine and metaphysics link actions to the whole and yield to incoming aggression. The resultant art is similar to aikido or tai chi in outlook and technique, and many practitioners studied these two gate arts before joining the Akashayana. Masters are said to be able to strike or throw an opponent from a distance by causing the universe to move in concert with their bodies.

Yung Chuan: The Li-Hai style of Do emphasizes freedom and creativity under the deceptive moniker of "Ordinary Fist." Masters of the style assess an individual student's needs and prescribe the techniques best suited for her. These need not be traditional martial arts movements — boxing, modern dance and Nietzsche are studied alongside traditional kung fu. Using the Eight Limbs as a framework, a Yung Chuan Tao-shih divests herself of attachment to a particular school or method. The art also follows Li-Hai ethics by emphasizing disarming and restraining. The goal is to stop violence rather than master it.

The Living Art: Systems

Previous versions of Do have presented it as a sort of "super kung fu," with a lot of power but not much variety. While the Akashic Brotherhood receives the finest training in the world (although not the most dedicated; see the Shih in **Demon Hunter X**), it has a diversity that goes beyond the ability to deliver killing blows and jump onto rooftops.

A new Akashic character can begin with no more than two dots of Do, even after spending Freebie Traits. Members of other Traditions may not begin with it at all and may only learn it if they can work magic in the Akashic paradigm and have the trust of a senior Brother (see **Initiates of the Art** for information on using multiple paradigms).

Do cannot be learned in isolation, because it is a synthesis of techniques gathered under the Akashic paradigm. To successfully grasp it (and fill out those dots on your character sheet!) a Brother must have twice as many levels in Abilities that belong to limbs other than the Dharmamukti (unarmed combat) as the level of Do the character is trying to learn. These must be spread out over a number of limbs equal to the required levels of mastery.

For example, Sai Fong is trying to master the fourth level of Do. To do this, she needs to have eight levels in other limbs, spread out among four limbs other than the Dharmamukti. She has Crafts (clothes dyeing) 2, Melee 3, Academics (Buddhist Philosophy) 1 and Athletics 1. She has studied the Karma, Shastamarga, Prajna and Tricanmarga limbs by learning these Abilities, so her skills are broad enough, but she falls slightly short in terms of sheer knowledge. She learns a level of Medicine from a Sleeper acupuncturist and begins to see the common links between Do and the healing arts. After a period of intense training, those insights allow her to learn that fourth level.

Furthermore, individual Sihings and Sifus often have their own standards beyond the minimum. Jou Shan always insisted that his students be as skilled in mediation and rituals as the fighting arts. The Jade Dragon reportedly accepts only students who master a skill that he himself doesn't know (considering that he's nearly eight hundred years old, that's no easy feat), so that the Fallen Brother's agents will have a diverse array of skills.

Do Basics

In its basic form, Do uses the same maneuvers as the Brawl Talent. However, hard training and Awakened instruction means that these movements have more accuracy and lethality than those used by a street fighter or most martial artists. Remember also that Do, Brawl, and Martial Arts (for those using **Kindred of the East** or other Year of the Lotus books) are separate Abilities. If your character has 2 dots of Do and 4 dots of Brawl, you have to choose between the better dice pool and the nifty abilities. You can't mix and match to get the best of both.

These are the core benefits that Do provides as soon as it is learned:

Lethal Attacks: Damage from unarmed Do maneuvers is lethal due to the Tao-shih's facility with pressure points or focused power. She can choose to reduce it to bashing (changing damage types is a reflexive action that can be declared at any time before the player rolls to see if she hits).

Hardened Defense: Similarly, Brawl or Melee attacks that cause lethal damage can be blocked while unarmed by rolling Dexterity + Do, difficulty 5 (see below for the reason for the reduced difficulty). Iron-hard limbs either stop the weapon, or the character is quick and fluid enough to make contact safely by catching a blade between her hands, blocking at the forearm instead of the weapon, etc. This cannot be used against projectiles or bullets.

Well Trained: Because of the intensive mental and physical training that Tao-shih go through, the difficulty to use Do in combat is always one less than its Brawl counterpart. For example, A Tao-shih using Do to punch an opponent would do so at difficulty 5, while a kick would be difficulty 6.

These benefits make Do an awesome fighting art, but Akashic Brothers should (as usual) restrain their egos. Given an equal amount of time to study, a mundane martial artist can become more accomplished in less time, because he doesn't have to study anything outside of fighting to grow. Do, on the other hand, gains its strength by learning the lessons of many fields, promoting adaptability and making the whole more than the sum of its parts.

Do in Mind's Eyes Theatre

In **MET**, Do is greatly simplified. **MET** games should have a minimum of combat in any case. Plot and character development should be the order of the day.

Nevertheless, Do is a potent combat ability. No Akashic can start with more than two Ability Traits in Do, and no other character can possess it without securing tutelage in game. As stated elsewhere, a non-Akashic must be able to use magic in the Akashic paradigm to qualify for Do training and must demonstrate loyalty to the Sangha. Sleeper students must be utterly devoted to the Brotherhood as well.

Anyone who learns Do must have twice as many Ability Traits in related Abilities (the ones listed under Do's Eight Limbs) as the number of Do Traits the player intends to have when she spends Experience Traits. These must be spread out over as many limbs as the level of Do to be purchased.

Do cannot be used in the same conflict as the Brawl or Martial Arts Abilities. While using Do, a character can choose to deliver lethal or bashing damage with unarmed strikes. He adds one Trait to her Physical Traits during combat challenges so long as she has any remaining levels of Do, just like using a specialty.

Furthermore, an Akashic can choose special maneuvers, as described below (each special maneuver has a **MET** equivalent). Every level of Do learned permits one special maneuver.

If the Storyteller is using Dragon Rules (**Laws of the East**, p.193) then Do grants the same benefits as Brawl, Martial Arts, or Melee when determining extra damage.

Do training is time-consuming. An Akashic Brother must spend one hour per Do Trait per day training, or her skills diminish. This can be handled during downtime but hampers the character's ability to maintain Influences, Contacts or the like. As a rule of thumb, Storytellers can rule that Do Traits are added to a Brother's total Influences when determining the maximum number of Influence Traits the character can retain at any given time. A Brother can choose to ignore the time-consuming aspects of Do training, but a Storyteller should reduce the lazy Tao-shih's Do Traits accordingly.

Movements of Mastery: Maneuvers

If you are using the system presented in **Kindred of the East** (p.140-142) and the **Kindred of the East Companion** (p.131-134), allow a practitioner of Do to learn any of the maneuvers presented in those books, as long as the character can find a teacher. Martial artists typically know a number of techniques but only specialize in a few. A teacher can usually pass on a number of maneuvers equal to her Do or Martial Arts + Intelligence, including the maneuvers she has elected to specialize in herself (and has selected as maneuvers as per the rules for Do and Martial Arts). Please note that if you use the rules in those books, the **Well Trained** benefit is *never* used with the attack difficulties listed in **Kindred of the East**, p.140. It always uses the base difficulty for Martial Arts maneuvers; the benefit already compensates for the special effectiveness of those martial techniques.

If the character already has a maneuver as part of the Martial Arts Ability, she can elect to learn it again as part of her Do, as long as her Do Ability is equal to her Martial Arts

Ability. She doesn't need a teacher for this because she is essentially learning to look at an old technique a new way. Besides these, there are a number of techniques that a Tao-shih alone can specialize in.

Because of the intense training Akashic Brothers receive, they may select more Martial Arts or Do maneuvers than other fighters. For each level of Do beyond the first, the player may pick one maneuver. Magic may enhance or defend against these tactics, as noted below.

Butterfly Palms: The Tao-shih trains the off-hand side of her body and practices complex katas that stress simultaneous attack, defense and movement. If she performs multiple actions, she gains a bonus die on any one Dice Pool after they have been reduced. **MET:** When using the Two-Gun Mojo rules (see **Laws of Ascension**) unarmed (or with a weapon in which you have the Weapon Art maneuver), you suffer one less penalty Trait for your off hand.

Weapon Art: Applying the lessons of Do to weapon use, the Tao-shih gains the **Well Trained** benefit, reducing his difficulty by one when using a familiar weapon (as a rule of thumb, assume that a character has one "familiar weapon" per level of Melee), and the **Lethal Attacks** benefit while using familiar weapons that normally only do bashing damage.

The character can also use the following Do maneuvers with a familiar weapon: **Butterfly Palms**, **Arrow Cutting** (this cannot be used to catch missiles with a weapon) and **Broken Rhythm**.

While using this benefit, the Tao-shih's Dexterity + Melee dice pool cannot be higher than his Dexterity + Do. Most Wu Chuan masters teach this fighting technique. **MET:** You gain the Do specialization bonus (one bonus Trait on resolution) with a melee weapon of your choice.

Peaceful Way: The Tao-shih learns to view other arts with the same mindfulness as Do, applying unexpected solutions to problems based on his holistic view of the world. The character gains the **Well Trained** benefit for a single skill that is listed under the Eight Limbs. The character's dice pool cannot be higher than the appropriate attribute + Do to gain this benefit.

While the character can create beautiful works of art and perform marvelous feats of body control and concentration, the source of his extra insight reveals itself to anyone who looks closely enough (roll Perception + Do or Awareness, Difficulty 8). You paint like a warrior, and you meditate with a fearsome scowl. Another martial artist may even be able to roughly gage your character's ability by watching her at work or even looking at the things she's worked on. **MET:** You gain a Do specialization bonus on one other Ability of your choice.

Arrow Cutting: Named for a technique common to Japanese kenjutsu and naginatajustu, the Akashic can deflect and catch missiles with her bare hands. If you succeed on a roll of Dexterity + Do (difficulty 7), your character can block an incoming missile no faster than an arrow (no bullets!). At difficulty 9, she can catch missiles and use them in combat during her next action. Akashic warriors often opt for multiple actions to return the "gift" to their attackers, a la Jack Burton versus Lo Pan at the end of *Big Trouble in Little China*. **MET:** If you take a two-Trait penalty on your defense against an arrow, crossbow bolt, thrown knife or the like, you can choose to catch it instead of deflecting it.

Broken Rhythm: Derived from Lost Track Kung Fu, Fencing and Boxing alike, this favorite of the Yung Chuan school is the result of training to music and learning *not* to follow the beat. The fighter can now attack at unpredictable moments.

In any turn in which she wins the initiative, a Tao-shih can step in and strike while the enemy is still readying a defense or relaxing his guard. While the attack is sloppier than normal (+2 difficulty), the defender applies the difference in initiative ratings as a penalty to any attempt to block, dodge or counterattack that turn, up to a total of +3. If the Tao-shih performs multiple actions, this maneuver can only be used once a turn. If an enemy has active Time perceptions, this maneuver becomes useless, although an attacker with Time 2 or 3 might be able to counter this. **MET:** You must bid an additional Trait to make a Broken Rhythm strike. If you hit, the opponent cannot use any Abilities for a retest.

Iron Shirt: Common to the Lohan Chuan style, Iron Shirt involves punishing drills in which the forearms, shin and torso are repeatedly exposed to strikes with fists, feet and poles, as well as special breathing exercises and postures designed to collect Chi in the bones, muscles and sinews.

At the end of this training, the character gains a number of bonus soak dice equal to his Do rating versus bashing damage *only* (even if you use the Cinematic Damage option from **Mage:**

The Ascension, p.238). The character will always take one level of damage if there is no way it could all be soaked by his normal Stamina. For example, if an Akashic Brother with a Stamina of 3 is struck for 5 levels of bashing damage, he still takes one level even if the total number successes for Stamina + Do roll to soak is 6. Life magic can enhance this power in a number of ways, from enhancing soak capabilities to healing the damage after it has occurred. **MET:** You suffer only half damage from all bashing attacks (round fractions up).

Iron Hand: Iron Shirt's counterpart is used in the Wu Chuan style. Punishing the hands and using herbal treatments to strengthen them as they heal allows the Tao-shih to break freestanding objects (as opposed to the specially braced and prepared bricks and boards that martial artists usually break) and strike with enough power to bypass armor and bone — one soak die is ignored from a target's pool, either from armor or Stamina. Unfortunately, the Tao-shih's hands are permanently numbed, imposing a +1 penalty to Perception or Dexterity rolls involving fine motor coordination or tactile sensitivity. Entropy 2 and Forces 2 can both be used to strike weak points, doing one additional level of damage per success. Many Akashics disdain hand conditioning in favor of learning the magical method instead. **MET:** When striking an armored target, one level of damage from your attack always penetrates the enemy's armor. This does not bypass magical defenses, though.

Kiaijutsu: Hsien Chuan teaches the use of the voice as a weapon of terror and deception. With this maneuver, the character has mastered those techniques. Once per combat, the character may frighten an enemy with a deep shout by rolling Manipulation + Do, with a difficulty equal to the opponent's Willpower + 3. Each success increases the difficulty of an enemy's actions by one for the next turn, to a maximum penalty of +3. Furthermore, if the Tao-shih scores more successes than the enemy has Willpower, then she may immobilize him for the next round or cause him to flee (Storyteller's choice).

An Akashic may also use the power more subtly, changing the timbre of her voice and "holding the shout in," so as to be filled with fierce energy. Rolling Charisma + Do (difficulty 8), the Tao-shih can add successes to her Performance, Leadership, or Intimidation rolls for the scene. This tactic has the same problem as **Peaceful Way**: A perceptive observer can deduce what you are capable of.

This tactic is useless against the basic mental defenses granted by Mind 1, but it may be used as a focus for Mind 2 or 4 effects to control an enemy's mind. **MET:** If you take an action to channel your shout at an opponent and win a Social Challenge, you cause the victim to suffer one penalty Trait on all challenge resolution in the next turn.

Jou Chuan: Emphasized in Shen Chuan, the Soft Fist allows a skilled Akashic to redirect an unarmed or melee attack to another assailant or even return it to the attacker. If the player rolls Dexterity + Do (difficulty 7) and scores more successes than the attacker, the Tao-shih can injure a nearby enemy (including the original attacker), doing damage equal to the attacker's Strength + weapon dice and adding any extra successes beyond what was necessary to accomplish the maneuver. Alternatively, the character can seize the weapon, in which case it is automatically ready to use the next turn. Typically, this enhanced by the rote **Rolling Hands**. **MET:** If you defeat a melee attacker in a challenge, you may attempt a followup Static Challenge. The difficulty is the same as for the prior test, but the enemy doesn't risk any Traits. If you win, you can redirect the attack into that enemy or into anyone else attacking you in melee. This is reflexive and does not take an action from your turn.

Escape Arts: The mysterious Lin Shen learn to defeat locks and knots and dislocate their joints painlessly. Anyone who learns such arts can escape being tied up by an amateur without a roll. If restrained by a cop, hojo-jutsu expert, or a BDSM enthusiast, the Akashic must roll Dexterity + Do, with a difficulty ranging between 5 for a quick handcuffing to 7 or 8 if the captor binds all of his limbs and sets him in a deliberately awkward position. With Life 3 body alteration, most such escapes are accomplished automatically. Exceptional cases require one or two successes at most. **MET:** You automatically escape from normal rope bonds with no challenge. If handcuffed, expertly tied or otherwise secured by someone with *Security*, *Torture* or similar Abilities, you can still test your Physical Traits against the captor's Mental Traits, using *Do* for a retest. If you win, you escape. This takes a full minute/conflict.

Plum Flower Blossom: By training while balanced on the top of the stumps of trees — set higher and farther apart as training progresses — a Tao-shih learns to perform amazing leaps and acrobatic feats. Rolling Dexterity + Do (difficulty 6),

the character may double his jumping distance or bounce from object to object for one turn, plus one for every two successes. If one of these leaps is an attack, it is penalized as an additional action and has its difficulty increased by one but adds two extra damage dice. Forces 2 and Correspondence 3 can enhance leaping distances to levels seen only in the most fantastic Hong Kong wuxia films. **MET:** If you make a Static Physical Challenge (difficulty 6) you may make a leaping attack. You can move up to six steps and still attack with your *Do*, though you suffer a two-Trait resolution penalty on the strike.

Ten Thousand Weapons: The Tao-shih learns how to use any object as a melee weapon, from a paperclip to a rolled-up newspaper. Any object she holds, throws or spits (such as that paperclip) with violent intent always does her Do in dice of bashing damage. If an object was normally capable of doing that amount of damage, the damage becomes lethal, as the objects is accurately aimed to weak points and used in unexpected ways. If the object does lethal damage, it does an extra die of it in this character's hands. Entropy and Forces can make such weapons strike even harder.

The ultimate limit to this ability is the imagination of the player; if he cannot describe how the character would use the object as a weapon, then it cannot be done. Particularly awkward objects (such as a large television set) may impose an increased difficulty, but it should never be as high as for someone who doesn't know this maneuver. **MET:** You can cause a normal object to inflict bashing damage and a bashing weapon to inflict lethal damage. Anything not specifically designed as a weapon automatically has the Negative Trait *Fragile* and may also be *Clumsy* or *Heavy* at the Storyteller's discretion.

The Mandala of Motion: Do Rotes

Aside from using magic to enhance Do, Do can be a focus in its own right. Any of the Eight Limbs can be used for this, but to successfully act as a focus, the Ability must be properly used. Typically, this means that the applicable roll must score at least three successes. Anything less means that the Brother's concentration is not complete. This is balanced by the fact that the focus can typically be used in the same time the magic is being performed, giving Brothers an edge in combat and other time-sensitive situations.

The following rotes use Do as a focus. Many variations exist, and players and Storytellers should feel free to add to or modify the list given here.

Purifying Step (•• Forces or •• Spirit)

Japanese Tao-shih developed this technique to harness the stomping movements now found in modern sumo and Shinto ritual. A focused blow to the floor can have its power channeled to a foe, upsetting her balance or causing injury.

The movement can also draw the attention of local spirits who respond to the shaking of the earth and air. In an area where an Akashic is likely to attract sympathetic spirits, this can be a blessing.

Clapping and vigorous chanting can also have the same effect.

System: With Forces, this rote transmits the energy created by stomping through the ground to a target. This can either cause direct injury (standard damage, less one success for affecting another target) or push the target three feet per success in any direction, where she will most likely lose her footing. The target may roll Dexterity + Athletics, Martial Arts or Do (difficulty 7) to keep her footing. Each success reduces the displacement by a foot; three successes allow her to remain standing).

As a Spirit effect, the rote is a quick version of **Call Spirit** (**Mage: The Ascension**, p. 187). This is most often used when a Brother is defending a Bodhimandala, and she can easily attract friendly spirits where the Gauntlet is weak.

As an attack, this rote — while usually vulgar — can be made coincidental with the application of a little creativity. The Spirit version may be coincidental or vulgar depending on what the summoned spirits do.

MET: Initiate *Forces* **or** *Spirit.* You make a vigorous stomp or clap. You may use this rote to summon spirits, just like the *Spirit* magic described in **Laws of Ascension**, or you may direct it as an attack. If you use it as an unbalancing attack, make a challenge of your Mental Traits against the enemy's Physical Traits (the enemy uses Athletics to retest). If you win, the foe falls to the ground and must take an action to stand. *Grades of Success:* Each grade of success allows you to strike an additional opponent.

ROLLING HANDS (• FORCES)

Also known as sticking hands, push hands, or trapping, this technique becomes even more potent in the hands of an Awakened Tao-shih. Making contact with an opponent's body (usually by touching his guard at the forearm or elbow), a martial artist can react to an enemy by sensing and redirecting force. With Forces senses, this practice becomes easier and more effective.

System: Each success reduces the difficulty of a parry or block by one, to a maximum of -3. If the Tao-shih strikes in the same turn, he can divide successes between both the attack and a parry or block. This effect is coincidental.

MET: Apprentice *Forces.* You sense the forces involved in your strikes and your enemy's counterattacks. As a result, you gain a one-Trait resolution bonus on your next attack or defense. This lasts for one turn. *Grades of Success:* Each grade of success extends the duration by one grade. For one grade you may grant these senses to another person.

CINNABAR TEARS (••• LIFE, •• MATTER)

This vicious form of internal alchemy transforms a Brother's bodily fluids into dangerous toxins. By ingesting a small amount of the substance to be created and moving into a series of special postures, an Akashayana can distill and release this substance without harming herself. An Akashic can sweat cyanide, cry acid or envenom a knife with cinnabar (mercury sulfide) "blood" by drawing it along her arm.

System: Akashayana are immune to the poisons they create with this rote. Generally, a toxin does one health level of damage per success on top of an unarmed or weapon attack. Envenomed tools or body parts last for as long as successes are spent to retain the toxin, but they cannot be made permanent. Really exotic or artificial substances cannot be created with this rote, which is usually vulgar.

MET: Disciple *Life,* **Initiate** *Matter.* With a successful Arete challenge, you transform a bodily fluid into a toxic or venomous liquid. This fluid inflicts one health level of damage as a poison when it strikes — this can add to the damage of a weapon coated with it, though some toxins may also be acidic and damage your weapon. Anyone who bites you similarly suffers a level of lethal damage. The toxin isn't cumulative. You can't put multiple toxins on a weapon to add more than one level of damage. The toxin retains its potency for one minute/conflict, or until it's used. Each use allows you to treat one weapon or make one venomous strike. *Grades of Success:* Each grade of success increases the duration by one grade.

IRON SNAKE (•• CORRESPONDENCE, •• FORCES, ••• MIND)

Developed by the kusarigama master Shishidi Baiken, this rote gives a flexible weapon such as a chain, rope or even a length of cloth the power to entrance an enemy and strike from many directions at once. Twirling the weapon in special patterns enhances its force and speed. It can create optical illusions, appearing distant when it is just about to strike.

System: A Tao-shih needs to have at least six dice in her Melee dice pool to use this rote and must spend a turn weaving the pattern of rope, chain or cloth. If successful, the rote reduces an opponent's unarmed and Melee dice pools by one per success (after a success is spent to affect the target). The target's ability to sense the distance and position of the weapon is effectively scrambled by Mind and Correspondence magic. Forces magic allows it to strike with full force at angles that wouldn't normally allow the Brother to land a hard blow. By spending an additional success, a sash or piece of cloth can be turned into an effective weapon (inflicting bashing damage) through the precise channeling of kinetic energy. In addition, the rote is often combined with Time, allowing multiple attacks to strike a relatively defenseless opponent. This rote is usually coincidental, except for creating iron-hard lengths of cloth.

MET: Initiate *Correspondence,* **Initiate** *Forces,* **Disciple** *Mind.* While using a chain, rope or length of cloth, you cause the opponent to suffer a one-Trait penalty on all challenge resolution against attacks. This effect lasts for one minute/conflict. *Grades of Success:* Each grade of success extends the duration by one grade. For one grade, you may use a piece of cloth or similar nonlethal object as a weapon scoring bashing damage for the full duration.

RIGHTEOUS FIST (••• LIFE, •••• MIND, •••• TIME)

By striking a Metal Element pressure point while chanting portions of the Drahma Sutra, members of the Hsien Chuan and Lohan Chuan schools can key the injury of the blow to the target's thoughts and actions. If the victim performs a proscribed act or thinks a dangerous thought, his meridians channel destructive forces throughout his body.

System: Three successes must be spent to affect the target, contact his mind and bind the condition with Time magic, before spending successes on damage and the duration of the effect. This allows the Brother to stipulate a single thought or action that injures the target. Successes may be spent to add further conditions. Damage is an aggravated Pattern attack, which takes the form of a sudden illness. Successes can be used to spread the injury out over time, making it coincidental.

MET: Disciple *Life*, **Adept** *Mind*, **Adept** *Time*. You must score a physical strike on the opponent (with a Physical Challenge), though it need not inflict any damage. You then set one proscribed condition no longer than a single sentence of up to twelve words. If the subject violates that condition, he must make a Static Challenge (difficulty of your Physical Traits at the time of the strike) or else suffer one aggravated health level of damage. This lasts for one minute/conflict. *Grades of Success:* Each grade of success allows you to extend the duration by one grade, or add three words to the conditional sentence.

Arashi-Waza (•• Correspondence, •• Forces, ••• Time)

The Japanese Vajrapani invented the "Storm Technique" rote during the Kamikaze War. A fast spinning kata gathers internal power and then releases it in circle of lacerating fists, feet and weapons. When the whirlwind comes to a halt, a tired Warring Fist may have several slain enemies at his feet.

System: This rote increases an Akashic Brother's speed, and then channels his movements to affect any target in his line of sight. Each success spent either adds to his effective combat dice, or allows a target that normally would be out of range to be affected. The Brother uses multiple actions as per the standard combat rules but benefits from the increased dice pool. Weapons can be used with this rote. It is usually vulgar.

MET: Initiate *Correspondence*, **Initiate** *Forces*, **Disciple** *Time*. You may strike at one target outside of your normal hand-to-hand range with an unarmed attack, making a Physical Challenge as usual. *Grades of Success:* Each grade of success allows you to attack an additional target at the cost of a one-Trait resolution penalty on *all* attacks for each target beyond the first. These targets don't necessarily have to be out of range.

The Final Blow (•••• Entropy, ••• Life, ••••• Mind, ••• Prime)

This famous Do rote allows a warrior to hold on to life long enough to fight for a few seconds more. The rote is brief, requiring only that the Brother steady her breathing and focus on the task at hand with every iota of her concentration, so that she literally doesn't realize that her life has ended until the battle is done.

System: Entropy holds back physical and metaphysical decay, Life allows the body to keep operating, Mind allows the Brother's consciousness to thrive in a dead brain and Prime provides the energy to maintain the Brother without the natural supply of Quintessence that permeates a living thing. Each success adds an extra health level, called "Dead," which, when used in conjunction with a Willpower point, allows the Brother to fight on after physical death. Additional successes must be spent on duration. If the magic ends, and the character is wounded down to "Dead," she perishes. Any magic used to heal "Dead" health levels must be vulgar Life/Matter effects.

MET: Adept *Entropy*, **Disciple** *Life*, **Master** *Mind*, **Disciple** *Prime*. You still your breathing for a moment (taking a full turn to cast the effect) and then resist the effects of death itself. You may cast this before injury or even while Mortally Wounded (so long as you use a Willpower Trait to perform an action during incapacitation), or even immediately after taking an injury that would kill you! If you succeed on the rote, you gain an additional Dead health level. Functionally you're dead, but by spending Willpower Traits you can ignore its penalties like any other health level. Damage beyond this one level tears your body apart too severely to maintain. This rote lasts for one minute/conflict. Healing spells used on you while "dead" must also include *Matter* levels equal to the *Life* levels used, and are vulgar. *Grades of Success:* Each grade of success extends the duration by one grade, or adds one additional "Dead" health level. You cannot make this rote permanent.

84,000 Dharma Doors: Rotes and Foci

Akashic Magic is not an Art that is wrestled into place by confidence and will, but arises when an individual puts his own desires in harmony with the All. Just as the cells of a body simply act instead of willing the body to be, the Akashayana act as reflections of the whole body of the All.

The Sword That Cuts Through Illusion: Rotes

As Awakened power is supposed to be a byproduct, rather than a goal, of spiritual training, most Akashayana prefer spontaneous magic. However, to learn the nature of the Dharmas, a Brother must practice their forms. The following is a short selection of what that discipline includes.

Internal Obligation (•••• Mind, ••• Prime, •••• Time or ••• Life, ••• Prime, •••• Time)

The Shi-Ren use this rote ensure dedication in their bodyguards. The Jnani use it as a therapeutic technique to prevent emotional excesses in the undisciplined. Using advanced acupuncture techniques, a Brother alters a subject's Chi flow to engender a set response whenever a certain event occurs. Shi-Ren often incorporate a trigger phrase while they're intensifying the Fire energy of duty, while Jnani merely describe a condition that might arise while provoking the equanimity of the Metal soul.

When the condition arises, the subject does whatever the conditions require, from having a certain set of emotions to committing murder. Variants alter the subject's Chi balance to give him certain strengths or weaknesses when the event arises.

System: The threshold for this rote is five successes plus the duration according to the guidelines listed in **Mage: The**

Ascension, p. 209. Because of the use of Prime, the mage need not concentrate on the effect once cast. The Mind version can control memories, actions, and emotional states, which the subject experiences as if they are his own. The Life-based version simply moves the subject's body like a marionette. He might shoot someone or fall unconscious when the stimulus occurs. Combining both versions, the mage can weave a contingent **Better Body** effect or reduce a Physical Attribute. Extra successes must be spent on these variations, however. The rote is usually coincidental on the sorts of people that it's typically used on, but for the average person, it's vulgar.

MET: Adept *Mind*, Disciple *Prime*, Adept *Time* or Disciple *Life*, Disciple *Prime*, Adept *Time*. You use acupuncture or massage (both governed by the *Medicine* Ability) on a subject for at least a full scene. You then describe a condition consisting of one sentence of up to twelve words in length and an action that would take no more than a single turn to complete. When that condition arises, the subject must defeat you in a Static Mental Challenge for the *Mind* version, or a Static Physical Challenge for the *Life* version. Each challenge is against the Traits you had at the time when you cast the rote. You should make a specific card with the conditions and difficulty upon casting and give it to the subject for later reference. If the subject fails, he must perform the action you have described. The subject is under the conditions of the rote for one minute/conflict. *Grades of Success:* Each grade of success extends the duration by one grade, adds 3 words to the sentence you use to describe the condition or adds one grade to the duration during which the subject must act in response to the condition being triggered. You may also combine *Life* and *Mind* to increase or reduce the subject's Physical Traits. Each Trait affected costs one grade of success.

AUSPICIOUS DIALOGUES
(••• MIND OR •• ENTROPY, •• MIND)

Originally created by the Kannagara, the Li-Hai perfected this rote in their work to modernize the Brotherhood. **Auspicious Dialogue** translates slang, body language and emotional nuances for a Brother and allows him to replicate them in return. By concentrating and holding her hand in the mudra for Compassion, she learns the real meaning behind street slang, vocal embellishments and corporate newspeak and can use the same gestures in reply. She opens her mind to other perspectives and the knowledge arises spontaneously.

System: While this rote doesn't translate directly, the character can understand and use any slang and dialect from a language that she speaks and use it in return. Thus, the character can get her point across — and look good doing it — to a Syndicate board meeting or a house full of Scottish heroin addicts who constantly refer to Sean Connery's Bond films (or both at the same time, if necessary). Each success lowers Social difficulties by one for one specific subculture or speaking style, to a maximum of three. The rote is coincidental. A Paradox Backlash usually signals some horrible gaffe or misunderstanding.

MET: Initiate *Entropy*, Initiate *Mind* or Disciple *Mind*. You make a mudra (a special hand gesture — *Subterfuge* can be used to disguise it as normal body language). You gain one bonus Social Trait when talking to a group of people who have

the same cultural background (a rough guide is that they would all be covered by the same *Influence*). This lasts for one minute or until you lose the Trait by bidding it. *Grades of Success:* Each grade of success extends the duration by one grade, adds one additional Social Trait or adds one group that you gain this benefit with. You must be able to speak the same language as the people you're using this rote on.

DRAHMA PROTECTOR
(•••• MIND, •••• SPIRIT)

The Jnani use this rote to convert spirits to the Drahma. These beings guard Bodhimandalas and assist the Brotherhood because of their sincere belief in the truth of Akashic teachings. At heart, that is the ideal situation in which Drahma Protectors are enlisted. In fact, many spirits are bound to the Akashic way whether or not they voice an obvious need for salvation through the Sangha.

Drahma Protector convinces a spirit to see the Akashayana as the true path to inner peace. Such a spirit protects Akashic Brothers wherever they may be found. Unwilling protectors may rebel, but that is merely a sign of its own struggle with the truth. A Jnani chants wisdom from the Akashic sutras after purifying herself, so that the spirit may know the will of the All.

System: This rote has a threshold equal to the sprit's Gnosis + Willpower. The rote turns the affected being into a loyal servant of the Akashayana for as long as successes are spent on duration. The spirit will do anything in its power to assist the Brotherhood, as long as that assistance doesn't violate Akashic ideals or the spirit's essential nature. Such spirits guard a number of Jnani-controlled Bodhimandalas.

MET: Adept *Mind*, Adept *Spirit*. After ritually purifying yourself for at least 10 minutes, you chant for a full turn. This summons a spirit, who is then converted to Akashic beliefs. The spirit takes the initiative to help and protect you for one minute/conflict, as long as you are true to the Akashic philosophies it now believes. *Grades of Success:* Each grade of success extends the duration by one grade.

SHINOBIJUSTU
(••• CORRESPONDENCE OR ••••• ENTROPY OR ••• FORCES OR ••• MIND)

Many Akashics know the art of invisibility, from the subtle Lin Shen to the graceful Sulsa. These rotes vary greatly from sect to sect. Some use special walking techniques, others bizarre mudra, and still others feel that visibility is selfishness and that formlessness can be cultivated with an enlightened mind.

System: All of these rotes use different methods to make the user unseen. Correspondence 3 warps a pocket space around the mage, so that light travels around him. Forces 3 creates a physical illusion, while Mind 3 creates a mental one; the latter can affect several people at once, while the former requires concentration to affect multiple minds, but deceives all five senses.

The most advanced version is used by Euthanatoi killers — called "Closing Shiva's Eyes," it destroys the *idea* of the mage's presence; as such, it cannot be resisted with mental

defenses or extrasensory powers such as a vampire's Disciplines or a Garou's Gifts. Only careful Prime and Entropy magic stand a chance. Even then, the mage can spend successes to penalize the attempt.

MET: Disciple *Correspondence* or Master *Entropy* or Disciple *Forces* or Diciple *Mind*. You make a special gesture and step. This renders you invisible (and you should cross your arms over your chest as usual) for one minute, although with every version of this rote except for the one using *Entropy*, you can be detected normally by any supernatural powers that would allow it. In addition, the *Mind* version allows you to be caught on film, videotape of other recording media (although the image can't be seen by anyone looking at it while you are invisible and in his presence). Unlike the other versions, the *Entropy* version *cannot* be detected by cameras *or* sphere powers, with the sole exception of Entropy senses or Prime magic that is used to detect your Resonance. *Grades of Success:* Each grade of success can extend the duration by one grade or extend the invisibility to one other person.

Tumo (•• Life, optional •• Forces)

Tumo is a form of yoga where the practitioner learns to master her body temperature. The magical variety of the skill was developed by Chabnagpa and Karmachakra Brothers as a tool to withstand Tibet's fierce winters. Through this special practice, they can endure ascetic hardships or reach sacred places normally barred to mystics by subzero temperatures. In southern climes, Brothers use a variant to resist the effects of high temperatures, preventing sunstroke and dehydration. Pushing the limits of body control, Awakened Tumo can also stand against fire and temperatures that freeze flesh stiff.

Taoist Akashics use gentle movements, while other Brothers concentrate on mastering a complex breathing pattern. Whatever the method, it takes only a moment to yoke the body to the mind.

System: With Life alone, a Brother can withstand cold or heat that does no immediate tissue damage. Her body regulates its temperature perfectly. With Forces, Antarctic temperatures and bonfires have little effect; each success reduces the damage of a temperature-based attack by two health levels. Meditating on a mountain on a clear day or walking on coals is coincidental; shrugging off a flamethrower or immersion in liquid nitrogen most certainly isn't.

MET: Initiate *Life*, optional Initiate *Forces*. By sitting in a meditative posture and breathing deeply for one turn, you can resist extreme cold or heat. With Life alone, you can resist any extreme of temperature a human being could survive in. With the *Forces* variant, you can even resist being plunged into the middle of a bonfire or being frozen solid by liquid nitrogen. You gain an additional *Resilient* Physical Trait that can be used against either heat- or cold-based attacks (you must choose one) and you may bid Stamina-related Traits such as *Resilient* to resist lethal or aggravated heat- or cold-based attacks. This rote does not allow you to resist any other form of damage and lasts for one turn. *Grades of Success:* Each grade of success allows you to extend the duration by one grade.

BALANCING THE FURIES (●●● OR ●●●●● PRIME)

This dangerous rote allows an Akashic Brother to temporarily overcome his Resonance or impart it upon another being. Yin, Yang and Heaven all flavor a being's Chi. Through a variety of methods, an Akashayana can adjust the balance between the three forces. For example, a Brother with excessive Yang (Dynamic) Resonance may impose Heavenly (Static) Resonance upon it by meditating in a Confucian library, or retire to a dank cave to erode it with the Yin (Entropic) essence. Herbs, diet and exercises may all be used to adjust his Chi balance.

The rote can also forcibly adjust another being's Chi balance by striking at vital points, chanting special mantras, or using certain Do postures. This can cause a mortal to rapidly sicken. This rote also impairs the powers of other supernatural beings.

This is a dangerous practice. Internal harmony is meant to come from enlightenment, not magical control, and it is inauspicious to alter the furies in another without their permission. Still, it happens; in fact, there is said to be a secret technique that allows the balance to be adjusted permanently. However, Masters are few and far between these days. For now, it remains a legend.

System: This rote is always penalized for opposing a mage's Resonance. It can be used to temporarily shift personal Resonance; this requires two successes for every Resonance Trait altered. These Traits can never be eliminated, but three Entropic Traits could be shifted into two Entropic and one Dynamic, or one of each kind. This has a number of uses: It can keep the mage from being recognized by Prime senses or reduce the difficulty of a subsequent effect.

Used against other mages, it can warp an enemy's magic, make him appear to be an impostor to friends using Prime senses and break his bond with anything he has linked to his own Pattern. Used therapeutically, it can serve as a last stand against Quiet, Jhor, or Clarity, by distributing dangerously high Resonance through the three furies.

Kuei-jin, Shih and other beings with quantifiable levels of Yin and Yang Chi have their temporary Chi balance altered by one per success (after one success is spent to affect another target). Other creatures are affected at the Storyteller's discretion. While being infused with Yin may have little effect on a vampire, a werewolf might be crippled by an Entropic infection, which his friends might take for an unhealthy taint.

The Prime 5 version of this rote can permanently alter a subject's Resonance and temporarily adds Resonance Traits to the subject's total. There is no known way to eliminate Resonance without destroying the part of a Avatar it's attached to.

MET: Disciple or **Master** *Prime.* You must touch the subject three times within one minute/conflict. In combat this requires three successful Physical Challenges, but it need not do any damage. You may then alter one of the subject's Resonance Traits for one turn. This severs any connections between the subject and any people or objects he has bonded

to his Pattern by using the *Prime* Sphere. You may also alter the Resonance of a being who normally does not possess it in quantifiable terms; the Storyteller determines the effects. You may use the rote on yourself, but you are always penalized for working against your Resonance.

If a creature has Yin or Yang Chi ratings (see **Laws of the East**), you may change one point of Yin Chi to Yang Chi, and vice versa. This also lasts for one turn. With Disciple level *Prime*, this rote affects the creature as if his Chi balance has been temporarily altered. With Master *Prime*, the creature acts as if his permanent Chi balance has been altered (although this does not affect the duration of the effect). *Grades of Success:* Each grade of success can extend the duration by one grade or alter one additional Resonance Trait. Master *Prime* can make the effect permanent at the Storyteller's discretion. Using Master *Prime*, you may also add entirely new Resonance Traits; these cannot be made permanent, and you must spend one additional grade of success for each Trait you add.

FLOWER GESTURE (●●● MIND, ●●● TIME)

The Buddha Sakyamuni lifted a flower at the conclusion of his final sermon. With a gesture he imparted the essence his teachings to Mahakasypa.

With this rote, a Brother can transfer her ideas in an instant. Like Mahakaysypa's enlightenment, it comes as a sudden burst of inspiration. Kannagara elders and Shi-Ren scholars use mudras and brief phrases to transmit a burst of thought, said to arise from Akashakarma itself.

System: This rote is essentially rapid telepathy. After one success is spent making contact, each success thereafter multiplies the speed at which information arises in the target's mind. The information is immediately understandable.

MET: Disciple *Mind,* **Disciple** *Time.* After using a mudra or a koan (an unanswerable riddle), you may telepathically contact a subject and spend up to one minute communicating with him, despite the fact that only one turn passes in the game. *Grades of Success:* Each grade of success adds another effective minute of communication to a turn or extends the actual duration of the telepathic link by one grade of success. Storytellers should ban the use of this rote as an out-of-character stalling tactic.

AUSPICIOUS ACTS: FOCI

The following foci are commonly used by the Brotherhood:

Asceticism and Abstinence: Fasting, rigorous exercise, poverty and celibacy free a Brother from materialistic, selfish urges. Universally used by the Kannagara, all sects practice ascetic disciplines to a certain extent. Since they are not as inconvenient as other foci (whether or not you're celibate won't affect most combat scenes), it is recommended that no more than two Spheres use this practice as a specialty focus. **MET Ability:** None — you cannot retest asceticism; either you did or you didn't.

Breath: Yogic breathing, Taoist reverse-diaphragm breathing and breaths with specific durations adjust an Akashic's inner balance and refine her perceptions. Exhalations express power, while inhalations absorb it. This rote requires some uninterrupted time to perform. **MET Ability:** *Meditation.*

Bodywork: Massage, acupuncture, moxabustion, and energy balancing therapies all serve as useful methods to refine and channel Chi. A skilled acupuncturist also knows where the body's weaknesses are, and can exploit them with a needle, a finger or even a thought. Manipulating the body can also affect the mind, spirit, and even karma. **MET Ability:** *Medicine*.

Calligraphy and Poetry: Both discipline the mind and enact the primal stages of creation, when the initial chaos of the universe combined into meaningful patterns. Classical Chinese and Kaja are the keys to the Akashic record. Unfortunately, only the Kuei-jin have retained mastery of the language. The ability to write or understand Kaja is known only to a very few Kannagara, Jnani and Wu Lung.

Poetry is writing that points to a greater meaning outside of itself. Poetry inspires new insights into the universe and serves as a common focus for Mind, Time and Sprit Arts. **MET Ability:** *Expression* (Poetry and/or Calligraphy). The character must also know how to read and write the language appropriate to the effect used.

Chanting and Singing: From simple mantras to portions of the Vedas, song and voice are more than noise. Akashics agree that the primal expression of the Akasha was a word whose sacred vibration led to the Ten Thousand Things. Whether that was the Om, the Shinto kotodama, or a mysterious sound represented only by a dead Kaja character, a voice is breath invested with intelligence — life itself. **MET Ability:** *Performance* (Singing).

Crafts: Right concentration can be perfected by performing an act as perfectly as possible. One channel for this practice is the production of pieces of superb craftsmanship and artistry. The act of creation inspires the Awakened mind to put a little magic into the final product. **MET Ability:** *Crafts*.

Drums: Japanese Akashics claim that kami live in their traditional drums, and some Chinese Brothers use drums to train their warriors' sense of timing and increase their emotional energy. Spirit, Mind and Entropy Arts often benefit from the vibrations created by drumming — they reverberate in both the mortal and invisible realms. **MET Ability:** *Performance* (Drums).

Eyes: The eyes reveal everything about a person. Eye contact begins many Mind rotes, and a certain gazes can frighten or misdirect. **MET Ability:** None. You must make eye contact with the target in game.

Food and Herbs: A mainstay of ancestor worship and spirit magic, rice, butter, ginseng and incense serve as pleasing offerings to Heaven's inhabitants. Furthermore, the metaphysical properties of herbs and food allow them to create or destroy health. Whether inhaled, smoked, eaten or imbibed, the Chi balance of a substance invariably intermingles with the person consuming it, allowing for a variety of effects. **MET Ability:** *Hobby/Professional/Expert Ability* (Cooking).

Kata and Dance: A kata is a set of prearranged movements designed to perfect the techniques of a martial art and transmit a symbolic message. "Do kata" (also called hyung or chuan) connects a Brother to the forces of the Wheel itself. Dance has a similar function but also tells a story about the Sangha or describes the beings that populate the spirit worlds by mimicking their actions. **MET Ability:** *Do, Performance* (Kata) or *Athletics*, but not more than one of these, as each represents a different approach to kata.

Mandalas: A mandala is a diagram of the mystical structure of the Tapestry. It can be created with silk, sand, gardens or even temples or cities. Do is sometimes described as a mandala of movement. Spirit and Correspondence effects often use a mandala. Some designs are passed on for millennia, and others are personal creations. **MET Ability:** *Expression* (Drawing or Painting).

Mudras: The Akashayana use these sacred hand and finger positions to invoke a variety of effects These also act as a sign language. Each word and phrase is patterned after the mystical significance of a given gesture. Mudra include the defensive postures of Do and kuji-kiri, the finger-weaving passes used by Yamabushi mystics and their ninja cousins. **MET Ability:** *Linguistics*.

Mountains and other sacred sites: Aside from being potential wellsprings of power, mountains give the Akashayana a primal connection with Meru. Dragons reside in the shapes of mountain ranges, and, as rivers, begin in their snowy heights. **MET Ability:** None. You have to travel to the site in question, though for arduous journeys, *Survival* might be appropriate.

Sex: While few outsiders are aware of it, sexual rites have been a part of the Akashayana's methods throughout the Tradition's existence. The difference is one of emphasis. While most sex magic involves harnessing the orgasm, the Brotherhood directs carnal desire toward a passion for enlightenment. The Chabnagpa and Blue Skin factions use these rites the most. **MET Ability:** None. Check with your Storyteller before selecting or using this as a focus. It may not be appropriate for all venues.

Weapons: The Vajrapani favor swords and spears. Most Japanese Brothers have at least picked up a katana, and the Sulsa construct swords of their own. Less combative sects use extremely complex weapons that belong in a dojo instead of on a battlefield. Nine-bladed tridents and flexible swords require precision to use, honing the Brother's mind and spirit for any number of purposes. Some Kannagara and more peaceable Vajrapani use simply wooden staffs. Weapons in harmony with their users can be used for both belligerent and peaceful magic. **MET Ability:** *Melee*.

THE WAY OF THE ARTISAN: WONDERS

The Akashayana are loathe to rely on external tools. When enlightenment can be reached in this very body, why should material objects be so important? Still, Akashic Brothers create their Wonders; swordsmiths forge blades with the imprints of their souls, and calligraphers write words that stir hearts for a thousand years. Creation hones the mind.

AUSPICIOUS SISTRUM

Arete 2; 5-pt. Talisman

This staff is topped with three interlocking rings, representing either the Three Fires of Greed, Ignorance and Hatred that must be overcome, or the Three Jewels of the Buddha, his teachings and his monks. When rattled, it wards off danger and summons benevolent beings to come to the wielder's aid. The rattling of the three rings alerts all to the staff holder's beliefs.

System: An Entropy 3, Mind 3 effect attracts friendly people, who are well disposed to the wielder, or repels those that would wish her harm. Some sistrums are also enchanted with a Spirit 3, Entropy 1 effect that calls friendly spirits and repels harmful ones. The staff has an effective Arete of 2, but it can be used for two consecutive turns as part of a ritual. The sistrum's magic is usually coincidental.

THE TWINS

Special Artifacts

Legends ascribe the creation of these swords to the Eight Immortals, several Emperors of China and the Japanese smith Muramasa. They may all be correct, as the two blades have been destroyed and recreated several times in several nations. Whenever created, they are of the finest craftsmanship — they are the weapons of nobility, whether they are Chinese jianns, Korean gums or Japanese katanas. At least two Akashic weapon-makers have forged them in the Brotherhood's history.

One blade glows with Yang. The other crackles with Yin. Aside from their quality, each weapon channels Chi into its wielder and horribly wounds shen. And each carries a curse, for the swords seek a balance through their owners. When a warrior possesses one, he is compelled to seize the other. Unfortunately, a horrible fate comes to anyone who has both. Only those who never use the blades are immune to the curse.

System: The swords inflict aggravated wounds and inflict an additional die of damage due to their superior quality. Each provides five dice of countermagic against magic of an essence opposite to its own. For example, the Yin blade counters fire magic, and the Yang blade counters cold. Each acts as a level-two *Node*, each with a Resonance to match its temper. Quintessence from the Yin sword has the Entropic Resonance Traits *Icy* and *Metallic*. The Yang blade's Chi is Dynamic, *Fiery* and *Energetic*.

Holding a weapon allows the Resonance to affect the user. The curse is a simple Mind 3 effect that can be resisted normally. However, when Paradox backlashes occur from magic that harnesses the swords' Quintessence, they are immediately put into a Quiet pool that compels the user to seek out the other sword. The "doom" spoken of simply comes from the fact that both swords, when brought close together, lose their magic; they attain a harmony between them that silences their powers. This usually manifests when the swords are about to be used.

These swords are often made while in the throes of Quiet, or as part of a Seeking. They seem to be keyed in to the basic pattern of the Tellurian or else they "reincarnate," almost like mages' Avatars....

The Truth

Peter saw a sudden streak of orange. He smelled a predator. *She's looking through my thoughts*. A brief impression of a fang and claw slipped through his thoughts. Standing in the rain before him, she smirked, as if to say, *You're no danger to me*.

Then, the tiger in Peter's thoughts crept into the Alaya mind, into the memories of his past lives. Smoke Tiger broke contact, and her hard smile vanished.

"General…"

Smoke Tiger took off her dark cotton jacket. Behind the stiff collar was a dark blue tank top. Her arms were brown and wiry (*Like Sataghni's*, Peter thought). She turned around. She removed her shirt to show her back.

It was scarred. A sharp blade had cut dozens of Kaja characters into it. Peter knew the sounds they represented, but not their meanings.

"It's a grievance," she said. "There's a legend that, long ago, a poor family sent their daughter to the Emperor, with a grievance cut into her back. They carved the characters with care and skill, to attract his attention."

"I know it," said Peter. "She fought her way into the Son of Heaven's presence to ask for aid against the barbarians, and he was so impressed with the beauty of the writing that he dedicated his troops to her cause."

She ran a finger along a scar that meant "man" and said, "This will take us to the part of the Record we wish to go, won't it?"

"Yes," he replied. "Sit with me."

She dropped into a half lotus posture. Peter sat behind her and chanted what was written in her back. Smoke Tiger began to sing as well, and they found a kind of harmony as ancient sounds were wrenched from the human throats never meant to contain it. The sound became light; a place bordered by swiftly moving characters that fell with the rain. Shimmering streams of thought surrounded them. They were swept into the current, turning with the Wheel. Ahead, a smoky light beckoned. Peter remembered the Bardo Thodol; such lights were the entrances to dark rebirths as the hungry dead or hell-beings. They were the lives where darkness lay.

They fell through. The red mists parted.

Peter had a sword again. It tugged on a thick leather belt as he left his tent.

A young boy ran to him. The mountains' thin air hadn't been kind to him. When he arrived, he leaned on his staff, gasping. "General Chan?" the boy said. "Luo Fu sent me to tell you that the prisoner is ready."

"I know, Heng. Bring her to the Kannagara's tent."

Heng sucked in a deep breath and ran off to relay the message. Peter's — Chang Ng's — eyes followed his path up to the mountains that loomed in the mist behind him.

The center of the camp was noisy. Eight Vajrapani moved through weapon drills together, shifting and stabbing with their spears in perfect time. He smelled rice stew cooking on the fire, bitter from the scraggly mountain plants that had been added for taste. He stepped to one side to avoid Heng, who ran from the large tent before him with a new errand, grabbing the falling entrance flap to let himself in.

Three Kannagara sat inside, red robes tucked under their knees. Luo Fu and a small, dark-skinned man in a threadbare cloak flanked them.

In the center stood the prisoner. She didn't look older than 12 or 13, but her hands and feet were shackled by iron chains, staked to a post near Luo Fu, her jailer. She scowled at Peter as he sat down.

"This is Lu Ying," said Luo Fu. "She killed three people in Turtle Valley."

"A Dacoit and her two servants," interjected the girl. "I recognized them from my last life. Why am I in chains?"

Lou Fu frowned. "The area is wracked with fighting now. Handura are looking for her and clashing with Vajrapani patrols along the way. Some of the death-priests have been fighting for several lifetimes." He gestured at her. "They won't rest until they carry her body back to Kali."

Lu Ying clenched one fist and raised it, shaking the chain. "I've done my duty." She peered into Peter's eyes. "I don't understand why I've been confined, General. You heard Luo Fu — it's time to finish them off, while they're spread thin looking for us."

Peter opened his mouth, and Chan Ng's gravelly voice spoke. "You're a child, Lu Ying. You need to live a child's life. Many things have changed since your last incarnation. You— "

"I'm ready *now*." She did not look down from his gaze, the way a child would. "I remember the fighting arts, and the Dharmas do my bidding. I'm as ready to kill for the Sangha as I ever was."

"You don't understand. The war has served its purpose. It only continues because angry Brothers like you cling to it."

"No, it hasn't. Our enemies still live and they still kill. Luo Fu saw them massacre the sick and their holy men still consign the weak to toil in their next life." She was not blinking. He'd seen that mad stare in many Vajrapani. Luo Fu glanced from her to him, lips pursed as if he was about to speak. He remained silent.

"When this war started, we were one people, traveling among many scattered voices. In this country, the people were divided among the rivers, mountains, and jungles. Their Awakened were unified by a belief in the Great Wheel, but they couldn't even see their own similarities. They were ignorant of each other. Have you heard of the Night of Fana?"

"No." Lu Ying stood up and paced in a tight circle, as far as her chains allowed.

"Our Brothers found Samadhi through the common truths in our ways and those of the Darwushin, a foreign cult. To see your own enlightenment in a stranger's teachings — Drahma revealed itself to us in a new way."

"Your mistake was attacking them in one stroke, General Chan. Otherwise, they would still be scattered and the Chakravanti would not plague us today."

"I asked him to strike at us that way," said the dark-skinned man.

Lu Ying spun to face him and leapt, snarling. The chains pulled her to the ground. Both of her wrists broke when the shackles smashed against them.

The three monks raised the mudra for peace. Lu Ying's eyelids drooped and her breathing slowed. The dark man chanted softly, and her swollen wrists healed.

"I am a prophet, girl," the Chakravanti said. "I have been one for many turns of the Wheel. I saw your strong Brotherhood cross the mountains, and I cast the bones to see how we could make that future for ourselves."

Lu Ying lifted her head to regard him.

"Kali's priests say that the Age of Iron is coming to the world. The people in ten directions will fall to false teachers, and the true keepers of the Dharmas will go into hiding. I saw that time, child. The world was choked in metal, and fearful people burned the temples of the Wheel. The survivors were from strong fellowships. The Akashi were one such people; now the Chakravanti stand by their side.

"The survivors of Fana chart the ways in which all return to the All. Without their work, the hidden sages of the coming age will never learn to share the sacred places or work the miracles that guard our wisdom.

"Do not misunderstand me. Your Vajrapani still thirst for my blood. Our doctrines are *not* the same, and you are not the only one here who thinks that the holy Wheel demands my death." He glanced to Luo Fu. "But my visions are pure. We will survive the Age of Iron, because you have driven us to unite, and the driven Ahl-i-Batin to discover a new truth."

• • •

Peter mediated on the cliff's edge, feeling Chan Ng's body settle into the rough stone. He took slow breaths, exhaling mist that obscured the snow-covered peaks in the distance.

He heard footsteps. He rolled into a stand. Luo Fu approached.

"Is it true?" the muscular man asked. "It was never about avenging the dead, the oppressed? It was for… a dream?"

"A vision," the General replied. "An oracle. When the war began, I never wondered why the Kannagara would ask me to fight them all at once. You told us their crimes; how could a war be just punishment for one man's murders? But I was angry, Luo Fu. I thought of the Bodhicitta, kept from their Awakening by the knife of an arrogant sorcerer. It was only after the Batini came that I realized the truth."

Luo Fu's face tensed in exasperation. "But what they do *is* wrong! Every 'good death' kills someone who might have been a Bodhisattva! How can we be helping them, when their existence mocks Drahma itself?"

"We are fulfilling the Bodhisattva Vow. We are delaying our final Samadhi to save the world." He smiled. "Did you think it would be easy? You mustn't tell anyone else, Luo Fu. Nu Ying represents the last of the sickness that has caused this war to go on for so long. The truth can cure her madness, but it would turn the Sangha against itself. The Vajrapani would abandon the

Kannagara. They would fight the war alone, destroying the Chakravanti. And us."

"I can't believe that," said Luo Fu. He stumbled back. "We can't be dying and losing our chance at enlightenment for *them*. Even if the oracle is true, we could simply spread into their lands."

"We'd be petty conquerors and nothing more. Grasping for that power imprisons us in Samsara. If we reveal what we know, then the Sangha will crumble and the Chakravanti will fall apart when they realize that their unity is a contrivance. Then our brothers and sisters in the Batini will fall, for how can you postulate unity among the ruins?" He drew his sword in a single, smooth stroke. "But you don't believe me. I can see that in your eyes and the way your body moves."

"No, General. Please." He looked at the weapon in disbelief and fear.

"I am so sorry, my friend. I— "

The General looked at Smoke Tiger, trembling before him. He knew what happened next—Luo Fu would drop to his knees and let Chan Ng strike the fatal cut.

The past is an illusion. It can change, if we change the eternal Now with it.

He tossed the sword off the cliff. It glittered in the sunlight and fell into the mist.

"The truth is the essence of Drahma," he said to Smoke Tiger. "The truth about ourselves and what we've done, be it to save others or to condemn them.

"Go and tell the truth now."

But when he looked down, Smoke Tiger was dead. Her head rested near him. There was still a bloody sword in his hand. Peter regarded the weapon that had returned from the abyss. Chan Ng's hands shook with guilt, with sadness and horror. Or they had, in this memory.

There was a shimmering and the world vanished, as if it had been unraveled by the tug of a cosmic thread.

Peter was in Bangkok again. The rain had stopped.

His knees were soaked in bloody water. In front of him, Smoke Tiger was slumped forward; the blade of a wakizashi sprouted from her shoulders, marring the perfect scar for "justice."

Masako was curled up, inches away. Her left leg was distorted and swollen from the fall, and she had the raccoon mask bruises of a severe concussion. Her chest rose and fell, but she didn't stir, as Peter stood.

He looked to his teacher and wept into the still water.

THE AKASHIC RECORD

The Akashayana's Mind prowess is more than the result of a simple organizational decision by the Council. The Akashic paradigm claims that perception and thought lie at the root of all phenomena. For this reason, the Brotherhood has cultivated the Akashic Record — the imprint of thought upon the Tapestry.

WHAT IS THE AKASHIC RECORD?

The Akashayana believe that karma turns the Great Wheel of cause and effect. That karma begins with thought. The Brotherhood claims that all phenomena ultimately derive from the minds of sentient beings. Mortals, devils, gods and Awakened beings inspire the flow of the cosmos with their own awareness.

The form that all phenomena takes is impermanent but comes from the basic revelation of being itself. This primal form is called Akasha, the "void." Akasha is not a substance or a power, like Chi, but is the field of pure awareness that Chi and matter travel along.

This primal emptiness is shaped by thought. Like a valley to the river running through it, Akasha determines the shape that events take and the path that Chi flows. Confucian Akashics liken it to Li, the refined power of Heaven's will.

The first Akasha (the name the Brotherhood also uses for its Ascended members) is said to have dismembered himself at the foot of a waterfall. This act symbolized breaking the barriers between the flow of thought and karma and the egoistic conception of the self. By radically demonstrating the fragility and mortality of his body, he identified its dissolution with the constant flow of the Great Wheel.

The imprint caused by desires, beliefs and actions is known as Akashakarma. It is the imprint from which all karma expresses itself. While this should theoretically cause it to touch all phenomena, the Awakened can only touch a part of it without reaching Samadhi. Thus, Akashayana can usually only sense mental impressions from Akashakarma, and only those impressions most similar to their own.

The traces Akashakarma leaves have many names; the Merumandala and Akashakaya are common designations, but in modern times, it is simply known as the Akashic Record. Many outsiders believe that it is some sort of telepathic network, but the Sangha doesn't believe in energy transferring from mind to mind. Instead, when a Brother quiets his conscious babble, he can sense the vast emptiness from which karma and thought arises. He is no longer limited to the thoughts that come from a particular body, time or place. These thoughts *are* his, so much as he can be said to be a discrete, thinking being in the ocean of the All.

The Record is symbolized by language, specifically writing. Just as Akashakarma guides the Wheel of Ages, so too does language guide thought, acting as a vessel that contains and shapes their concepts. The Akashic Record is not a combination of books and minds. The act of reading and chanting sacred texts resonates with the Akasha itself. Thus, most foci for Akashakarma take the form of the written word. These may be ancient records preserved from the Shaolin Temple, or in the case of progressive Li-Hai, web-based documents waiting to be called up on a palmtop computer. They include the Akashic sutras as well as sacred books and songs from every country the Brotherhood has ever called home.

The Record as a Paradigm Element

Akashic Mind Arts rely heavily on the idea of the Record. The mushin principle is the argument that the ego blinds an Akashayana from the turning of the Wheel. Quieting the mind gives a Brother access to all minds, as they are no different from his own. To the Brotherhood, consciousness is a santana, or "stream," that simply follows the grooves imprinted by Akashakarma. When a Brother lets go of his ego, he is no longer bound by the impression created by his fears, hopes and habits. That stream flows outwards in all directions, sensing but never bound to the impressions of other minds.

Akashic Awareness (1- to 5-pt. Supernatural Merit)

Rinpoche, who have been Brothers for many incarnations, often have an unusually strong connection to Akashakarma. This is both a blessing and a curse. While it can be a font of information, the Akashic Record is no substitute for experience. Furthermore, the minds of others can be addictive or dangerous. A foolish Brother might depend on the insights of others instead of listening to the Bodhicitta within.

This Merit represents an exceptional attunement to the Akashakarma. It works in conjunction with magical effects (see Reading the Endless Scroll, below) that join the Brother's mind to the Record, and with the Brother's *Past Life*. For each point the character has in this merit, the player rolls one die (difficulty 6). Each success reduces the difficulty of an effect by one (to the standard final modifier of -3). A botch traps the character in the Record for as long as the Storyteller deems fit.

This benefit can never be used for magical attacks or defenses. It only applies to informational spells that are routed through the Record. However, this can aid attempts to steal secrets from unwilling minds and overcome wards placed over certain places or things, so long as the attempt is made within the Record.

The *Akashic Awareness* Merit also reduces the difficulty of other Brothers attempting to access the character's thoughts or memories. While this is useful when networking minds, it can also make unwanted intrusion easier. This applies only to effects that would normally gain the benefits above and generally doesn't apply to effects generated outside the Record or the Akashic paradigm. What constitutes an "Akashic Brother" is ultimately determined by the paradigm of the individual in question. Thus, an Akashic *barrabus* can make full use of Akashakarma so long as he believes in a twisted form of Drahma.

MET: Each Trait in this Merit gives you a one-Trait bonus to the resolution of all magic related to the Akashic Record and its rotes (below). However, any other member of the Akashic Brotherhood gains bonus resolution Traits on any magical Mental Challenge against you.

Reading the Endless Scroll

While the paradigm of Akashakarma is very flexible, accessing the Record itself is less so. For game purposes, the Akashic Record is limited to the collective minds of the Brotherhood, their memories and histories. Reading the minds of outsiders and using physical magic (such as the Pattern Spheres) must follow the standard **Mage** rules. The following rotes are the standard methods used to read Akashakarma. Other rotes may benefit from the *Akashic Awareness* Merit at the Storyteller's discretion.

ISHIN DEN SHIN
(•• CORRESPONDENCE, •• MIND)

"From my mind to your mind." This rote allows an Akashic Brother to sense the current emotions of local Sangha, including any physical sensations such as pain or excitement. The Brother breathes deeply and visualizes a sphere of awareness expanding to encompass his comrades.

System: After spending successes to affect another target, and for Correspondence range on each person sensed, the character must spend one success on each subject to successfully sense them.

MET: Initiate *Correspondence*, Initiate *Mind*. After spending a turn or more in meditation, you forge an empathic link (or a telepathic link, if all parties are willing and you have Disciple *Mind*) with one subject who is not in your line of sight. If both of you are Akashic Brothers, you do not need to be aware of the identity or location of the subject; you can just declare that you're trying to contact another Brother. This link lasts for one turn. *Grades of Success:* Each grade of success allows you to extend the duration by one grade or add another subject to the mindlink.

TURNING THE WHEEL OF AGES
(•• OR ••• MIND, • SPIRIT, •• TIME)

Euthanatoi, who call it Shruti and use it outside of the Record, also use this rote. By reading ancient texts in conjunction with meditation, an Akashic Brother experiences the past of another member of the Sangha, even to the extent of recalling their past lives. Some events, such as the Himalayan War and the moments of Samadhi, cannot be accessed in this fashion.

System: Mind plumbs the subject's thoughts. Spirit allows her Avatar to be tracked through many lives, and Time pushes those perceptions into the past. This rote typically has a threshold of five successes, plus those spent to explore the Avatar's past. Mind 3 is used on a willing subject or a member of the Akashayana. Mind 4 is required if the Brother is studying an unwilling subject, unless she is also a Brother. The *Akashic Awareness* Merit does not grant any benefit when the character explores the Avatars of outsiders.

MET: Initiate or **Disciple *Mind*, Apprentice *Spirit*, Initiate *Time*.** You spend a minute or more reading from the Stone Sutra. This allows you to experience one of the past lives of a single subject. Disciple *Mind* is required when you are exploring the past lives of an unwilling subject, unless they are also members of the Akashic Brotherhood. *Grades of Success:* Each grade of success allows you to explore one additional past life.

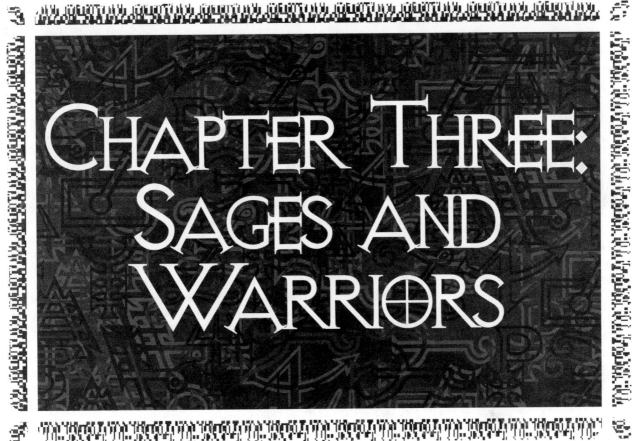

CHAPTER THREE: SAGES AND WARRIORS

He took a face from the ancient gallery
and he walked on down the hall.
— The Doors, "The End."

The Traditions think they know the Akashic Brotherhood. Shaved heads and flying karate chops make the Warring Fists easy enough to identify, don't they?

For every Kannagara monk or modern samurai, there is a Shi-Ren working his magic through bows and handshakes, and Jnani finding Meru's traces in a forest of skyscrapers. The Akashayana Sangha believes that each person has to find his or her own path to the Drahma. Outside the temple and dojos of the Tradition, subtlety and diversity thrives.

Even the Arts that other mages see are likely to be misinterpreted. While an outsider might see a self-torturing monk, the Brotherhood sees someone who is trying to wash away the stains of deception. While their actions might be obvious to all, the reasons remain a mystery to all but a few.

However, the path a monk or martial artist chooses isn't indicative of the whole of the Brotherhood. While the Akashayana Sangha values its defenders and spiritual leaders, the majority lead full lives outside the battlefield or the Bodhimandala. Shi-Ren know the power of money and cultivate business ties for themselves and their Brothers, and Li-Hai stalk the cutting edge of martial arts, politics and medicine. Even the Kannagara are more than cloistered Phoenix Robes; many direct charities promote Eastern philosophy in the media.

Part of the misunderstanding has to do with the approach Westerners take to Akashic beliefs. They see the Brotherhood as a mysterious, exotic entity, isolated from the world around them. While this might be true for many Western Bodhimandalas, the Asian Brotherhood is integrated into its native societies. Akashayana take an active, dynamic part in politics and culture, and the practices that seem so strange to Westerners are a part of everyday life in the East.

In the end, the fact is that many people don't *want* to believe in the Akashic way. They want to hang on to their egos and prefer to think that their errant, selfish thoughts can't escape their minds to perpetuate suffering. The Drahma challenges the very thing that other magi see as fundamental to their existence: that they are free agents who can control the All through their thoughts. Thus, the wheel of karma turns, and the mystics who need the Brotherhood's guidance the most take comfort in empty illusions.

WHISPERS FROM THE VOID: NOTABLE AKASHAYANA

The Akashic Brotherhood as a whole frowns on the notion that some of their number deserve a more exalted (or reviled) place in history than others. Still, the Sangha treasures its history; Brothers share their stories of teachers who inspired them and enemies who filled the path toward Samadhi with danger and suffering.

NU YING: RAGING EAGLE

Background: One of the few true Sifu remaining on Earth, Raging Eagle can trace his incarnations all the way back to the Himalayan War. This has left him with a burden that few Brothers would willingly bear.

Nu Ying discovered the truth about the war and worked to conceal it on the Sangha's behalf. To do this, he became a deceiver and an assassin, cutting down Brothers who remembered the war and refused to keep silent. He paid for his service with a karmic debt that dooms him whenever he leaves a Bodhimandala for more than a week. Some whisper that he has suffered in the Pit of Harmony, incarnating into Yomi's torture when the weight of his sins grew too heavy for a human birth.

Raging Eagle began his current life in 1950, when he was born to a working class family in Denver, Colorado. He took to sports as a child, becoming a skilled boxer by the age of 16. He Awakened after an intense sparring session when he easily defeated his stronger, more experienced, coach. Jou Shan arrived a day later, and took the boy as his apprentice.

At first, Nu Ying served as a Vajrapani at a mountain Bodhimandala near his former home. As he studied Akashakarma and learned about his past, he was entrusted with some of the

Ascension War's most dangerous missions. After the destruction of the Consanguinity of Eternal Joy, he retired to the Kannagara, but the secrets locked in his mind left little room for inner peace. Without the distraction of the Ascension War, he has been forced to face his past.

As a full Sifu, Raging Eagle does his duty for the Brotherhood, but he chooses isolation when he can, training in an ancient cave in the Garuda Valley. Occasionally, he'll teach a Sidai some of the secrets of combative Do, but these lessons go hand in hand with frequent mind reading and ethical lessons in order to ensure that a student doesn't misuse his potent teachings.

Image: Raging Eagle shaves his head completely. This makes his brown eyes appear darker and deeper. In this incarnation, he is a Caucasian with powerful rippling muscles. Although he's in his fifties, he looks about 20 years younger. This is less the result of magic than a disciplined and healthy lifestyle — he is capable of outperforming his juniors without one whit of supernatural assistance. He moves with assured precision and never fidgets. In combat, he specializes in simple, perfect and lethal movements.

On the other hand, he's a terrible dresser. When he must appear outside of his clerical garb, he wears a badly fitted blue suit or casual clothes that are 20 to 30 years out of date. He prefers comfort to style. He keeps a set of prayer beads with him at all times. These act as a Periapt worth 5 pawns of Quintessence, a gift to him from Jou Shan.

Roleplaying Hints: Don't waste words. Every utterance should be a lesson, a warning or a way to practice the Drahma. You rarely praise your students because you believe that they can find a deeper satisfaction in practice than from your attempts to stroke their egos. When you recall the mistakes of your previous lives, you are sometimes overcome with sadness and worry. In these situations, you return to your cave and train when you can. In conversation, you almost never show your emotions. When you must express your feelings, you do so with silence or practice. You despise violence, and sometimes give opponents longer than you should to compose themselves, but your superlative ability rarely allows this to become a problem.

Sect: Kannagara, formerly Vajrapani.

Essence: Questing

Nature: Penitent

Demeanor: Pedagogue

Attributes: Strength 4, Dexterity 5, Stamina 5; Charisma 3, Manipulation 2, Appearance 2; Perception 3, Intelligence 4, Wits 5

Talents: Alertness 4 (Sense Ambushes), Athletics 5 (Leaping), Awareness 3, Brawl 4 (Boxing), Dodge 5 (Multiple Attackers), Intimidation 3, Leadership 3, Streetwise 1

Skills: Crafts (Weaponsmithing) 3, Do 5 (Basic Movements), Etiquette 4 (Akashic), Meditation 4 (Silent), Melee 4 (Swords), Stealth 3, Survival 3

Knowledges: Academics (Akashic History) 3, Body Control 4 (Breathing), Cosmology 2, Enigmas 2, Investigation 3, Law 3, Linguistics 3, Medicine 3, Occult 4 (Asian), Strategy 3

Backgrounds: Arcane 2, Avatar 3, Destiny 4, Dream 3, Library 3

Arete: 7

Spheres: Correspondence 4, Entropy 3, Forces 3, Mind 5, Prime 3, Spirit 2, Time 3

Willpower: 9
Quintessence: 8
Paradox: 5
Resonance: (Dynamic) Explosive 1, (Entropic) Ruthless 1, (Static) Focused 2

Xiao Mengli: The Crossroads

Background: Mengli stands at the crux of many modern Akashic elements. She has no known past incarnations or karmic imprint in the Record, yet she takes to Akashic studies easily and naturally. She has a fierce temper yet remains fair and insightful even when angered. She's Chinese and quite traditional, yet she smoothly adopts modern conventions and customs when necessary. She is a reminder of what the Brotherhood was, and where it's going.

Mengli's still young, no more than 21 or 22 years old. Her exact age remains unknown, as she comes from a provincial agricultural community in China that kept few records. When she arrived at the Bodhimandala in Beijing, the startled monks took her in and asked why she'd come. "My feet came here because they knew the road already," was her reply.

As a student of the Kannagara, Mengli excelled in stealth, combat skills and the martial aspects of Do. She had a keen insight for the law. However, she remained rambunctious. Though she gave lip service to tradition and frowned at those who lacked patience or respect, she had little tolerance for excessive study. For a time she leaned in the direction of Li-Hai utilitarian philosophy before finally admitting to more Vajrapani tendencies.

Once she'd mastered the rudiments of Do and enough self-control to keep from getting into *too* much trouble, Mengli left the care of the Kannagara to "let her feet find the road again." She disappeared from view for about three months, showing up in the United States with an alternate identity and a few contacts among other mages there. Over the next two years, she ran a smuggling ring, moving valuable artifacts, weapons and even people — relieving the Chinese government of an item with mystic significance, bringing an expatriate back to the country or just shuttling relics from one Bodhimandala to another. Older traditionalist Akashics purse their lips and frown at her lack of propriety or respect for the law, but they must recognize her value to the Sangha. She's managed to evade Technocratic notice (for now) and every year comes up with some valued artifact or scrap of knowledge from the Brotherhood's history, even if she has no memory of any of it.

Where the road will carry Mengli next, even she doesn't know.

Image: Xiao Mengli has the features of a classical Chinese woman, young and earnest, still well honed and slender from her early rural upbringing and martial training. Her eyes are dark and piercing, flitting from point to point — she's always suspicious that someone might be on to her smuggling. In battle, she sizes up the enemy, strikes to cripple and then flees with incredible litheness. She keeps her black hair short and out of her eyes.

Depending on her surroundings, Mengli dresses either in a heavy overcoat and simple black shirt and pants, or else in a traditional Chinese dress. She learned early on the value of not standing out too much.

Roleplaying Hints: You're not really sure where you came from or where you're going — the monks tell you that you have

no past, a clean slate without any karma to weigh you down. The Kannagara would keep you chanting and praying for your whole life in hopes of achieving liberation without the weight of any previous incarnations upon you, but you haven't the patience for it. Better to be *doing* something!

While you agree (mostly) with the Brotherhood's beliefs, you find the philosophy of non-attachment annoying. Sure, it's simple to say that nothing really exists, but that doesn't help the millions out there who struggle and starve. You have to raise people past the need for subsistence before they can stand up and reach for enlightenment. That's why you do what you do: Not only is it a thrilling living, but it provides valuable tools and funds for the Brotherhood to help others.

And, of course, you're a world-class ass-beater when it comes down to it.

Sect: Vajrapani

Essence: Questing

Nature: Thrill-Seeker

Demeanor: Survivor

Attributes: Strength 3, Dexterity 4, Stamina 4; Charisma 3, Manipulation 4, Appearance 3; Perception 4, Intelligence 3, Wits 3

Talents: Alertness 4, Athletics 3, Awareness 2, Brawl 2, Dodge 4, Intimidation 1, Streetwise 4, Subterfuge 3

Skills: Crafts (Weaponsmith) 2, Drive 2, Etiquette 3, Firearms 1, Meditation 2, Melee 3, Stealth 2, Survival 2

Knowledges: Academics 1, Computer 1, Enigmas 1, Investigation 1, Law 1, Linguistics 3 (English, French, Japanese, Sino-Tibetan), Occult 1

Backgrounds: Allies 2, Arcane 2, Avatar 1, Contacts 5, Destiny 3, Influence 1, Resources 3

Arete: 3

Spheres: Correspondence 2, Mind 3, Time 2

Willpower: 7

Quintessence: 1

Paradox: 0

Resonance: (Dynamic) Unpredictable 1

THE BODY OF THE LAW: AKASHIC CHRONICLES

It's easy to fall into stereotyping with Akashic characters, or to ignore their cultural origins altogether and present them simply as Awakened martial artists. One way to prevent this is to give an Akashayana a distinct place in a multi-Tradition cabal.

Aside from their traditional roles as warriors, Akashic Brothers also excel as scholars (the Akashic Record is particularly useful for this), explorers (Jnani often pick up quite a bit of wilderness lore as a result of their lifestyles), mediators and mind-control specialists. This last is particularly worth mentioning, as it is an oft-overlooked capability. Shi-Ren tend to be the most proficient, although the Kannagara often alters thoughts to release people from cycles of destructive behavior. While few admit to it, some Akashayana have used their prowess with Mind Arts to implant devious suggestions that are worthy of NWO brainwashing in terms of their efficacy.

This doesn't mean that Akashic warriors should be overlooked! The Vajrapani are quite simply the finest warrior-mages that the Traditions have to offer. The price of this skill is constant, dedicated practice, as unmatched in intensity as its results are in effectiveness. This aspect of the Tradition is rife with roleplaying opportunities, as characters search for the Sifu who knows the secret of the Thunderbolt Kick or learn to paint a perfect landscape in exchange for a critical lesson. Athletic feats and sparring can portray the excitement of combat without letting it dominate the plot of the chronicle. Even in a story with little violence, a warrior can be an intimidating presence, and make the critical difference in the occasional melee.

THE ALL-AKASHIC CHRONICLE

Often overlooked, a cabal consisting entirely of Akashic Brothers can hold its own unique themes and rewards. This is a great way to avoid stereotypes, as each character must find a unique voice without the trappings of a Tradition to support being "original."

Akashic cabals can form for a variety of reasons, from simply being a group that trains together to specialized groups that protect the Sangha's financial, political, legal and even criminal interests. A Kannagara often leads an Akashic cabal, but there is no hard-and-fast rule that says this has to be so, or that there even has to be a leader.

One distinctive element of the Akashayana is their emphasis on the student-teacher relationship. A cabal often consists of pairs of Sidai and Sihing. The few Sifu often act as mentors for the entire

---

CONTROLLING DO

For a new Storyteller, Do can be an intimidating Ability. While it makes Akashayana incredible close-range fighters, it doesn't make them omnipotent. If your chronicle derails because Do always crushes the opposition, you have a number of options at hand to even the balance.

First of all, Do is remarkably ineffective when your opponent is on a rooftop with a rifle. What Technocratic operative *doesn't* carry a gun? Even with Correspondence enhancements, Do doesn't deal with range as well as the mundane alternative.

Secondly, Do is a time-consuming practice. If training isn't incorporated into the chronicle, the Storyteller has every right to tell the player that she can't spend experience to increase her Do skill. The Storyteller might even reduce the character's Do rating if training is constantly ignored.

Finally, Do — even its peaceful applications — marks the character as a trained fighter. Once a throat is torn out or a hand unconsciously makes a perfect fist, the other side knows that trouble is coming. Thus, they're less inclined to be fair. If someone sees a Tao-shih in action, they're likely to try to outnumber and outgun him at their next encounter.

Why have Do at all? The reason is that in the World of Darkness, the Brotherhood's teachings lie at the root of the martial arts. They systematized barehanded combat when bronze tools were in their infancy. They incorporated Do into their paradigm more fully than any other Tradition or Craft. Their reward is that they can truly master those arts, but as firearms become cheaper, deadlier and more commonplace — and people turn away from honor — Do's utility fades. This doesn't bother the Akashayana; Do was always meant to be more of a vehicle for enlightenment than a way to train warriors.

VIOLENCE AND HORROR

In an action-packed chronicle, there's going to be a fair amount of violence. Add Do, and broken bones and bloody hands might quickly become standard fare.

Don't let this happen. While the denizens of the World of Darkness might be a little more hardened to the ugly side of life, violence should still have an emotional impact. A woman who can kill with a single punch is more than a good fighter. She's horrific like an animated corpse or a demon-binding sorcerer. The fiction in this book tries to emphasize the fact that a battle is more than rolled dice and body counts. When someone is murdered before your eyes, the trauma may never go away.

There's only one type of person who can witness killing without the accompanying emotional trauma. These people are called sociopaths. Sociopaths don't Ascend (although the Nephandi provide an alternative route for a psychotic willworker's search for magical understanding). Letting a player's character act like one betrays the overarching theme of **Mage**: to become a wiser person.

This doesn't mean the characters have to cry and moan whenever a body hits the floor. The reaction can be subtle, from increased callousness to nightmares. A Vajrapani may try to live with her bloody duties while maintaining a sense of caring. It won't be easy, but wisdom never is.

Give violence the weight it deserves. It's a potent Storytelling tool, but violence in the game, like in real life, should carry internal as well as external consequences. While this advice is especially pertinent for Akashic chronicles, it applies to any game where deadly combat takes place.

group. Akashic Brothers consider learning to be a lifetime endeavor, and few believe that they will outgrow the need for external guidance.

An Akashic Brotherhood chronicle can center around the characters' struggle to practice and learn. Such games are more than sitting around a monastery chanting and breathing; learning to balance material and spiritual needs can be a challenge. Who pays for said monastery? How do the monks feed themselves? The answers to these questions could be more interesting than you might think. When Technocrats trace a Bodhimandala through their property records and Nephandi slip a little something extra into the groceries, a Chantry's mundane side becomes an important consideration.

Exploring the Brotherhood's mundane ties can also make for a subtle story. It's easy to make the right decision when the Yama King Emma-O sends shikome assassins through the Bodhimandala's gate, but when the Confucian scholar who teaches your Sidai classical Chinese is also a drug addict, the waters get a whole lot muddier. Akashic-run martial arts schools can bring up issues of violence and responsibility, as Sleeper students use and misuse their skills in the world outside the dojo. The idea isn't to ram a certain opinion down your players' throats but to allow the characters to deal with these issues.

A traveling chronicle can also open up several opportunities for Storytellers. Imagine the culture shock that might occur when a band of cloistered Asian Kannagara travel to New York to pick up a tulku. Misunderstandings can arise between Akashayana and members of other Traditions, or even between Akashayana from opposite ends of the globe. Play up the differences between the Brotherhood's calm, healthy lifestyle and the bizarre affectations of other mages.

Traveling Brothers might be on a mission for the Sangha or the Traditions, or they might simply be searching for a Sifu who can teach them a critical Ability or Sphere. Jnani in particular make themselves hard to find, both to preserve their lifestyles and test prospective students. Missions include finding lost Wonders and dragon nests, spy missions or even paramilitary operations in which the Brotherhood's combat skills come in handy.

If you plan on running an Akashayana chronicle in Asia, the Year of the Lotus books, particularly **Dragons of the East** and the **Kindred of the East**, provide an invaluable guide to the atmosphere and supernatural forces at work in the Middle Kingdom.

MIDNIGHT OCEAN: AN AKASHIC CABAL

 Midnight Ocean is an example of how the Akashic Brotherhood has adapted to the 21st century without straying from its roots. The Akashayana has always emphasized training, and most cabals form around a common method that its members prefer.

In the case of Midnight Ocean, their path to the Drahma is an unusual one: piracy. The cabal began when a group of Li-Hai took to the seas to steal from Dalou'laoshi junks and selfish merchants. The proceeds were funneled to the Sangha and needy Sleepers. Today, the members of Midnight Ocean have forsaken the sea for the streets, the stock market and the Internet. Wherever the enemies of the Drahma profit, Midnight Ocean is there to humble them and spread the wealth to those who really need it.

HISTORY

Midnight Ocean traces roots to the middle of the 13th century. The founders, all Li-Hai from Fujian, China, originally served as guards on the merchant vessels that plied the trade routes between India, Okinawa, Vietnam and China. In the Mohist tradition, the five founders defended their charges from Japanese wako, fierce storms and greedy imperial bureaucrats.

Over time, the founders realized that many of their employers were no better than the pirates who attacked them. The gold they guarded bought mercenaries and bribes, or came from roping honest folk into debt-slavery. Faced with the hypocrisy of their position, they chose to take the initiative and decide for themselves who deserved the riches that floated across the South China Sea. They stole a boat from a slaver they had once protected and began a career of noble piracy. In the rough-and-tumble ports of Shuri and Hong Kong, they recruited other Akashayana and quite a few Sleepers as well. Soon, Midnight Ocean was practically a Bodhimandala with sails. Two dozen Brothers and more than a hundred Sleepers scoured the waters for justice and profit.

Midnight Ocean's numbers declined throughout the Ming and Qing dynasties. Both were insular, punished travelers and discouraged trade with the "barbarians." When Western ironclads came to China during the time of the Qing dynasty, Midnight Ocean was forced to reduce itself to one vessel staffed by six Brothers and a Sleeper crew. During the Opium War, they were the scourge of British vessels from India, but this soon brought British — and Technocratic — retribution. Midnight Ocean's last vessel was blown to pieces, and the survivors made it to shore only by stowing away on the Technocrats' metal ship.

On land, the cabal allied itself with the Golden Dragons and began to pursue other ways to perform their sworn mission. They insinuated themselves into smuggling and fraud, updating their methods as time passed and new members added their insights. The West proved to be an easy mark; the complexity of international banking and trade opened up opportunities to funnel the ill-gotten gains of others into more-worthy projects. Shi-Ren naturally gravitated to the new Midnight Ocean, creating tension with the Li-Hai who had inherited the cabal from their masters. This divide persists to the present day.

Now, Midnight Ocean rarely stages the bold raids that were the bread and butter of the cabal's seagoing days. Modern members specialize in computer fraud, blackmail and industrial espionage. Nowadays, direct theft is reserved for those times when the cabal needs a quick influx of cash.

PRACTICES

Midnight Ocean's members keep separate homes in New York, London, Hong Kong, Tokyo, Bangkok and New Delhi, monitoring the flow of wealth in every city. Each of these dwellings doubles as a base of operations when the cabal gathers for a mission.

Bishop Chen, based in Hong Kong, has the authority to begin an operation, although he rarely does so without consulting Lucy Hark. Members are expected to discover everything they can about local financial events and the secret interests that set them in motion. During the Ascension War, they monitored wealthy Technocrats. In the 21st century, the cabal goes after anyone who knowingly profits from the suffering of others.

When they find a target, Midnight Ocean members gather as much intelligence as possible and use this to decide what type of action to take. The next step is a practice run, in which they try their plan out against an institution similar to the victim's without carrying it to the point of actually stealing. Finally, the operation itself commences. Members usually coordinate their actions through Mind magic but use other effects sparingly, to conceal their Awakened nature.

Midnight Ocean robs banks, armored cars and the like to either send the mark down a false track or make the best of a situation in which they haven't gathered enough information to use subtler means. When doing so, they use Mind magic to minimize the trauma that security guards and tellers might experience when they're confronted with a holdup. The cabal has one ironclad rule: If a member kills an innocent during an operation, she must leave the cabal.

The cabal prefers indirect attack to open conflict. Chen is an expert hacker and Hark's business connections and dynamic personality allow her to pry secrets from a mark's closest confidantes.

THE WHITE JADE ISLAND

Midnight Ocean's history is filled with stories of adventure and wonder. One such story is that of the Jade Island.

In one of the last adventures of the Ming dynasty, a Midnight Ocean vessel took the Walker Wing Chao to the West. When he failed to return from his tour of the foreign lands, Captain Au Chin-Fu and his crew scoured the seas for their former passenger. Captain Au searched the Akashic Record and dreamed of Wing Chao standing on a cliff of white jade.

Following his vision, he traveled to parts of the sea that no human ship had ever disturbed. He found a jade island, but it was black and cold. Its masters were Wan Kuei pirates, who harried Captain Au's ship. The leader of the undead fleet offered to take them to the White Jade Island — if they would give one of the crew to them. Captain Au volunteered; it is said that his screams echoed across the misty sea as the crew sailed away.

When the crew finally reached the White Jade Island, they found it in ruins, as if it had collapsed from the inside. In the wreckage of an Akashic Bodhimandala, they found a folded orange robe and a bowl full of ashes. With heavy hearts, they charted a course for home, and took the robe, the bowl and a piece of white jade.

A hundred years later, a young girl was shown the bowl, and exclaimed, "You've found Wing Chao!" She Awakened in that instant, full of Captain Au's memories. The west wind blew the ashes out of the bowl even as she put on the robe. When she was old and wise, she took a small boat out to the open sea. She left the piece of jade with a Sidai, and said, "If you need me, throw this into the ocean."

Nobody knows where the piece of white jade is today, much less the island it came from. However, one thing is certain — Au Chin-fu has not reincarnated since then.

When they have stolen whatever they can and made life as difficult for the victim as possible, they retreat back to their individual homes. Midnight Ocean keeps ten percent of the take and divides the rest between donations to the target's victims, charities and cash-strapped Bodhimandalas around the world. The Golden Dragons usually handle these payments for the group through their own formidable network.

USING MIDNIGHT OCEAN

While Midnight Ocean brings in lots of money, the group itself lives fairly modestly. The majority of the money they take finances the cabal's homes, transportation and equipment. An Akashic Brother can't hit them up for a loan without providing someone for the cabal to take the money from or waiting for the cabal to hit pay dirt itself.

However, Midnight Ocean follows a mission to just about anywhere. On two occasions, they've even returned to raiding the seas. Another cabal might run into them as they rob a common antagonist (or might even *be* the target if they've callously let others suffer on the path to power).

The cabal has adapted much of its magic to modern technology. While it is still Akashic to the core, quite a few members have found ways to use the Dharmas that would startle a Sifu born at the turn of the century. This makes them invaluable mentors as well as examples of how Akashic Brothers can adapt their magic to a changing world.

Midnight Ocean's membership also rotates on a fairly regular basis. A Brother might be able to join the group if she isn't violent or impulsive, and has a keen eye for detail. Financial skills are a bonus, but most new members are trained by Hark to shore up any gaps in their knowledge.

Members: Bishop Chen (Li-Hai, Sihing), Lucy Hark (Shi-Ren, Sihing), Miwako Kabayama (Jnani, Sihing), Quentin Kolinsky (Vajrapani, Sidai), Suchart Jones (Li-Hai, Sidai), Jean Fountain (Shi-Ren, Sidai)

BISHOP CHEN

Chen Shiu-yik grew up in a family of Chinese immigrants in New York City. He started calling himself "Bishop" when teachers at the Catholic school he attended couldn't pronounce his name. While it started off as a joke, he used it for so long that he eventually stopped responding to his birth name. This irritated his family to no end. All the same, they appreciated his easygoing and generous nature.

An uncle quickly noticed Bishop's Awakening and tutored him in the Akashic Arts. Bishop had always had an interest in computers and quickly incorporated them into his magical style, storing the Drahma Sutra on disk and creating virtual prayer wheels and digitally rendered mandalas to assist his concentration. When his uncle retired to the Kannagara, Bishop took his uncle's place in Midnight Ocean. After using his innovative Arts to raise the cabal to new heights of efficiency, he was recognized as its leader.

Bishop is an easygoing leader and a genuinely nice person. In his spare time, he concocts secret schemes to make other people happy. He treats this as seriously as his work for Midnight Ocean and considers it a part of his spiritual practice. He might spy on someone for weeks in order to find the best way to anonymously help him. The most important thing is to arrange it so that he can't be thanked in return. That way, he won't get too proud of himself.

As Midnight Ocean's leader, he decides what missions the cabal undertakes and coordinates the group as a whole. He prefers nonviolent missions that are loosely planned so that he can improvise with little risk to others. Lucy Hark has been pressuring him to plan with a little more structure and organize missions by their potential payoff. They've agreed to disagree for now, and Bishop recognizes that the two of them need to find a happy medium.

Image: A man in his early 30s, Bishop Chen stays in shape by jogging and cycling. He ties his hair back in a ponytail to hide a creeping bald spot and dresses in black athletic casuals, preferring shorts to show off his chiseled calves and take attention away from his barrel chest. His one vice is running shoes; he owns a dozen pairs of expensive high-tops in an array of loud colors. His voice has a light South China accent.

Roleplaying Hints: Talk about your ideas constantly. Think of a new way to use Akashic magic every day. Swagger and play the role of a modern pirate one moment, and launch into a discussion on modernizing the Drahma the next. All of your talking is a ruse to cover up the fact that you care about the people around you. You want to help them behind the scenes, rather than play the role of a conquering hero.

Sect: Li-Hai

Essence: Dynamic

Nature: Caregiver

Demeanor: Gallant

Attributes: Strength 3, Dexterity 3, Stamina 3; Charisma 3, Manipulation 2, Appearance 2; Perception 3, Intelligence 4 (Natural Technician), Wits 4 (Grace Under Pressure)

Talents: Alertness 2, Athletics 4 (Running), Do 4 (Flying Kicks), Dodge 2, Leadership 3

Skills: Firearms 1, Meditation 3, Stealth 2, Technology 3

Knowledges: Computer 4 (Hacking), Enigmas 2, Investigation 3, Law 2, Linguistics 2, Occult 2, Strategy 3

Backgrounds: Avatar 1, Library 3, Resources 3

Arete: 5

Spheres: Entropy 2, Forces 3, Mind 4

Willpower: 7

Quintessence: 5
Paradox: 1
Resonance: (Dynamic) Enthusiastic 1, (Static) Humble 1

LUCY HARK

Lucy Hark loves Hong Kong. She loves the busy streets, the profits to be made, and most of all, she loves being Shi-Ren. Her father was a Golden Dragon. She spent her childhood dreaming of the day she would Awaken and join the Dragons herself, even though he called it a foolish fantasy.

She did Awaken — at her father's funeral, after Triad killers gunned him down in his own office. Thousands of people came to pay their respects. Lucy felt a burst of enlightenment come when she realized the invisible connections that bound all of these people to her father. She felt the power the coursed beneath the tears and handshakes and wanted a part of it.

Her mother refused to let her take up the mantle left by her father but realized that Lucy had an obligation to use her gifts to help others. With her mother's reluctant blessing, Lucy entered a monastery in Taiwan but found the Kannagara's ways stifling. After her mother passed away, she sought out the Golden Dragons.

However, the Gam Lungs were reluctant to disobey her mother's wishes. They trained her, but only sent her on the simplest errands. She joined Midnight Ocean to prove herself capable enough to *not* suffer her father's fate. She replaced a Shi-Ren member who had died robbing a Zaibatsu-backed bank, and took on his duties enthusiastically.

Lucy handles Midnight Ocean's finances, including their contributions to the Akashayana and certain Sleepers. However, she still serves the Golden Dragons in a secret capacity, ensuring that much of the money the cabal distributes finds its way into the Gam Lung's coffers. She rationalizes her actions by reasoning that enough money goes to other causes to justify her skimming a little off the top for them. Whenever Midnight Ocean makes another score, she wrestles with her conscience, but the struggle between her cabal and her ambitions has yet to resolve itself.

As the cabal's de facto second in command, Lucy Hark organizes the details that Chen's creative plans often overlook. She frequently chides him to make more rigorous preparations. While she's subverting the cabal's stated goals, she still cares about her Brothers and wants things to run smoothly.

Image: A statuesque Chinese woman in her late 20s, Lucy Hark walks confidently and looks people straight in the eye. She's fond of simple gold jewelry and wears business attire with bright, solid colors. When she's in the field, she wears impeccably maintained army surplus uniforms, a black baseball cap and a bandoleer of sharpened coins to use as throwing weapons. Her long hair is usually kept in a bun.

Roleplaying: Explain something over and over again until you're sure everyone understands. You know that people are weak and prone to error, and it's your responsibility to account for those flaws. You're ambitious; if you ever got enough power in your hands, you could do great things for the Brotherhood. The only problem is, you don't know how to get that power without cheating people who've put their lives on the line for you. You'd make a bid for the leadership of the cabal, but you know that Chen is really the best choice. The two of you are a good team — between his crazy ideas and your thoughtful execution, Midnight Ocean could do anything.

Sect: Shi-Ren
Essence: Questing
Nature: Autocrat
Demeanor: Director
Attributes: Strength 3, Dexterity 3, Stamina 2; Charisma 3, Manipulation 4 (Trustworthy), Appearance 3; Perception 3, Intelligence 4 (Precise), Wits 3
Talents: Alertness 3, Athletics 2, Do 4 (Misdirection), Dodge 3, Intimidation 2, Leadership 3, Subterfuge 4 (Lies)
Skills: Drive 2, Etiquette 3, Meditation 2, Stealth 3
Knowledges: Body Control 1, Investigation 2, Law 3, Linguistics 3, Science 4 (Economics), Strategy 2
Backgrounds: Avatar 2, Dream 2, Resources 4
Arete: 4
Spheres: Entropy 4, Mind 2, Time 2
Willpower: 7
Quintessence: 6
Paradox: 0
Resonance: (Static) Ornate 1

Meru's Children: Templates

Warriors who master the killing arts. Honorable ascetics who blind themselves to the flesh. The Akashic Brotherhood suffers from the illusions perpetrated by the West and even by themselves. At its core, the Akashayana is composed of men and women who believe they can save themselves from suffering and guide others along the road to greater self-understanding. This is more than a quiet reflection on the nature of being — it's an adventure that tests bodies and souls.

Everyone has to follow the middle way between sacrificing himself to the Wheel and succumbing to its empty pleasures and persistent pains. The following templates represent the way in which the Sangha struggles to keep that balance.

Thunderbolt Warrior

Quote: *I accept my death; you don't accept yours. That is why you will lose.*

Prelude: You've always known what you were meant to be. As a child, you trained in the fighting arts under an Akashic Sifu, preparing for the front lines of the Ascension War. Your family had done so for generations, and every part of your upbringing was meant to prepare you for life in the Vajrapani. You heard the stories of heroes like Chang Ng and Kwan Te. Your parents pulled you out of school and filled your mind with the Drahma Sutra and Asian philosophy.

In your teenage years, the facade of normalcy became difficult hard to maintain. Bruises and broken bones from your intense training made your friends suspect abuse. When that happened, you were ordered to find new friends. While the Sangha's allies were everywhere, you sometimes felt the urge to get out into the world and discover things for yourself. Sometimes, you'd run away for days at a time, just to take in the outside world without the pressure of your heritage weighing upon you.

That was foolish thinking. When Metal Dragons killed your parents, you realized that the Akashayana was more important than your own egotistical needs. You returned to training with a vengeance, dedicating every movement and every breath to defending the Brotherhood. When you practiced with this kind of sincere devotion, you thought you could feel yourself slip beyond the bonds of your selfish ego.

You finally Awakened one night after nightmares about your parents forced you out of bed. You went to the family altar and chanted a mantra to calm yourself, but the image of your parents grew brighter and brighter. You cried and screamed, but the apparitions didn't vanish. You reached for a sword — who knows what you were going to do with it? — and then you were bathed in a golden light. You knew the phantoms for what they were — emanations of the Bodhicitta. You appeared at the Bodhimandala the next day, relieved to take the next step to Samadhi.

Concept: A Vajrapani through and through, you are ready to give your life to serve the Brotherhood. You are a warrior whose rough violence has been polished into the shining facets of a scholar, poet and dutiful retainer. You are the modern incarnation of ronin and wuxia heroes, ready to fight without any fear or hesitation. Unfortunately, you don't have much of a life outside that. Your grim demeanor is a facade to hide a shy, underdeveloped personality.

Roleplaying Tips: Don't tolerate criticism of the Akashic Brotherhood. In another era, you might have been ready to kill over a slight on your tradition, but a stony silence is the best option these days. You are almost never afraid, because you have replaced panic with awareness through years of discipline. When danger comes, silently take a combat stance. When the fight begins, move like a whirlwind. Act aloof (actually, frightened and confused) when faced with personal relationships and everyday life.

Magic: You channel Forces and Prime through Do and an array of melee weapons. Mantras make up the bulk of your Mind training. When you are called on to touch the Dharmas, you do so with total commitment, heedless of the dangers of Samsara.

Equipment: Traditional and modern clothing, melee weapons (including a magical sword: a two-point Talisman), prayer beads and beautiful tattoos of the Three Ministers

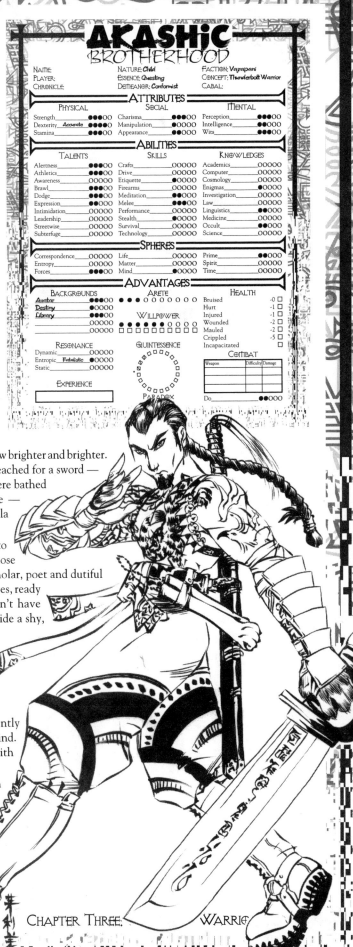

AKASHIC BROTHERHOOD

NAME: NATURE: *Child*   FACTION: *Vajrapani*
PLAYER: ESSENCE: *Questing*   CONCEPT: *Thunderbolt Warrior*
CHRONICLE: DEMEANOR: *Conformist*   CABAL:

ATTRIBUTES

PHYSICAL
Strength ●●●○○
Dexterity *Accurate* ●●●●○
Stamina ●●●○○

SOCIAL
Charisma ●●●●○
Manipulation ●○○○○
Appearance ●●○○○

MENTAL
Perception ●●●○○
Intelligence ●●○○○
Wits ●●●○○

ABILITIES

TALENTS
Alertness ●●○○○
Athletics ●●○○○
Awareness ○○○○○
Brawl ●●●○○
Dodge ●●●○○
Expression ●●○○○
Intimidation ○○○○○
Leadership ○○○○○
Streetwise ○○○○○
Subterfuge ○○○○○

SKILLS
Crafts ○○○○○
Drive ○○○○○
Etiquette ●○○○○
Firearms ○○○○○
Meditation ●●○○○
Melee ●●●○○
Performance ○○○○○
Stealth ●○○○○
Survival ○○○○○
Technology ○○○○○

KNOWLEDGES
Academics ○○○○○
Computer ○○○○○
Cosmology ○○○○○
Enigmas ●○○○○
Investigation ○○○○○
Law ○○○○○
Linguistics ●●○○○
Medicine ○○○○○
Occult ●●○○○
Science ○○○○○

SPHERES

Correspondence ○○○○○
Entropy ○○○○○
Forces ●●●○○
Life ○○○○○
Matter ○○○○○
Mind ○○○○○
Prime ●●○○○
Spirit ○○○○○
Time ○○○○○

ADVANTAGES

BACKGROUNDS
Avatar ●●●○○
Destiny ●○○○○
Library ●●●○○
○○○○○
○○○○○

ARETE
● ● ● ○○○○○○○

WILLPOWER
● ● ● ● ● ○○○○○
□□□□□□□□□□

HEALTH
Bruised -0 □
Hurt -1 □
Injured -1 □
Wounded -2 □
Mauled -2 □
Crippled -5 □
Incapacitated □

RESONANCE
Dynamic ○○○○○
Entropic *Fatalistic* ●○○○○
Static ○○○○○

QUINTESSENCE / PARADOX

COMBAT

Weapon	Difficulty	Damage

Do ●●○○○

EXPERIENCE

TRADITION BOOK: AKASHIC BROTHERHOOD

Sheet 1

ARETE

WILLPOWER

QUINTESSENCE/PARADOX

RESONANCE

DYNAMIC

ENTROPIC *Fatalistic*

STATIC

NAME:
CHARACTER: *Thunderbolt Warrior*
CHRONICLE:
FACTION: *Vajrapani*
ESSENCE: *Questing*
CABAL:
NATURE: *Child*
DEMEANOR: *Conformist*

BACKGROUNDS
Avatar x3
Destiny
Library x3

SPHERES
Disciple of Forces
Apprentice of Mind
Initiate of Prime

ROTES

PHYSICAL
Dextrous x2   *Wiry*
Quick x2   *Resilient*
Tough   SOCIAL
Charismatic
Commanding
Fearsome   MENTAL
Cunning   *Attentive*
Insightful   *Intuitive*
Reflective

ABILITIES
Alertness   *Melee x2*
Brawl x2: Do
Dodge x2

MERITS & FLAWS

Sheet 2

ARETE

WILLPOWER

QUINTESSENCE/PARADOX

RESONANCE

DYNAMIC

ENTROPIC

STATIC *Calm*

NAME:
CHARACTER: *Shaolin Monk*
CHRONICLE:
FACTION: *Karmagara*
ESSENCE: *Pattern*
CABAL:
NATURE: *Masochist*
DEMEANOR: *Perfectionist*

BACKGROUNDS
Avatar x3
Arcane x3
Dream x2

SPHERES
Disciple of Mind
Apprentice of Prime
Initiate of Spirit

ROTES

PHYSICAL
Quick   *Tireless*
Lithe   *Wiry*
Tenacious   SOCIAL
Beguiling
Charismatic
Persuasive   MENTAL
Insightful x2
Reflective x2
Wise x3

ABILITIES
Awareness   *Academics (Theology)*
Brawl: Do   *Enigmas*
Meditation   *Linguistics*

MERITS & FLAWS

SHAOLIN MONK

Quote: *There is nothing holy in the Drahma.*

Prelude: You never liked the outside world. Your family toiled ceaselessly for the trappings of status. Your fine clothes came at the expense of regular meals and time spent together. They said that they kept up appearances for your sake, but you knew that they merely clung to wealth as a way to measure their worth. Everyone else seemed to take this standard for granted, but since you'd suffered under it, you couldn't agree.

The circles you moved in through adolescence supported the same values. Name brands collided with vicious insults to the poor. When your secret got out — that despite the clothes and the private school you were worse off than any of them — you became a victim of their taunting. By the your late teenage years, you'd had enough of it.

You got involved in Eastern religions. Buddhism appealed to you because of its antimaterialistic stance. Against the wishes of your family, you went to Dharma Talks and meditation sessions. When the monks spoke to you, understanding flared in your heart. At the same time, the monks seemed all the more willing to talk to you. One day, you decided to shave your head and take monastic vows.

As a monk, you were free of the self-centered concerns of your family and the contempt of your peers. For the first time, you felt a sense of peace, but it seemed to be a different sort of peace than the Buddhist path described. You had visions, waking dreams of gods and devils that frightened you but filled you with a sense of wonder.

Your companions also seemed to have a special place for you. The abbot subjected you to grueling ascetic practices and kung fu training, saying that it was the surest way to pierce the wondrous, terrifying illusions that crept through your mind. The visions, he said,

were shadows of your pure inner nature and needed to be mastered to encounter your Awakened self. Physical training was ideal; it cultivated the leftover rage you felt from your childhood and freed your body from the distractions of illness and pain.

Over the next few years, you came to realize what the Kannagara and the Akashayana were, and you embraced them wholeheartedly. You are an Awakened monk, schooled in the Shaolin tradition. Although the temple is lost, you still pursue the same serenity and discipline that you spiritual ancestors cultivated hundreds of years ago.

Concept: You have wholeheartedly embraced the methods of the Kannagara Shaolin tradition. You're an ascetic, martial artist and priest who has devoted his life to rejecting the material world. You are willing to help others follow the same path, or simply talk to them in a comforting and humane fashion. You can leave your monastery, but cloistered physical practice lies at the heart of your training.

Roleplaying Tips: You're unfazed by wealth and power; those are fleeting things that bring more suffering than pleasure into people's lives. Steer people away from greedy or self-destructive acts. Contrast a quiet serenity with sudden ferocity when it's time to defend the Drahma or jolt people out of their comfortable illusions. Speak in koans, but don't overdo it.

Magic: Mind helps you transcend the false structure of the rational world, while Spirit allows to merge with the All itself. Prime comes about as a side effect of your Do training. Overcoming physical frailty, your body's Chi obeys your directions. You use traditional Kannagara foci.

Equipment: Robes, a razor, a begging bowl and a sistrum (a staff headed with three interlocking rings). That's it — you're an ascetic, remember?

AKASHIC BROTHERHOOD

NAME: NATURE: *Masochist* FACTION: *Kannagara*
PLAYER: ESSENCE: *Pattern* CONCEPT: *Shaolin Monk*
CHRONICLE: DEMEANOR: *Perfectionist* CABAL:

ATTRIBUTES

PHYSICAL
Strength ●●○○○
Dexterity ●●●○○
Stamina ●●●○○

SOCIAL
Charisma ●●○○○
Manipulation ●●○○○
Appearance ●●○○○

MENTAL
Perception/Concentration ●●●●○
Intelligence ●●●○○
Wits ●●●○○

ABILITIES

TALENTS
Alertness ○○○○○
Athletics ○○○○○
Awareness ●●●○○
Brawl ○○○○○
Dodge ●●○○○
Expression ○○○○○
Intimidation ○○○○○
Leadership ○○○○○
Streetwise ○○○○○
Subterfuge ○○○○○

SKILLS
Crafts ●●○○○
Drive ○○○○○
Etiquette ●●○○○
Firearms ○○○○○
Meditation ●●●○○
Melee ●●○○○
Performance ○○○○○
Stealth ○○○○○
Survival ○○○○○
Technology ○○○○○

KNOWLEDGES
Academics ●●●○○
Computer ○○○○○
Cosmology ●●○○○
Enigmas ○○○○○
Investigation ○○○○○
Law ●○○○○
Linguistics ●●○○○
Medicine ●○○○○
Occult ●○○○○
Science ○○○○○

SPHERES

Correspondence ○○○○○
Entropy ○○○○○
Forces ○○○○○

Life ○○○○○
Matter ○○○○○
Mind ●●●○○

Prime ●●○○○
Spirit ●●○○○
Time ○○○○○

ADVANTAGES

BACKGROUNDS
Avatar ●●●○○
Arcane ●●●○○
Dream ●●○○○
○○○○○
○○○○○

ARETE
● ● ○ ○ ○ ○ ○ ○ ○ ○

WILLPOWER
●●●●●○○○○○
○○○○○○○○○○

HEALTH
Bruised -0 □
Hurt -1 □
Injured -1 □
Wounded -2 □
Mauled -2 □
Crippled -5 □
Incapacitated □

RESONANCE
Dynamic ○○○○○
Entropic ○○○○○
Static *Calm* ○○○○○

QUINTESSENCE

EXPERIENCE

PARADOX

COMBAT

Weapon	Difficulty	Damage

Do ●●○○○

REINCARNATE

Quote: *If I've done it before, why do I have to do it now?*

Prelude: You were a weird kid. You never had many friends; they were put off by your vivid fantasies. Your teachers and parents were worried too, because the stories you'd tell them about your daydreams contained things that no child should be familiar with. You told them of bloody wars and supernaturally deadly swordsmen. Sometimes you'd chant for them in a strange language. Your family sent you through a gauntlet of child psychologists. Some of them recommended antipsychotic drugs and others asserted that it was a phase. In the end, your family kept you off medication and decided to wait and see if you'd settle down as you matured.

You didn't. Sometimes, you would have vivid nightmares, where many-armed gods confronted you in a vast, dark space. Word got around that you were a freak, and high school became a special hell for you. When you were 14, you came home from another day of taunts and beatings and you encountered your parents talking to a contingent of robed bald men. Something about them was eerily familiar; hadn't you dreamed about them?

Your parents told you that they had come all the way from Dharamsala, India, to meet you. They said you were a tulku, a reincarnated spiritual teacher from their homeland. You were stunned that they took this so calmly, and you went to set the bald men straight. You had your problems, but you didn't need another disappointing diagnosis.

Then they sang. You knew the chant — the alien language had been with you from childhood. Something arose from inside you, and you began to join them in reciting the Stone Sutra. Flustered by the experience, you sat with them, and they told you that they'd spent their entire lives looking for you.

The monks opened a bag and showed you a collection of rattles, bones and scrolls. The dreams whispered to you, and you picked out the artifacts that had belonged to you in your past life. Then they reached into the bag again and gave you one more thing — the jawbone from your previous body.

The past unfolded: your lives in the Akashayana, your deaths from war, disease and old age and the secrets of the Dharmas. You went with them, barely pausing to think, *What about my life? What about my family?*

Now in your late teens, you struggle between the life the Brotherhood has prepared for you and the life your family gave you. You miss them, and you now understand that they might not have let you go of their own free will. You chafe under the ritualistic routine that you follow, because — as much as you remember why the rituals are important — you want to move forward. You want enlightenment to come from this life, not the others.

Concept: You're a member of the Chabnagpa Jnani and a spiritual heir to Tibetan magic and spirituality.

You've spent many incarnations as a part of the jat, but you have a life that is more than the route prepared from you by hundreds of lifetimes. You want to adapt the Brotherhood's ways to your own experience, but you don't want to undermine ancient tradition. You know how important you are to the Sangha; tulku are the spiritual backbone of the Sangha. The living proof of their beliefs. You don't want to take that away from them.

Roleplaying Tips: Bridge the ancient and modern with your pronouncements. You're young, but you wield authority; use it to help the Brotherhood grow. You have "handlers" who revere you but regulate everything from your diet to how you dress. Try to pull a fast one on them from time to time, just to show that you aren't like your predecessors.

Magic: Mind and Time aptitude spring from your strong connection to the Brotherhood. Spirit comes your training with the Black Water Sect. You use ascetic practices, chanting and writing to touch the Dharmas.

Equipment: Robes, prayer beads, a bone rattle, a walking stick from your previous incarnation and a pair of sneakers you wear whenever your tutors aren't around

AKASHIC BROTHERHOOD

NAME:
PLAYER:
CHRONICLE:

NATURE: *Child*
ESSENCE: *Dynamic*
DEMEANOR: *Traditionalist*

FACTION: *Jnani*
CONCEPT: *Reincarnate*
CABAL:

ATTRIBUTES

PHYSICAL		SOCIAL		MENTAL	
Strength	●●○○○	Charisma	●●●○○	Perception	●●○○○
Dexterity	●●○○○	Manipulation *Sounding Profound*	●●●●○	Intelligence	●●○○○
Stamina	●●○○○	Appearance	●●●○○	Wits	●●●○○

ABILITIES

TALENTS		SKILLS		KNOWLEDGES	
Alertness	○○○○○	Crafts	○○○○○	Academics	●●○○○
Athletics	○○○○○	Drive	○○○○○	Computer	○○○○○
Awareness	●●○○○	Etiquette	●●○○○	Cosmology	●●○○○
Brawl	○○○○○	Firearms	○○○○○	Enigmas	●○○○○
Dodge	○○○○○	Meditation	●●●○○	Investigation	○○○○○
Expression	●●○○○	Melee	○○○○○	Law	○○○○○
Intimidation	○○○○○	Performance	●●●○○	Linguistics	●●○○○
Leadership	○○○○○	Stealth	●○○○○	Medicine	○○○○○
Streetwise	○○○○○	Survival	○○○○○	Occult	●●●○○
Subterfuge	●●○○○	Technology	○○○○○	Science	○○○○○

SPHERES

Correspondence	○○○○○	Life	○○○○○	Prime	○○○○○
Entropy	○○○○○	Matter	○○○○○	Spirit	●●○○○
Forces	○○○○○	Mind	●●○○○	Time	●●○○○

ADVANTAGES

BACKGROUNDS		ARETE	HEALTH	
Avatar	●●●○○	●● ○○○○○○○○○	Bruised	-0 □
Destiny	●●●○○		Hurt	-1 □
Dream	●●●●○	WILLPOWER	Injured	-1 □
Mentor	●●○○○	●●●●●●●○○○	Wounded	-2 □
	○○○○○	□□□□□□□□□□	Mauled	-2 □
			Crippled	-5 □
			Incapacitated	□

RESONANCE		QUINTESSENCE		COMBAT		
Dynamic	○○○○○		Weapon	Difficulty	Damage
Entropic *Vibrating*	●○○○○				
Static	○○○○○				

EXPERIENCE

PARADOX

Do ●○○○○

TRADITION BOOK: AKASHIC BROTHERHOOD

NAME: _____

CHARACTER: *Reincarnate*

CHRONICLE: _____

FACTION: *Jnani*

ESSENCE: *Dynamic*

CABAL: _____

NATURE: *Child*

DEMEANOR: *Traditionalist*

PHYSICAL
Agile _____
Athletic _____
Vigorous _____

SOCIAL
Charismatic / Friendly
Charming x2 / Ingratiating
Expressive / Witty

MENTAL
Alert / Discerning
Clever / Intuitive
Creative _____

ABILITIES
Academics (Theology)/Performance (Singing)
Brawl: Do / Cosmology
Meditation / Linguistics

MERITS & FLAWS

BACKGROUNDS
Avatar X2
Destiny X2
Dream x3
Mentor

SPHERES
Initiate of Mind
Initiate of Spirit
Initiate of Time

ROTES

ARETE

WILLPOWER

QUINTESSENCE/PARADOX

RESONANCE
DYNAMIC _____
ENTROPIC *Vibrating*
STATIC _____

TRADITION BOOK: AKASHIC BROTHERHOOD

NAME: _____

CHARACTER: *Prosecutor*

CHRONICLE: _____

FACTION: *Shi-Ren*

ESSENCE: *Dynamic*

CABAL: _____

NATURE: *Bon Vivant*

DEMEANOR: *Architect*

PHYSICAL
Energetic _____
Graceful _____
Tireless _____

SOCIAL
Beguiling / Expressive x2
Diplomatic / Persuasive
Eloquent _____

MENTAL
Attentive / Knowledgeable
Cunning / Observant
Dedicated / Rational

ABILITIES
Brawl: Do / Intimidation
Subterfuge / Investigation
Law / Streetwise

MERITS & FLAWS

BACKGROUNDS
Avatar
Contacts X2
Influence: Legal x3
Resources x3

SPHERES
Initiate of Entropy
Initiate of Mind
Initiate of Prime

ROTES

ARETE

WILLPOWER

QUINTESSENCE/PARADOX

RESONANCE
DYNAMIC *Sly*
ENTROPIC _____
STATIC _____

PROSECUTOR

Quote: *I can't convict someone who believes that the Buddha told him to do it. The state rests.*

Prelude: You weren't always a stickler for justice. The third child in a wealthy family, you didn't have to worry about carrying on the family business or marrying a powerful partner to carry on your parents' interests. That left you free to be the *enfant terrible*. You were kicked out of so many boarding schools that you stopped unpacking your bags every time you moved.

Adulthood brought more serious vices with it: alcohol, cocaine and prostitutes. You stopped making friends and started losing them to stable jobs and marriages. Your family stopped speaking to you, but so what? They still kept the checks coming.

That all turned around when you met her. She introduced herself by leaving an envelope with her phone number on it. Inside were photos of one of your drug-addled romps with two call girls. You phoned her and arranged to meet at a fancy uptown restaurant, the kind you hadn't been inside in years. A hard-looking woman with gray hair was waiting for you.

You smiled the way you always did to buy time before you lied, but she told you that she was a private eye, working for your family. You relaxed long enough to be caught unawares when she said that they'd hired her to blackmail you. You were given another envelope, filled with college registration forms. To your surprise, a prestigious Ivy League school had already accepted you.

At first, you went to college unwillingly, always looking for an angle to get back into your former life. At each attempt, the P.I. appeared at just the wrong place and time. You turned to your studies in the hope that it would all be over with when you graduated, and you fought off your addictions as best you could.

After a while, you began to actually enjoy your new life. You seemed born to the discipline of academic life; why hadn't you done this before? You had a natural grasp of the law, and in mock trials, you could reduce a witness to a shivering wreck. During your graduating year, you went back to your family to thank them. They didn't know what you were talking about; they'd never hired anyone to follow you, and they'd cut you off of your allowance years ago! You thought they were just ashamed to admit that they'd gone to such lengths to help you.

Reasoning that you'd be a great prosecutor because you knew how crime worked from the inside, you went to work for the state. One day, a steel-haired woman appeared on the defendant's box. You gave her a nod of recognition and got her off of half a dozen violent offenses. Your arguments failed subtly, neglecting obvious evidence and convincing everyone that you'd lost a fierce court battle. You were at the top of your form.

The woman approached you after the trial. She called your skills magic and introduced you to the Shi-Ren. You learned to master your speech and emotions, and you use them to get Brothers out of legal trouble and put dangerous criminals away.

Concept: You're a lawyer (and a good one at that), even though you aren't a law-and-order type of person. With your Awakened perspective, the law is just another facet of reality that a superior person can use to his advantage. You relish the ability to win or throw cases as you please. You're the Akashayana's eyes and ears in the courts, and you take care of Traditionalists when their cases come to court. As for run-of-the-mill criminals, you take pains to emotionally conquer them before calling for the maximum punishment possible.

Roleplaying Tips: You're wily but disciplined. Where you used to get your kicks being the black sheep, now you satisfy yourself by mastering the courtroom. Even when you lose on purpose, you get a secret thrill from putting one over on your colleagues. In truth, you need that emotional satisfaction to keep yourself from returning to your old vices. You prosecute drug-related charges with zeal, always reminding yourself of what the consequences would be if you fell to temptation once again.

Magic: You excel at Mind magic; it lets you find the truth, even wring it out of someone. Entropy can seriously mar or improve a police investigation. Prime is a natural outgrowth of your passion for what you do; you need to master your Chi to be the best.

Equipment: A well-appointed condo, a selection of simple, elegant suits and other clothes (you're a "khaki casual" kind of person), a Porsche you've had since you were a teenager, a leather briefcase and a tiny cellular phone

---

AKASHIC BROTHERHOOD

NAME: NATURE: *Bon Vivant*   FACTION: *Shi-Ren*
PLAYER: ESSENCE: *Dynamic*   CONCEPT: *Prosecutor*
CHRONICLE: DEMEANOR: *Architect*   CABAL:

ATTRIBUTES

PHYSICAL	SOCIAL	MENTAL
Strength ●●○○○	Charisma ●●●○○	Perception ●●●○○
Dexterity ●●○○○	Manipulation *Smooth* ●●●●○	Intelligence ●●●○○
Stamina ●●○○○	Appearance ●●●○○	Wits ●●●○○

ABILITIES

TALENTS	SKILLS	KNOWLEDGES
Alertness ○○○○○	Crafts ○○○○○	Academics ●○○○○
Athletics ●○○○○	Drive ●○○○○	Computer ●○○○○
Awareness ○○○○○	Etiquette ●●○○○	Cosmology ○○○○○
Brawl ○○○○○	Firearms ○○○○○	Enigmas ●●○○○
Dodge ○○○○○	Meditation ●●○○○	Investigation ●●●○○
Expression ○○○○○	Melee ○○○○○	Law ●●●○○
Intimidation ●●○○○	Performance ○○○○○	Linguistics ●○○○○
Leadership ○○○○○	Stealth ○○○○○	Medicine ○○○○○
Streetwise ●●○○○	Survival ○○○○○	Occult ●●○○○
Subterfuge ●●●○○	Technology ○○○○○	Science ○○○○○

SPHERES

Correspondence ○○○○○	Life ○○○○○	Prime ●●○○○
Entropy ●●○○○	Matter ○○○○○	Spirit ○○○○○
Forces ○○○○○	Mind ●●○○○	Time ○○○○○

ADVANTAGES

BACKGROUNDS
Avatar ●●○○○
Contacts ●●○○○
Influence ●●●○○
Resources ●●●●○

ARETE
●● ○○○○○○○○

WILLPOWER
●●●●● ●○○○○
□□□□□□□□□□

HEALTH
Bruised	-0 □
Hurt	-1 □
Injured	-1 □
Wounded	-2 □
Mauled	-2 □
Crippled	-5 □
Incapacitated	□

RESONANCE
Dynamic *Sly* ●○○○○
Entropic ○○○○○
Static ○○○○○

QUINTESSENCE / PARADOX

EXPERIENCE

COMBAT
Weapon	Difficulty	Damage

Do ●○○○○

Street Marshal

Quote: *Property is theft, and this is repossession!* (with a brick thrown through a Starbucks window for emphasis)

Prelude: You know what social inequality is. You grew up in a dirt-poor country and came from a dirt-poor family. You were working by the time you were six. When you were twelve, your hands went numb from operating a sewing machine in a factory that made shoes for North Americans. The pay was more money than your family had ever seen before, but it took four months' wages to buy a pair of the shoes you put together every day.

But seeing the fruits of your labor getting shipped away touched off your ambition. You were going to get your family to the "Gold Mountain." You studied at every spare moment. When you could get to school, you excelled. You finally made it to America on a government scholarship. They gave you enough for tuition and a meager income, but it was more money than you had seen in your entire life.

But the "Gold Mountain" wasn't all it was cracked up to be. Between racism on the street and the ignorance of the typical American about where his luxuries came from, it was enough to make you scream. People were still poor and justice was still rare. It just seemed like the oppression was better financed over here. You sent money back when you could and looked for work at your university. At the same time, you stayed close to immigrants from your homeland. They all answered your complaints with a weary, familiar nod, except for an older man who told you to keep on struggling. Over time, he became your close friend and mentor.

You wound up working for the campus newspaper, which was full of like-minded people. You learned to organize demonstrations with posters, graffiti and the Internet, and you learned how to keep a group of protestors together when the cops charged in with horses and tear gas. After these adventures, you debated with your mentor about the morality of your actions, and he challenged you to apply your antiauthoritarian beliefs to other aspects of your life.

At first, the self-defense skills he taught were what kept you coming back. Eventually, you looked forward to matching wits with him. You learned to refine your views after each argument.

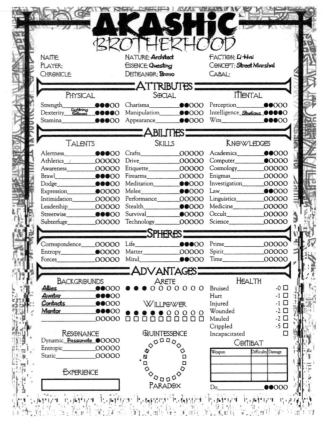

After clashing with police in Seattle, you led a defiant band into an area cordoned off by police. They didn't even seem to notice you until a plainclothes officer pulled up in a black car. He got out and pointed a strange handgun at you, and suddenly you were gone. In a blur, you were five blocks away in your mentor's arms.

Your teacher taught you what it was to be Li-Hai, but in your heart, you already knew. You're going to be the fist that smashes the clay feet of Western hegemony and lets its stored benefits topple down to the people you grew up with.

Concept: You're a revolutionary but not a terrorist. You believe in resistance, not violence, and don't condone the use of force except in self-defense. However, property is a fair target — the multinationals that run rampant over the world need to be taught a lesson. As a Li-Hai, you believe that *everyone* deserves equal treatment before Heaven.

Roleplaying Tips: Don't be patient — that's the counsel of authority figures who want to feed off the less fortunate for another day, another year, another decade. Respect ability, not position, and obey the Drahma by rejecting its outward form. You don't consider yourself to be a violent person — in a perfect world, you'd be a pacifist — but you have a simmering anger about the terrible things that the West takes for granted. Remind everyone of what those things are.

Magic: Mind puts an emotional punch into your speeches and Entropy keeps you in the right place at the right time during the chaos of protests gone wrong. Life gives you a needed boost when it's time to run or fight; you hone your Do skills to do just that.

Equipment: Ragged army surplus clothing, big black boots with blue laces, a black bandanna, political 'zines, body armor scavenged from half a dozen contact sports (1 die of protection), a laptop and a can of spray paint

AKASHIC BROTHERHOOD

NAME: NATURE: *Architect* FACTION: *Li-Hai*
PLAYER: ESSENCE: *Questing* CONCEPT: *Street Marshal*
CHRONICLE: DEMEANOR: *Bravo* CABAL:

ATTRIBUTES

PHYSICAL	SOCIAL	MENTAL
Strength ●●●○○	Charisma ●●●○○	Perception ●●○○○
Dexterity *Lightning Reflexes* ●●●○○	Manipulation ●●●○○	Intelligence *Studious* ●●●●○
Stamina ●●●○○	Appearance ●●○○○	Wits ●●●○○

ABILITIES

TALENTS	SKILLS	KNOWLEDGES
Alertness ●●●○○	Crafts ○○○○○	Academics ●●○○○
Athletics ○○○○○	Drive ○○○○○	Computer ●○○○○
Awareness ○○○○○	Etiquette ○○○○○	Cosmology ○○○○○
Brawl ●●●○○	Firearms ○○○○○	Enigmas ○○○○○
Dodge ●●●○○	Meditation ●●○○○	Investigation ○○○○○
Expression ●●○○○	Melee ●●○○○	Law ●●○○○
Intimidation ○○○○○	Performance ○○○○○	Linguistics ○○○○○
Leadership ○○○○○	Stealth ●●○○○	Medicine ○○○○○
Streetwise ●●●○○	Survival ●○○○○	Occult ○○○○○
Subterfuge ○○○○○	Technology ○○○○○	Science ○○○○○

SPHERES

Correspondence ○○○○○	Life ●●●○○	Prime ○○○○○
Entropy ●○○○○	Matter ○○○○○	Spirit ○○○○○
Forces ○○○○○	Mind ●●○○○	Time ○○○○○

ADVANTAGES

BACKGROUNDS	ARETE	HEALTH	
Allies ●●○○○	●●● ○○○○○○○	Bruised	-0 ☐
Avatar ●●○○○		Hurt	-1 ☐
Contacts ●●○○○	WILLPOWER	Injured	-1 ☐
Mentor ●●●○○	●●●●●○○○○○	Wounded	-2 ☐
	☐☐☐☐☐☐☐☐☐☐	Mauled	-2 ☐
		Crippled	-5 ☐
		Incapacitated	☐

RESONANCE
Dynamic *Passionate* ●○○○○
Entropic ○○○○○
Static ○○○○○

QUINTESSENCE

EXPERIENCE

PARADOX

COMBAT

Weapon	Difficulty	Damage

Do ●●○○○

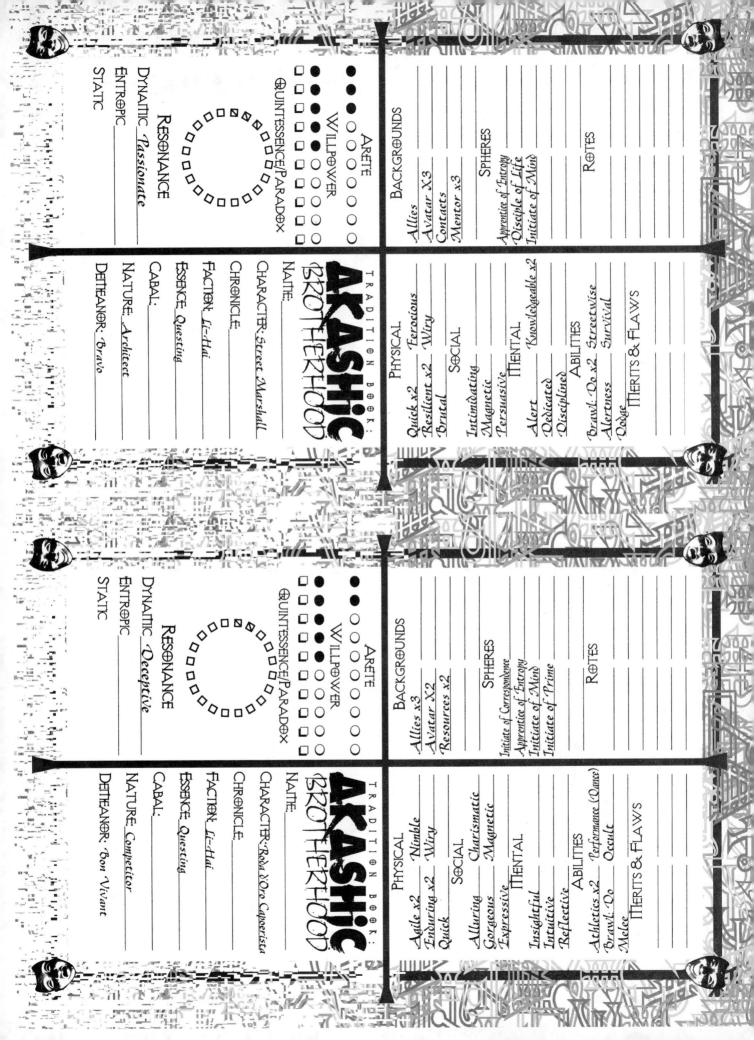

TRADITION BOOK: AKASHIC BROTHERHOOD

ARETE
WILLPOWER
QUINTESSENCE/PARADOX

RESONANCE
DYNAMIC: *Passionate*
ENTROPIC
STATIC

NAME:
CHARACTER: *Street Marshall*
CHRONICLE:
FACTION: *Li-Hai*
ESSENCE: *Questing*
CABAL:
NATURE: *Architect*
DEMEANOR: *Bravo*

BACKGROUNDS
Allies
Avatar X3
Contacts
Mentor x3

SPHERES
Apprentice of Entropy
Disciple of Life
Initiate of Mind

ROTES

PHYSICAL
Quick x2   Ferocious
Resilient x2   Wiry
Brutal   SOCIAL
Intimidating
Magnetic
Persuasive   MENTAL
Knowledgeable x2
Alert
Dedicated
Disciplined   ABILITIES
Brawl: Do x2   Streetwise
Alertness   Survival
Dodge   MERITS & FLAWS

TRADITION BOOK: AKASHIC BROTHERHOOD

ARETE
WILLPOWER
QUINTESSENCE/PARADOX

RESONANCE
DYNAMIC: *Deceptive*
ENTROPIC
STATIC

NAME:
CHARACTER: *Roda d'Oro Capoeirista*
CHRONICLE:
FACTION: *Li-Hai*
ESSENCE: *Questing*
CABAL:
NATURE: *Competitor*
DEMEANOR: *Bon Vivant*

BACKGROUNDS
Allies x3
Avatar X2
Resources x2

SPHERES
Initiate of Correspondence
Apprentice of Entropy
Initiate of Mind
Initiate of Prime

ROTES

PHYSICAL
Agile x2   Nimble
Enduring x2   Wiry
Quick   SOCIAL
Alluring   Charismatic
Gorgeous   Magnetic
Expressive   MENTAL
Insightful
Intuitive
Reflective   ABILITIES
Athletics x2   Performance (Dance)
Brawl: Do   Occult
Melee   MERITS & FLAWS

Roda d'Oro Capoerista

Quote: *The circle of life and death is too wide to limit the truth to any one culture. Come into that circle with me now.*

Prelude: You've always been a natural athlete. You excelled at almost every sport you tried, but you couldn't stick with anything for more than a few months. Maybe it was because you always wondered what "sport" meant, instead of how to beat the other team. When you dropped the winning basket in a game of three-on-three, you felt like you were wasting your time, but in the inner-city neighborhood you grew up in, there wasn't much else to do, and it earned the respect of your peers. Besides, your body felt like it *needed* to move. The only problem was that you wanted your mind to move with it.

You gravitated to combat sports in your college years. Boxing, fencing and wrestling allowed you to test your courage and make your own decisions instead of being confined by a coach or captain. You relished the opportunity to test your bravery, but you felt like that perfect moment where your body and spirit were united would only last as long as the bout.

You thought that martial arts might be the answer, but you found the traditions associated with them stiff and confining. You wanted a way to express yourself, not abase yourself to a black belt or master. Only one school seemed to have what you wanted. A fencing partner gave you the address — they taught a host of martial arts from around the world and emphasized a sense of camaraderie rather than authority. You picked up escrima and dumog quickly enough, but you fell in love with capoeira. The dance-like movements of the African-Brazilian art and its attitude — that the arts are a place for friendship instead of blind obedience — won you over completely. You Awakened in the roda (practice circle), spinning away from your mestre (teacher) to the beat of a drum. Suddenly, you saw the hidden pattern behind the pivots and cartwheels.

Your teacher took you aside and told you about the Roda d'Oro and its place in the Akashic Brotherhood. Now, you're a little more understanding of the Asian customs you once avoided, but you still wouldn't trade the sublime dance you've begun for anything.

Concept: Not all martial arts come from the East, and neither do all Brothers. You joined the Li-Hai through the Roda d'Oro, or "Circle of Gold," a fellowship of Akashayana who come to the Drahma through non-Asian physical pursuits. You follow Akashic beliefs but believe that every culture has seen those truths in their own unique fashion.

Roleplaying Tips: Smile warmly and shake hands with a gentle but firm grip. Friendship is the first lesson of the roda. The second lesson is deception; against your enemies, find the rhythm to which their spirits dance and attack between the beats. Never let them know if you are playing or moving in to finish them off. In the roda, you learn to discipline yourself and not to trust *too* easily.

Magic: Do, in the style of the arts you love, fuels your magic. Mind allows you to be a wily opponent, and Entropy enhances your unpredictability. Finally, Correspondence allows you to master the illusion of distance and gives you more to rely on than your eyes. For more elaborate effects, you might use a set of drums, or a Santeria ritual, but you translate these things through the Akashic paradigm.

Equipment: Loose, white casual clothes, Filipino knives, a set of drums, a motorcycle and an MP3 player

Yin-Crazed Alchemist

Quote: *The Tao regains equilibrium when it is shocked beyond duality.*

Prelude: Your father was an acupuncturist and herbalist. When he died, you were already versed in the secrets of internal power. He was a healer, but you were always more interested in improving yourself. You took over the family business competently enough, but your talents only really expressed themselves at night, after the patients were gone and you could pursue ancient experiments.

Mainstream Taoist texts called for moderation, but you found that path frustrating and fruitless. If it worked so well, why didn't you know any immortals? Instead, you looked for the Jade Elixir in old folktales. You studied the legends of the Ching Shih and the fox spirits who achieved eternal life by giving themselves over to darkness. Perhaps moderation wasn't the key. Maybe you had to give yourself over to Yin to stop the decay of your body and soul.

Your first experiments along these lines almost poisoned you, as you brewed potions that had long been thought toxic by Western science. You grew your hair and fingernails to enjoy the flow of unimpeded Chi and practiced exercises that forced dark power through your veins and bones. One by one, your patients disappeared, as if they could sense that your mind, body and spirit were undergoing sinister changes.

Finally, after a sleepless night, you discovered the Jade Elixir. In your unlit office, you brewed a potion of cinnabar, iron and bitter herbs. You drank it and went through the slow motions of the exercises that would force its energy through your body and soul. You Awakened to chilling, burning power, like an ebon dragon slithering through your meridians, and you knew that you had achieved your goal.

You came to the Jnani already set in your ways, looking for more knowledge so that you could take

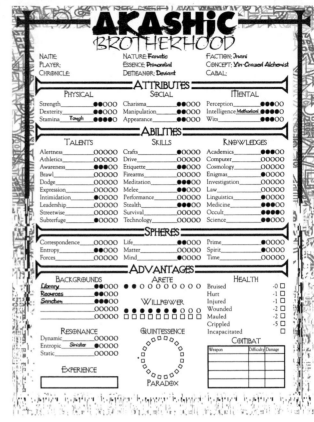

advantage of your new state. They taught you the refinement of Do and the way to final immortality, but you find their ethical debates tedious. Not that you disagree, but the goal of the Jade Elixir was to give you immortality, not to help every spiritually inferior being that crosses your path. The Jnani say that they want to rehabilitate you, but you are sure you took the right path.

Darkness awaits, and in the night, you will see the Drahma for the font of subterranean strength that it is.

Concept: You've rejected traditional Taoist beliefs to grab hold of the powers of legend. Instead of a perfect balance, your goal is to shock the self beyond it. By swinging wildly toward Yin, you separate yourself from the chaotic duality of the material world. You're not a bad person, but you do have a combination of wild-eyed fanaticism and callousness that fellow Brothers find troubling.

Roleplaying Tips: Dress in traditional robes and quote the classics. After all, you know that the tales of Chinese black magic are true, so why not go with it? Combine sinister, understated remarks with fanatical rants, as the passionate Yang sputters out of your body at unpredictable moments. Smile to yourself when you think of what you have accomplished and of the power that lies within your reach.

Magic: Spirit magic allows you to consort with the August Personage of Jade's lackeys and identify the gods that inhabit your own body and the bodies of others. Entropy allows you to channel Yin itself, and Life and Prime allows you to harvest Chi from your body. You use traditional Akashic methods with an emphasis on herbs and potions.

Equipment: Robes, a straight sword and a fully stocked herb shop and acupuncture studio

TRADITION BOOK: AKASHIC BROTHERHOOD

NAME:
CHARACTER: Yin-Crazed Alchemist
CHRONICLE:
FACTION: Jnani
ESSENCE: Primordial
CABAL:
NATURE: Fanatic
DEMEANOR: Deviant

PHYSICAL
Tough x3 _____
Quick _____
Brutal _____

SOCIAL
Fearsome _____
Beguiling _____
Intimidating _____

MENTAL
Rational x2 _____ Wise _____
Reflective x2 _____ Cunning _____
Intuitive _____

ABILITIES
Awareness _____
Brawl: Do _____ Stealth _____ Medicine _____
Medicine _____ Occult _____

MERITS & FLAWS

BACKGROUNDS
Library x2 _____
Resources x2 _____
Sanctum X3 _____

SPHERES
Initiate of Entropy _____
Initiate of Life _____
Apprentice of Mind _____
Apprentice of Prime _____
Apprentice of Spirit _____

ROTES

ARETE
WILLPOWER
QUINTESSENCE/PARADOX

RESONANCE
DYNAMIC _____
ENTROPIC Sinister
STATIC _____

TRADITION BOOK: AKASHIC BROTHERHOOD

NAME:
CHARACTER: Theologian
CHRONICLE:
FACTION: Kannagara
ESSENCE: Primordial
CABAL:
NATURE: Celebrant
DEMEANOR: Pedagogue

PHYSICAL
Tireless _____
Nimble _____
Stalwart _____

SOCIAL
Charming _____ Charismatic _____
Friendly _____ Persuasive _____
Expressive _____ Gorgeous _____

MENTAL
Clever _____ Dedicated _____
Alert _____ Insightful x2 _____
Attentive _____ Knowledgeable _____

ABILITIES
Brawl: Do _____ Occult _____
Etiquette _____ Academics (Theology) _____
Meditation _____ Linguistics _____

MERITS & FLAWS

BACKGROUNDS
Allies _____
Contacts x3 _____
Library X3 _____

SPHERES
Disciple of Mind _____
Disciple of Spirit _____

ROTES

ARETE
WILLPOWER
QUINTESSENCE/PARADOX

RESONANCE
DYNAMIC Joyous
ENTROPIC _____
STATIC _____

THEOLOGIAN

Quote: *I don't believe in a personal God. That would be selfish.*

Prelude: You were introduced to the church when your parents enrolled you in Sunday School. You always seemed to ask the wrong questions. How could a God of love send unbelievers to hell? How could He have a gender? Your teachers weren't impressed.

Still, you stayed an active church member throughout your teenage years. At first, you simply worked with charities and youth outreach programs, but the sexism and homophobia of some of your fellow parishioners left you wondering whether you were doing the right thing. To answer those questions once and for all, you studied to be a priest.

Unfortunately, seminary college didn't bring you any closer to being able to reconcile your faith with the tenets of your branch of Christianity. You refused holy orders because you didn't think you could support the Church you'd be asked to serve. Instead, you stayed in school and became a lay theologian.

You were introduced to Asian religion through your studies: when Thomas Merton discussed the similarities between Eastern and Western monastic traditions, he spoke to your belief that every culture must have some idea of the divine truth. You went to conferences where you met Buddhist monks and Taoist priests, and you were impressed by their wisdom, despite the fact that many of them felt that God couldn't offer you any special insights into your own spiritual condition.

Over time, your beliefs changed from worshiping a personal God who would answer your prayers to a designation for the absolute principle of reality. God was the love and justice that were intrinsic to the fabric of all things. You learned to see Nirvana or the Absolute as the way in which God had manifested for other cultures, just as He (or She) had through Jesus in yours.

You worked closely with Asian clergy, excitedly sharing your new beliefs with anyone who would listen. When you were invited to talk at a monastery in Japan, you quickly packed your bags and, brimming with ideas, you wrote your lecture on the flight over.

You talked to them for hours and felt a new sense of illumination build every time you

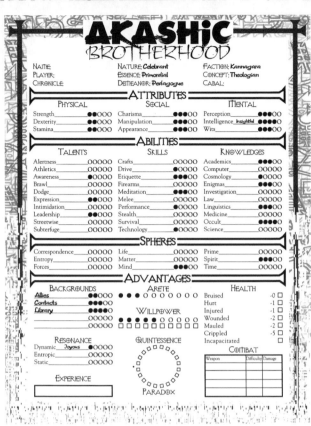

AKASHIC BROTHERHOOD

Character Sheet — AKASHIC BROTHERHOOD

NAME:
PLAYER:
CHRONICLE:

NATURE: Celebrant
ESSENCE: Primordial
DEMEANOR: Pedagogue

FACTION: Kannagara
CONCEPT: Theologian
CABAL:

ATTRIBUTES

PHYSICAL
Strength ●●○○○
Dexterity ●●○○○
Stamina ●●○○○

SOCIAL
Charisma ●●○○○
Manipulation ●●○○○
Appearance ●●○○○

MENTAL
Perception ●●○○○
Intelligence *Insightful* ●●●○○
Wits ●●○○○

ABILITIES

TALENTS
Alertness ○○○○○
Athletics ○○○○○
Awareness ●○○○○
Brawl ○○○○○
Dodge ○○○○○
Expression ●●○○○
Intimidation ○○○○○
Leadership ●●○○○
Streetwise ○○○○○
Subterfuge ○○○○○

SKILLS
Crafts ○○○○○
Drive ●○○○○
Etiquette ●●○○○
Firearms ○○○○○
Meditation ●●●○○
Melee ○○○○○
Performance ●○○○○
Stealth ○○○○○
Survival ○○○○○
Technology ●○○○○

KNOWLEDGES
Academics ●●●○○
Computer ○○○○○
Cosmology ●○○○○
Enigmas ●●○○○
Investigation ○○○○○
Law ○○○○○
Linguistics ●●●○○
Medicine ○○○○○
Occult ●●●●●
Science ○○○○○

SPHERES

Correspondence ○○○○○
Entropy ○○○○○
Forces ○○○○○
Life ○○○○○
Matter ○○○○○
Mind ●●○○○
Prime ○○○○○
Spirit ●●●○○
Time ○○○○○

ADVANTAGES

BACKGROUNDS
Allies ●●○○○
Contacts ●●●○○
Library ●●●●○
○○○○○
○○○○○

ARETE
●●● ○○○○○○○

WILLPOWER
●●●●●○○○○○
□□□□□□□□□□

HEALTH
Bruised -0 □
Hurt -1 □
Injured -1 □
Wounded -2 □
Mauled -2 □
Crippled -5 □
Incapacitated □

RESONANCE
Dynamic *Joyous* ●○○○○
Entropic ○○○○○
Static ○○○○○

QUINTESSENCE / **PARADOX**

EXPERIENCE

COMBAT

Weapon	Difficulty	Damage

---

brought up a new concept. The monks listened attentively, as you felt a light welling up within you. You finished by saying that God was the Wheel Turner, and the ultimate ground where reality was created and destroyed. By the end of your speech, you'd Awakened.

In your studies, you had come to identify a God that was no different from the Drahma, and the Kannagara were happy to teach you more of the Way.

Concept: Your religious quest has taken you to the Akashic Brotherhood. While you use a Christian framework to approach the Drahma, you don't believe that it is the best path for everyone. Unlike some of the monotheists of the Celestial Chorus, you don't see God as a being a personal redeemer as much as the bedrock that supports reality itself. Your God doesn't take sides and doesn't intervene as an individual but provides the world for humanity to live in and the gentle correction of karma to remind us of our duties to one another.

Roleplaying Tips: Point out the similarities between religious mystics but show respect for the different paths each one takes. Don't pray for other people; prayer is a way to train your mind to unite with the godhead, and it would be rude to demand your own values in others. Never tolerate discrimination or immorality, but accept that these are a necessary part of God. Even suffering is part of a greater whole. God is always changing, but that change is the force that circulates justice through the All.

Magic: Mind opens you to others' beliefs and Spirit lets you see their embodied forms. You use prayers from many cultures, meditation, and the study of sacred texts in your magical workings. You aren't invoking God but trying to see the divine will firsthand.

Equipment: African crucifix, prayer beads, comfortable, unpretentious clothes and a huge array of religious texts from all over the world

Epilogue: After the Rain

Dreams.
— The final teaching of the Zen Master Takuan

Peter looked at the sky. The rising sun had turned the clouds into a red ceiling. Water rolled off the roof below him. He was tired, like a man who only realizes the weight of his shackles after he has dropped them.

"P— Peter." It was Raging Eagle.

"Sifu." He knelt to face his master. "Smoke Tiger's dead. She told me the truth." Peter looked to Masako. She was still unconscious, but Peter noted that none of her wounds were serious enough to be threatening.

Raging Eagle touched his arm with a shaky hand. "We brought you here, General, because you would remember the truth." He gasped in pain as he spoke. "You know the danger… you must keep the secret, or the Traditions… fall."

Raging Eagle smiled. "I will die, now, Peter. Karma… "

"No, Sifu, "Peter said. "You won't. You're free from that now." He put his hands over the bloody holes on Raging Eagle's abdomen and felt the warm welling of Yang Chi — life — gather at his fingers. The beads rose out of Nu Ying's wounds and rolled into Peter's hands as the flesh knit. "You will live, Sifu, because things will be different this time."

Raging Eagle blinked, his face a question. He put a hand down to steady himself and grimaced as he sat up. He shivered. The sun warmed his face.

"Peter, how did you — "

"Things will be different now. We've forgotten that people can change, Nu Ying. None of us are slaves to the Wheel. Not the Akashayana, not the Chakravanti, not anyone.

"We saw the war fester inside us, even after it had done the good that we had all intended it to do. I saw you with bloodlust in your eyes, Sifu. I saw myself cut down a man whose only crime was to have a conscience. So many of us are still locked in the cycle, waiting for the chance to confront our actions and make peace with them. How can we do that when we keep the truth a secret?"

"No, Peter." As Raging Eagle spoke, his face hardened. He crawled closer. "You can't. The Sangha will collapse. The Vajrapani will— "

"We will not fall, Sifu. We've fought and died for the Bodhisattva Vow for so long, I think we've forgotten that Samadhi exists. But it is there, within us, yearning to arise. Every life lived since the Himalayan War is the Bodhicitta trying to burst forth from a prison we built for it. We have learned the lessons of the war, and now we need to learn the truth. It's the key that opens our souls to the Akasha."

Raging Eagle pulled his broken leg in front of him to stand. He was still weak, and he shook with the effort of pushing off the ground. "I have to stop you. Please, reconsider."

Peter smiled. "You could stop me at any moment, Nu Ying, but you won't. You're alive because you failed to stop the truth from arising. You've given up your duty and gained your freedom." He stepped toward the roof. "The Wheel doesn't chain you to death anymore."

Raging Eagle stood up. He ran his hands along his shaved temples. His skin shone golden in the dawn's light. Water droplets fell from him and sparkled in the sun. He took a deep breath. His face was filled with impassioned concern. He walked to Masako and checked her pulse with a callused finger. Her eyes opened a little, and Peter saw them exchange the mudra: *Peace*.

He was at the very edge of the rooftop when his Raging Eagle turned to him and asked, "What will the truth give them, Peter?"

"Emptiness," he replied. "Nothing holy."

He stepped off the roof and into the world.

REFERENCES

The Akashic Brotherhood is inspired by a number of different Asian belief systems, but don't confuse what you read herein for the real thing. Buddhism, Taoism, Confucianism and the thousands of other faiths that make up the Asian cultural mosaic deserve respect. If you want to learn about them to enhance a character with those beliefs, the following references provide a starting point. If you want to study them to find a path to spiritual growth, find a good teacher. This advice applies doubly to people who want to study the martial arts; learning from a book isn't just useless. It's dangerous.

Books

Oxford World Religions: Eastern Traditions. An indispensable (if expensive) resource that banishes many of the myths about Asia's religions.

Bubishi: The Bible of Karate. An English translation of a text that influenced the beginnings of karate. It explains philosophy from a warrior's perspective, hand in hand with techniques and medicines. A warning: Don't even think of using any of the methods and recipes it lists; they're provided for informational purposes only and haven't been edited to reflect our modern understanding of the body.

Living Buddha, Living Christ. Thich Nhat Hanh, Nobel Peace Prize nominee, monk and activist, explores the similarities between Buddhist and Christian teachings, and provides a powerful argument for ecumenicism.

The Bodhisattva Warriors. While you should take Terrence Duke's history with a grain of salt, this book discusses the relationship between esoteric Buddhism and the martial arts in useful detail. No matter what you think of it, it's chock full of ideas that fit the Akashic Brotherhood.

The Inner Athlete. Dan Millman incorporates Eastern philosophy into Western sport. He explains concepts in the kind of plain language that would befit a Li-Hai.

The Tao Te Ching. Practically required reading, for too many reasons to go into here. One thing worth noting is that it is a relatively minor text in the Taoist religious canon.

The Art of War. Military strategy from the dawn of the Legalist Renaissance. Any Shi-Ren worth her salt should be able to quote it from memory.

The Book of Five Rings: Its author, Miyamoto Musashi, is widely considered to be Japan's greatest swordsman. There are several translations of the book, which uses swordsmanship as a model for battlefield strategy and life itself.

Musashi: Eiji Yoshikawa's novel about Musashi is an excellent resource for players and Storytellers looking to detail the Japanese Brotherhood, or even for a chronicle set during the dawn of the Tokugawa regime.

Films

The following films have been chosen because they're relatively easy to find. However, Asian films now attract an international audience. Do some looking around and see what you can dig up.

Iron and Silk. The true story of Mark Salzman's martial arts and life experience in China. Salzman plays himself in the film, along with teacher Pan Qingfu, the "Iron Fist." A gentle introduction to an important and fascinating culture.

Kundun. Martin Scorsese directs this film about Tibet and the Dalai Lama. **Mage** players should watch for the sequences where the Dalai Lama consults Nechung, the state oracle.

Once Upon A Time in China. This Jet Li epic is set during the beginning of the Boxer Rebellion. Dazzling martial arts action and cultural clashes ensue.

Star Wars Episode One: The Phantom Menace and *The Matrix*. Both movies provide visual inspiration for Do. Take away the lightsabers and the VR, and the characters could easily be using Akashic magic.

AKASHIC
BROTHERHOOD

NAME:	NATURE:	FACTION:
PLAYER:	ESSENCE:	CONCEPT:
CHRONICLE:	DEMEANOR:	CABAL:

ATTRIBUTES

PHYSICAL
Strength _____ ●OOOO
Dexterity _____ ●OOOO
Stamina _____ ●OOOO

SOCIAL
Charisma _____ ●OOOO
Manipulation _____ ●OOOO
Appearance _____ ●OOOO

MENTAL
Perception _____ ●OOOO
Intelligence _____ ●OOOO
Wits _____ ●OOOO

ABILITIES

TALENTS
Alertness _____ OOOOO
Athletics _____ OOOOO
Awareness _____ OOOOO
Brawl _____ OOOOO
Dodge _____ OOOOO
Expression _____ OOOOO
Intimidation _____ OOOOO
Leadership _____ OOOOO
Streetwise _____ OOOOO
Subterfuge _____ OOOOO

SKILLS
Crafts _____ OOOOO
Drive _____ OOOOO
Etiquette _____ OOOOO
Firearms _____ OOOOO
Meditation _____ OOOOO
Melee _____ OOOOO
Performance _____ OOOOO
Stealth _____ OOOOO
Survival _____ OOOOO
Technology _____ OOOOO

KNOWLEDGES
Academics _____ OOOOO
Computer _____ OOOOO
Cosmology _____ OOOOO
Enigmas _____ OOOOO
Investigation _____ OOOOO
Law _____ OOOOO
Linguistics _____ OOOOO
Medicine _____ OOOOO
Occult _____ OOOOO
Science _____ OOOOO

SPHERES

Correspondence _____ OOOOO
Entropy _____ OOOOO
Forces _____ OOOOO
Life _____ OOOOO
Matter _____ OOOOO
Mind _____ OOOOO
Prime _____ OOOOO
Spirit _____ OOOOO
Time _____ OOOOO

ADVANTAGES

BACKGROUNDS
_____ OOOOO
_____ OOOOO
_____ OOOOO
_____ OOOOO
_____ OOOOO
_____ OOOOO
_____ OOOOO

ARETE
● O O O O O O O O O

WILLPOWER
● ● ● ● ● O O O O O
□ □ □ □ □ □ □ □ □ □

QUINTESSENCE

OTHER TRAITS
Do _____ OOOOO
_____ OOOOO
_____ OOOOO
_____ OOOOO
_____ OOOOO

PARADOX

HEALTH
Bruised	-0	□
Hurt	-1	□
Injured	-1	□
Wounded	-2	□
Mauled	-2	□
Crippled	-5	□
Incapacitated		□

RESONANCE
Dynamic _____ OOOOO
Entropic _____ OOOOO
Static _____ OOOOO

EXPERIENCE

AKASHIC
BROTHERHOOD

MERITS & FLAWS

Merit	Type	Cost	Flaw	Type	Bonus

MAGIC

PREFERRED EFFECTS

ROTES

COMBAT

Maneuver/Do Technique	Roll	Difficulty	Damage/Effect

Weapon	Difficulty	Damage	Range	Rate	Clip	Conceal

ARMOR:_____

DO STYLE:_____

AKASHIC BROTHERHOOD

EXPANDED BACKGROUND

ALLIES

_____
_____
_____
_____

LIBRARY

_____
_____
_____
_____

CONTACTS

_____
_____
_____
_____

MENTOR

_____
_____
_____
_____

DESTINY

_____
_____
_____
_____

NODE

_____
_____
_____
_____

INFLUENCE

_____
_____
_____
_____

RESOURCES

_____
_____
_____
_____

POSSESSIONS

GEAR (CARRIED)

_____
_____
_____
_____
_____

EQUIPMENT (OWNED)

_____
_____
_____
_____
_____

FOCI

_____
_____
_____
_____
_____

WONDERS

_____
_____
_____
_____

FAMILIAR

_____
_____
_____
_____

PAST INCARNATIONS

_____
_____
_____
_____
_____
_____

AKASHIC
BROTHERHOOD

HISTORY
AWAKENING

_____
_____
_____
_____

GOALS/DESTINY

_____
_____
_____
_____
_____

SEEKINGS:_____   QUIETS:_____
_____   _____
_____   _____

DESCRIPTION

Age:_____
Apparent Age:_____
Date of Birth:_____
Age of Awakening:_____
Hair:_____
Eyes:_____
Race:_____   Appearance/Nature of Avatar:_____
Nationality:_____   _____
Height:_____   _____
Weight:_____   _____
Sex:_____   _____

VISUALS

CABAL CHART   CHARACTER SKETCH